DENTAL SCHOOL DEBACLE

A New Orleans Adventure
Part One

JIM P. SANDRAS, D.D.S.

Copyright @2021 Jim Sandras

All rights reserved. No part of this book may be reproduced or used in any manner without the prior written permission of the copyright owner, except for the use of brief quotations in a book review.

To request permissions, contact the publisher at jimpsandrasauthor@gmail.com.

Paperback ISBN: 978-1-7378604-0-2
Audiobook ISBN: 978-1-7378604-1-9
E-book ISBN: 978-1-7378604-2-6

First paperback edition 2021.

Cover art by Harbinger Design.

Facebook @jimpsandrasauthor

To my beautiful, sweet wife Cari, who advised me not to publish this, saying it would ruin my good reputation and lucrative dental career. I love you and I'm sorry.

And to my two awesome, college-educated children, Destin and Lauren, I love you and I'm extremely proud of you. Remember, all of this stuff happened way before you were born. Do as I say, not as I did.

Contents

Introduction 1
Pre-Dentistry 3
   Black Cow 5
   Bad Hair Day at the Country Club 23
Freshman Year 41
   Tennis Anyone? 43
   Happy Birthday Benedict 61
   A Gross Night at the Hyatt 79
   The Love Boat 113
   The Forgotten Tomato 127
   First Annual End-of-the-Year Party 147
Sophomore Year 159
   Microscopically Dead 161
   Plates 195
   Dinner at Brennan's 221
   High Speed Fun 243
   Second Annual End-of-the-Year Party 257

Acknowledgments

There have been many people who have helped me, encouraged me, and inspired me to write this book over the past 25 years.

First, I must thank my parents, Jimmy and Joyce, who encouraged me to be a dentist and supported me financially, emotionally, and spiritually throughout college and dental school. Thank you for paying all the bills so that I didn't have to work. And thank you for praying that I would stay out of jail (it only happened twice), not kill myself, or end up in a mental institution.

I'd also like to acknowledge my close friends who hung out with me growing up and influenced my debacle behavior: Sam "Zar" Sannasardo, John "Rat" Remy, Robert "Nip" Jones, Ryan Cheramie, Peter Connick, and Steve "Boulon" Wofford. I love you guys! I would also like to acknowledge my dental school classmates who inspired me to write this book: Robert Laville, Chris Mott, Barney Harper, Bart Barre, Allen Rodgers, Tommy Hillman, Todd Babineaux, Mark Schott, Pat Lonergan and the notorious Carl Zimmerman. Sorry I couldn't mention everyone. I can't tell you how much I enjoyed spending those four years with you.

Finally, thank all of you who helped with the editing and typing of this book, including Kim Salvaggio, Carol Ann Holley, Peter Connick, Octavio Nuiry, Krissy Martin, Emily English, Sam Nash and most importantly my 'Roll Tide' wife Cari. Without you I would have never published this book. Thanks for all your ideas and encouragement, and mostly for loving me. Last, but not least, I'd like to thank my brother, Johnny, and my sisters Kim and Joni, for putting up with me all these years and always being there for me.

Introduction

D*ental School Debacle – A New Orleans Adventure* is a fictional story based on real events that took place in New Orleans during the 1980's. Only the names and timeline have been changed to protect the innocent. It is a comical account of the lives of three college students who have been accepted into one of the top dental schools in the country. These three guys, Destin, Mike and Bobby, came from completely different social-economic backgrounds, yet became best friends due to a common denominator they shared: to complete the next four, difficult years of dental school without going psychotic or being convicted of a felony. Together they go on a hilarious, exhausting adventure in one of the craziest cities on earth. This book was not written with lots of medical jargon, or in terms which only those in the medical field can understand or relate to: although those people will enjoy and appreciate it immensely. On the contrary, this book was intended for anyone who likes a story about achieving the "American Dream" and wants to laugh out loud at the same time. But most importantly, it's for anyone who has ever sat in a dental chair. I promise, you will never look at your dentist the same. This book has been a labor of love of mine for over 25 years. I hope you enjoy reading it half as much as I've enjoyed writing it.

Jim P. Sandras, D.D.S.

CONTENT WARNING: IF YOU ARE POLITICALLY CORRECT AND HAVE NO SENSE OF HUMOR, PLEASE PUT THIS BOOK DOWN NOW!!

I would also like to apologize in advance to PETA. These events happened long ago when I was just a kid and you guys were nowhere around. I do not encourage or recommend that anyone repeat these heinous crimes against humanity, especially since now there are cameras everywhere.

Pre-Dentistry

1980 something...

NOVEMBER 5, 198?

DEAR MR. SANDRAS:

ALL REQUIRED MATERIALS HAVE BEEN RECEIVED, AND YOUR APPLICATION IS NOW COMPLETE. YOU WILL BE CONTACTED FOR INTERVIEW AT A LATER DATE. IF THERE HAS BEEN A CHANGE IN YOUR TELEPHONE NUMBER SINCE APPLYING, PLEASE CONTACT THIS OFFICE.

OFFICE OF ADMISSIONS
LSU SCHOOL OF DENTISTRY
1100 FLORIDA AVENUE
NEW ORLEANS, LOUISIANA 70119

Black Cow

The adrenalin was flowing at lot #35 in Mr. B's Trailer Park. Something sinister, of epic proportions, was about to transpire on this cold February night in Southwestern Louisiana. As was his routine, Boulon was at Destin and Fred's "luxury" mobile home distracting them from doing homework. And as usual, all three were sitting on the sofa with their feet on the coffee table, drinking cheap wine out of the bottle, watching television. But there was something different about this night, besides the full moon. Tonight, they were not paying attention to the television, but were instead daring one another to try and pull off a very rare, extremely illegal, and dangerous act – cattle rustling. They had been joking about it for the past few semesters, but tonight they were serious.

"I know we can do it," said Destin. "Just think, we could eat free steaks and hamburgers every day for the rest of the semester!"

Boulon was shaking his head. "Mais, you college boys aint got no clue what ya talkin' 'bout. How do ya plan on katchin a cow and bring it bach here?"

Jim P. Sandras, D.D.S.

"Boulon, don't you have a high-powered rifle?" asked Fred.

Boulon shook his head. "You city dudes is dumma den you look. Fa one ting, ya cood hear my turty/turdy a mile a-way. Dat farma wood be on us like a pit bull on a cat befo dat cow hit da grown."

"Then we'll use that German pistol you just bought," said Destin. Then he took a swig out of the $2.69 bottle of wine. "All we have to do is shoot it behind the ear once. That'll kill it. I should know. I have a minor in cow and cat anatomy."

"It's a lot harda dan ya tink," insisted Boulon. "Dem tings are sum heavy."

"We're big boys," said Fred flexing his muscles. "We can do it!"

Destin and Fred were both big boys, but Boulon was almost twice their size.

"Yeah! Let's do it!" yelled Destin. "Tonight's the night!"

Boulon hesitated, thought for a second, and then took a big swig of wine. "Mais, you guys are luc-key I ben drinkin' dis MD 20/20 wine all nite, otha wise I wooden even tink 'bout it. Jus promise me dat wen you daddy's come bail ya out of dat jail, dat day bail me out, too."

"Don't worry, Boulon," said Fred, as he snatched the bottle out of his hand. "We won't get caught."

Boulon stood up and folded his arms. "Let me ax you two intell-la-gent college stew-dants one question befo we go get dis cow. How do ya plan on gettin dat ting bach here?"

Fred jumped up. "We can tie it behind my Grand Prix and drag it back."

"Dat is da dummist ting dat I done ever heard," said Boulon as he reached back for the bottle. "If we get lucky e-nuf to get away

Dental School Debacle

wit dis I want me sum good meat, not no beef jer-key." He hesitated and thought. "We can use my motha-in-law's '67 Impala. I'm done finish workin' on dat ol ting. We cood put a bull in dat big trunk."

"GREAT!" said Destin as he jumped up. "Go get it and meet us in front of my trailer. And don't forget your pistol."

***

Fred and Destin were seniors in college, only a few months from graduation. They were both from upper class families in New Orleans and had been friends since childhood. They were very popular around the city, not only because of their families' money, but because they were also great high school football players. While they were seniors in high school, the two friends decided it would be in their best long-term interest to move away from home for college, preferably a small town where no one knew them. They could get away from their reputations, but mostly they could escape all the trouble they had gotten into with the law, their parents, the neighbors and numerous ex-girlfriends. Now they were living in a trailer park surrounded by soybean fields in Lafayette, Louisiana, 150 miles from home, daring one another to steal a cow. Boulon, their trailer park buddy, was a 41-year-old, full-blooded Cajun, married with two daughters. He grew up in the swamps of Louisiana and lived in the Atchafalaya Basin on a floating house before moving to Mr. B's Trailer Park. Boulon never made it past the eighth grade and had such a strong Cajun accent that the two students often had a hard time understanding him. He now worked offshore, rough-necking for a drilling company, and lived in the trailer next to Destin and Fred. Boulon met them several years ago while the two were outside boiling crawfish. They instantly became best of friends.

***

The two students were standing outside shivering in the cold waiting for Boulon and his mother-in-law's old car. Fifteen minutes later he pulled up in a dented '67 Chevy Impala with bondo mixed with white paint. Boulon was steering with his knees, shifting the gears with his right hand and holding a wine bottle with his left. Fred opened the squeaky door and saw that Boulon was wearing camouflage clothes and a camouflage hat, and had black shoe polish all over his face. On the front seat there were two hats—a full-faced black ski mask and an original WWI Red Baron hat.

"I want the ski mask," said Fred as he got into the car.

"You're really getting into this now, huh, Boulon?" asked Destin as he put on the Red Baron hat. All three squeezed into the front seat.

"Mais, I still tink dis is a bad i-dea." Boulon pulled away and started down the dark country road. "But we mite be jus able to pool it off."

Fred grabbed the almost empty bottle of wine from Boulon, finished it off, and threw it out the window successfully smashing it against a speed limit sign. "Let's go get some beef!" he yelled.

"How far do we have to go?" asked Destin.

"Faw. All most to New Iberia," replied Boulon as he shifted the old car into fourth gear. "We gonna need to stop and get us sum mo wine."

***

The temperature was dropping fast as the three rustlers drove deep into the country to a farm where Boulon knew there were

Dental School Debacle

hundreds of cows. The first thing they did was ride around the large property several times to scope it out. The farmer's house was an old wooden building that sat behind a small, shallow pond full of cypress stumps. After several minutes of careful observation, there were no signs of life in or near the house, just an uncomfortable quietness. The only light came from a 20-foot utility pole next to the pond. About 100 yards away sat a huge, well-built, two-story barn made entirely of cypress. By the time they found a secluded place to park, it was almost 1:00 a.m. They quietly got out of the car. Boulon reached into his pocket and handed Destin a can of black Kiwi shoe polish.

"Rub dis on you faces. It gonna make it hard fo da farma to shoot ya." Destin applied it to his face as they walked up to the barbed-wire fence and surveyed the situation.

"Mais, I got me a bad feelin in ma bones," said Boulon, staring at the farmer's dark house in the distance. "I tink dat guy gonna hear dat pistol. We betta fo-get 'bout dis. I tell you, we cood get 12 years of dat jail time if we go get caut. I want a done seen my dawda's go treu pube-atee, not jus hear bout it bee-hine bars."

"Nonsense," insisted Destin. "Then we'll have to get a cow some other way. We have to do it, tonight! We're already here and primed up. Besides, me and Fred have been planning this ever since we got kicked out of the dorms."

"That's true, Boulon," added Fred. "I have an idea." He ran to the car, opened the back door and pulled out two old, wooden carpenter's hammers and a tire tool and ran back. "I saw these in the back seat."

"Now we're talking!" said Destin with a gleam in his eyes. "I want the tire tool."

Jim P. Sandras, D.D.S.

Boulon shook his head and laughed to himself. "Na I kno you city boys are missin sum of dem brain cell. You neva gonna kill you a cow wit a hamma, all ya gonna do is get dat ting mad."

This got Fred's attention. He didn't know how mad a cow could get. He had never been around animals. The only time he'd seen a cow was while watching rodeos on cable TV. He kept thinking about how those mean "cows" attack those poor cowboys after being thrown off. "Do you think a cow might really attack us?"

"Don't listen to Boulon," said Destin. "They're like pet hamsters. All they do is eat, crap and sleep. A cow won't attack you, even if you hit it with a tire tool. Boulon thinks we can't do this, that we're just a couple of wimpy city boys. Come on, Fred, we've gotten away with a lot worse things back home. I say we do it."

Destin jumped the barbed wire fence and took off running at the cows while waving the tire tool over his Red Baron hat. He looked like a Marine landing on the beach of Normandy. Fred was getting excited watching Destin, so he pulled the ski mask over his face, jumped the fence and took off running after him, waving his hammer. Boulon went back to the car, opened the wine bottle, sat on the hood, and started laughing as he watched the two college students try to catch a cow. The two ran around the pasture for 30 minutes trying to corner one, but they couldn't even get close. Then out of frustration, Fred threw his hammer at a nearby cow, hitting it in the side, not even phasing the large bovine.

"Nice going, Thor," said Destin gasping for air. "I think Boulon was right. We're just fartin' in the wind."

Dental School Debacle

Fred raised his ski mask. "I think you're right."

The two discouraged, out-of-breath hunters walked back to the fence and looked at Boulon sitting on the hood of the Impala shaking his head.

"I didn't know cows were so fast," said Destin.

"Dere not," said Boulon as he worked his way off the hood. "Day jus ain't ben drinkin dat Mad Dog all night. Let me sho ya how dats done." He reached in the car, grabbed a flashlight and hammer, jumped the fence, and started creeping towards the cypress barn. "I know myself dar got to be sum cows in dere— dey not all runnin round outside at dis time of de nite."

The three entered the dark, quiet stables and looked around. The first thing they noticed was it's very low ceiling, less than five feet high—just tall enough for the cows. The loft above was full of hay. To get around, they had to crawl on their hands and knees while they quietly searched the stables with the dim flashlight looking for an innocent cow victim. Just when they realized they were crawling through six inches of cow manure, a black cow came running out of a stall and charged right at Boulon. Instinctively, Boulon reared back and swung the hammer with all his might, hitting the cow between the eyes with such a blow that the wooden handle broke in half. The stunned cow instantly dropped to its knees and fell over.

"MY GOD, BOULON! Look what you've done!" yelled Fred, leaning over the cow. "You killed it!"

Boulon picked up the top half of the hammer, looked at the cow lying on its side and said, "I didn't mean to... but maa, dat ting ran rite at me."

"Good job, Boulon," said Destin, patting him on the back.

Jim P. Sandras, D.D.S.

"You made it look easy. Now let's get this cow out of here."

Fred and Boulon quickly grabbed two legs while Destin grabbed the tail to drag the cow out of the stable toward the car. They were so hurried and scared, not paying attention to where they were going, that they backed into the drinking trough and fell in the water, making a huge splash. It took them a minute to realize what happened. Trying to ignore the cold, nasty water they were sitting in, Fred and Destin just looked at each other and smiled.

"If only my parents could see me now," said Destin.

"I'm sure they'd be proud of their prodigy," added Fred.

Boulon pushed himself up, wiped off his butt, and looked at the two college students sitting in the water trough joking around.

"Will you two gerls get up n help me drag dis cow out of here?" He extended his hands and pulled them out. "I am sho you daddy's wood done have baut you a cow if ya were ax him."

"It's the feeling of accomplishment that I thrive on," replied Destin, in his soaking wet clothes.

The three got serious again and began dragging the cow. After a hard struggle they finally reached the fence. Boulon walked over and easily pulled four creosol fence posts out of the ground. His adrenalin was flowing. Then they dragged the cow over the downed fence toward the road. Boulon quickly replaced the fence posts, and then he and Fred took off running for the car while Destin stayed with the cow. Seconds after the two left, the cow unexpectedly started moving and kicking its feet. After it made some strange gurgling sounds, the cow lifted its head and stood up. Destin's eyes popped wide open.

"Oh my God! It came back to life." He anxiously started

Dental School Debacle

backing up and talking to the cow. "It's OK, Mr. Cow, I know you're upset...and I'm sure you have a terrible headache. Don't worry, we're going to bring you to a vet. He'll give you something strong." The cow just turned his head and started walking towards the barn. Destin was determined not to let the cow get away, whatever it took. The only thing he could think of was to knock the cow down like he used to knock down running backs when he played linebacker in high school. He stood about 10 feet from the cow, got in a three-point stance, and then took off running as fast as he could with his head down, hitting the animal in its side. They both made grunting noises when they hit the ground. Just then Boulon and Fred drove up in the car and saw Destin lying on top of the cow. Boulon hopped out of the car and walked over with a grin.

"Destin, I tink it's time fa you to done fine a girlfriend."

"I thought it was dead," replied Destin, sitting on the cow's side. "As soon as y'all left it stood up and started walking. I didn't want it to get away, so I tackled it."

"I done toll ya, ya can't kill a cow wit a hamma," replied Boulon. "I prob-lee jus done nock it out."

As soon as Destin got up, the cow stood up too, although it was a little wobbly. This made Fred nervous. He was staring at the cow as he backed up toward the car.

Destin shook his head. "I can't believe a big guy like you, Fred, is scared of a little cow. Now get your ugly self back here and help us get this cow in the trunk." Fred cautiously walked towards the cow while Boulon opened the trunk. The two students each grabbed an ear and directed the unsteady animal toward the car. Boulon grabbed a front hoof and placed it on the

Jim P. Sandras, D.D.S.

rear bumper. Then to their surprise the cow climbed in the trunk the rest of the way by itself.

Destin was in awe. "That was easy."

"It mus tink it's some kine of livestock traila," replied Boulon.

While they were standing there in amazement, Fred grabbed the trunk hood and slammed it shut with every ounce of strength he had, knocking the cow on its side, again. The three quietly stood there for a second listening for any noise from the trunk, but heard nothing.

"I can't believe dat," said Boulon, "we done did it." Just as he said that the lights in the farmer's house came on.

"Fred mus have done woke him up when he slammed de trunk. Let's get out of here, fast." The three jumped in the car and took off. Boulon was driving like a maniac down the dark muddy roads. As soon as they got back to Highway 49 and on their way home, they started to relax, but only a little. Boulon was the most nervous. He had a family to support and was still worried about getting caught. He unscrewed the wine cap and started drinking again. "OK, my brave cow rustlers, what do ya suggest we gonna do wit dis ting now?"

"We'll cook it after class tomorrow," said Destin, rubbing his hands together in anticipation. "I'll take my TV antenna down and create a rotisserie spit. We can use those two police barricades we stole last semester to rest it on, and light a fire underneath it."

"Yeah," said Fred. "I'll cook a pot of beans, macaroni and cheese, grits…"

Boulon abruptly interrupted. "Wat da hell do dey teach you fools at dat dere college? You caint go cook a cow wit out guttin

Dental School Debacle

it and takin' off dat skin... and you kno we can't go lite a fire in da traila park. Da landlord wood kick us out rite nah."

"Screw Mr. Babineaux, and his stupid daughter," Destin angrily replied.

Boulon smiled. "Mais, I kno his dawda's mad like heck at chew and she dumped ya, but dat's no good re-son to go get kicked out."

"Hey look, I'm graduating in a few months and moving back to New Orleans.... and hopefully starting dental school this summer," said Destin. "I should hear from them any day now. But either way, I won't be anywhere around here."

"I dun got me a idea," interrupted Boulon. "We can put dis cow in my dawda's playhouse. I jus ran me sum lite to it. I can put my tarpaulin down on de flow, den we cood skin and gut it in dere. Mais, I know it mus be as cole as one of dem deep freezers in dat ting. Den tomorrow I cood bring it to my butcher friend, Ron Guidry, at Veron's." They agreed it was their best option.

It was almost 3:00 in the morning when they pulled into Mr. B's. The three were barely breathing as Boulon slowed down to the required 5 mph speed limit. It was so quiet in the trailer park that the only noise that could be heard was the hum of the mercury vapor streetlights. Their nerves were getting edgy as they approached Boulon's trailer. He slowly stopped in front of his neighbor's lot, put the car in reverse, and cautiously backed up to the 8x10 pink and white playhouse that he had just built. As soon as Boulon turned off the car the cow started moving, moaning and kicking the trunk with loud thuds.

Boulon freaked out. "MY GAWD! It's trying to get out! It's gonna wake up dis whole traila park! I'm dead! Twelve years in

Jim P. Sandras, D.D.S.

dat jail! I'm gonna mis my dawda' first communion!"

"Relax, Boulon," said Destin, "let's just hurry and get the cow out of the trunk."

Boulon grabbed the bottle of wine and finished it. "I can't bee-leave I let you boys talk me into dis."

"Don't worry, Boulon," said Fred. "Go inside and get your electric knife. Destin and I will take care of the cow."

Just then they heard two more loud thuds. Boulon quickly ran inside while Fred and Destin proceeded to open the trunk. As soon as it popped up, the cow instantly rose to its feet as if it were mounted on a spring. Destin grabbed the cow by the tail and pulled hard. It lost its balance and fell halfway out, leaving only its head in the trunk. Fred saw an opportunity to put the poor cow out of its misery. He jumped up, grabbed the hood of the trunk, and slammed it as hard as he could.

He looked at Fred standing over the cow. "Your technique is crude, Fred, but very effective."

"I didn't know what else to do," he replied.

Destin walked up to the cow and shook his head. "Look at this thing. It's bleeding all over the place. Let's hurry up and drag it into the playhouse before someone sees us. The two boys struggled, but eventually got the cow into the playhouse. They turned the lights on and looked around. It was fully equipped with a tea set on a small table, and toy appliances. Fred walked over and opened the little, pink refrigerator.

"What the heck are you doing, Fred?"

"Looking for food. I'm starving."

A few moments later Boulon walked in carrying a rolled-up tarpaulin, his electric carving knife, and an ax saw. His jaw

Dental School Debacle

dropped when he looked at the floor. The blood covered the entire playhouse floor. Then he saw the cow. He dropped everything and grabbed his head. "My Gawd! What da heck dun happen here?"

"You should've seen it Boulon—it was great," replied Fred. "Destin grabbed the cow by the tail and pulled it out of the trunk."

Destin interrupted. "Yeah, then Charles Manson here slammed the trunk on it."

Boulon was still holding his head looking around the small room accessing the damage. "Dis ting is ruined...and I jus built it. Jennifa is gonna kill me. I jus done told her we were skinin a few rabbits we done shot. I aint neva gonna get dis ting clean."

Fred tried to cheer him up. "Just tell Jennifer we shot a 200 pound jackalope."

Boulon mustered up a smile. "I'm la-fin, but it aint funny."

"Let's get busy," said Destin as he picked up the saw. "I have a biochemistry class at 8:00, and I have to go. We're getting our first test back and the professor won't give us the results unless we're there."

"That stinks!" said Fred. "Is this the same professor whose house you went to the night before a test and let the air out of all her tires because you didn't feel like studying?"

"No, this is the woman who looks like Fred Flintstone."

Boulon was getting impatient. "Will you guys quit talking bout dem ugg-lee teachers and let's clean dis stupid cow dat you talk me into stealing."

"We didn't steal this cow," Destin corrected. "It was self defense."

Jim P. Sandras, D.D.S.

"Yeah, it attacked us, remember?" added Fred. He then tried to take the saw away from Destin. The two students briefly wrestled for the saw before Boulon broke them up.

"You two are act-ting like lil' kids," he said as he took the saw away. "Do ya know how to skin a cow?"

"I skinned a cat in comparative anatomy," said Destin.

"I've cleaned speckled trout before," replied Fred.

"Yawl are sum useless," said Boulon. He picked up his electric knife and plugged it in the wall of the playhouse. "Dey ought to let me teach at dat dere college." He laid the tarpaulin down next to the cow and kneeled. "I done use to watch my Paw-Paw butcha dem cows when I was little. I tink I remember how to, but I for sure am gonna need yawl to help me."

"This looks like fun," said Destin as he kneeled in the blood.

The three started cutting, pulling, and sawing like drunken orthopedic surgeons. Finally, they had everything skinned, gutted and cut into quarters just as the sun was coming up. They had a garbage can full of guts and skin that Boulon said he'd give to his cousin who raised hogs. They washed off the meat, hosed out the playhouse, and then brought the fresh meat to Destin's trailer so Boulon's wife wouldn't know what really happened. As soon as Destin walked in, he looked at the clock.

"It's 7:30!" he yelled. "I have to go to class, now!"

"Don't worry, Destin," said Fred. "Go to your Biochemistry class. I'll stay here and help Boulon. I've only missed three classes this week."

Destin ran to the bathroom, brushed his teeth, tried unsuccessfully to get the shoe polish off his face, grabbed his keys, hopped in his 1980 Fiat Spider, and rushed to campus. He

Dental School Debacle

arrived at the chemistry building at 7:50, parked illegally, walked into the large auditorium, and sat in the second to last row, instantly falling asleep. Minutes later students started walking in. Every student that sat near Destin made a putrid face, pinched their noses, and moved to another seat. All the other students were talking about him.

"The dude's covered with blood!"

"He smells like he lives in a barn."

"He might be a serial killer."

"What's that all over his face?"

At 8:00 sharp the professor walked in and noticed that the whole auditorium was full, except for the desks around Destin. She just ignored the situation and went about her business.

"I have the results from the first test," said the manly looking woman. "Overall, the grades were pretty good, although they could've been better. The highest grade was a 97, with the lowest being a 16. I'm going to hand out the tests starting off with the highest and work my way to the bottom. I like to recognize hard work. Topping off the class with the 97 is Destin Dufrene. Mr. Dufrene..." The professor stood there waiting, but no one responded.

Then out of the silence someone yelled out. "He's sleeping in the back."

"Can you please wake him up and tell him to come get his test?"

"No way!" said the student. "He's covered with blood...and stinks."

"Then I'll give it to him myself." The professor walked up the auditorium steps and approached the snoring student. When she

Jim P. Sandras, D.D.S.

got within two desks of Destin, the stench hit her. She quickly took a deep breath and tapped him on the neck—the cleanest part of his body.

Destin jumped up and yelled. "I didn't mean to kill it! It attacked us!" He looked around, remembered he was in class, and quickly sat down.

"Relax, Mr. Dufrene," said the professor. "I have your test results; you made a 97—the highest in the class. Congratulations." Then she leaned over and whispered in his ear.

"If I were you, I would definitely improve my hygiene. You'd have more friends." Destin slowly got his bearings and smiled. "I had a rough night." He stood up, grabbed his test paper, and ran out of the auditorium to his car. Minutes later he was pulling into the trailer park. As usual, he stopped at the group of mailboxes at the entrance. In his box was a message from Mr. Babineaux, the landlord. It said he needed to see him. Destin instinctively thought the worst. Either it was about his daughter, or he had found out about the cow. He reluctantly pulled up to the portable metal office and walked in.

"Hi, Mr. B," said Destin politely. "You wanted to see me?"

"Yes, Destin, I sure do," replied the overweight man in his blue Sears jumpsuit. "I received a certified letter for you yesterday, but you were nowhere to be found, so I signed for it."

"Thank you very much, Mr. B." Destin snatched the envelope from his landlord and quickly opened it. Seconds later he threw the letter in the air and started jumping up and down with his hands in the air.

"YES! I DID IT! I'VE BEEN ACCEPTED INTO DENTAL SCHOOL! YES!" He grabbed Mr. Babineaux, who he so heartily

Dental School Debacle

disliked, and gave him a big hug.

"Congratulations, son," he said. "I guess that means you'll be moving soon?"

"Yes! Finally! New Orleans, I'm coming home!" He ran out of the office towards his car, hesitated, and looked back at Mr. B., remembering how he had given him such a hard time the past four years. This was his chance to get him back. He walked back into the office and looked his landlord in the eyes.

"By the way, Mr. B., tell your daughter there's no way her baby can be mine." Destin slammed the door and ran to his Fiat. Mr. Babineaux came running behind him.

"What are you talking about? My daughter's pregnant?"

Ignoring his landlord, Destin pealed out, throwing rocks against him and his metal building. He pulled into his small, narrow, oyster shell driveway doing 20 mph, stopping just inches from the barbeque pit where Boulon and Fred were cooking extremely fresh ribs. They both had to jump out of the way to avoid being hit.

"What's the matter with you?" asked Fred. "You almost hit us!"

"He mus-ta failed da test."

Destin jumped out of his convertible without opening the door, waving his acceptance letter over his head. "No, I made a 97, the highest in the class. But even better, I've been accepted into dental school!"

"Dude, you did it!" yelled Fred. He was happy for his old friend. "I knew you could do it."

"You real-le dun did it," said Boulon. "You summa gun, you." He walked over and hugged him. "Mais, I feel sor-ree for dem

Jim P. Sandras, D.D.S.

people at dat dare dentist school. Da place is neva gonna be da same."

Destin jumped on Boulon and started wrestling, but Boulon easily pinned him down. The two were laughing out loud as they wrestled in the driveway, knocking over the barbeque pit, rolling under the trailer into the air conditioning duct. Fred was just standing there shaking his head. He looked at the cooked ribs scattered over the driveway, and then looked at Destin, shoe polish on his face, his arms bloody from rolling in oyster shells, and laughing so hard he was drooling.

Fred smiled. "He's going to make one heck of a dentist."

Bad Hair Day at the Country Club

That same day, across the state, Mike was replacing a broken toilet in the ladies' restroom on the sixth hole at the Shreveport Country Club. He desperately hated plumbing work and knew very little about it. Every time he leaned over to connect the water line his long hair fell in his eyes making it difficult to see what he was doing.

"I'd rather wash dishes at Shoney's than do this," he grunted, bending over in a very uncomfortable position. He was finally about to finish the dirty job when he realized he needed a larger wrench. Besides, his knees were hurting so badly he had to stretch. As he stood up, he banged his head hard against the sink of the small outdoor restroom. He fell to his knees and threw the pliers against the wall, yelling obscenities.

While he was kneeling there rubbing his head, an elderly female golfer walked into the restroom. She saw Mike's long blonde hair and assumed he was a woman.

"Excuse me, I didn't know anyone was in here," said the

Jim P. Sandras, D.D.S.

woman, as she lowered her skirt. "I have to use the bathroom SO bad. I should've gone before the first hole, but my husband was in such a damn hurry. My heart doctor put me on these damn pills, and I swear, I almost need to wear a diaper."

She finally noticed the toilet was disconnected. "What's wrong with this damn thing?"

As soon as Mike turned around his eyes went straight to the lady's white, polyester underwear. The woman turned bright red when she saw Mike's goatee.

"This toilet's not working," he said while still rubbing his head. "You'll have to use the men's room."

The embarrassed woman quickly pulled up her skirt and walked out. A few seconds later she walked back in. "Young man, there's no toilet in there."

"Oh yeah, I forgot," replied Mike unsympathetically, "both toilets cracked in that hard freeze we had last night. I'm working on it now, Ma'am. I should have them both replaced by this afternoon."

The woman bent over and grabbed her stomach. "What am I supposed to do?" she grunted. "I need to go, NOW!"

Mike thought of a way to add a little humor to this miserable day.

"Use the urinal," he replied seriously.

The woman looked confused. "The urinal?"

"Sure," he insisted, "just sit on it backwards."

"Is it safe?"

"Absolutely. My sister does it all the time."

Mike finally smiled.

The woman hesitated, but having no other option, headed for

Dental School Debacle

the men's room. Mike had to witness this event. He rushed to the back of the small cinder block building, quietly stood on a garbage can, and peeked through the vent at the top of the wall. He didn't think she would do it, but there she was —an old, rich, white woman sitting backwards on the dirty urinal relieving herself. Just then her impatient husband walked up and went into the woman's restroom looking for her. When he didn't find her, he started calling her name.

"Joyce! Where the hell are you? The group behind us is about to catch up!"

Mike jumped down and walked around to the front to greet the man. "Can I help you, sir?" he asked innocently.

Mike could see the tension in the old man's face. He adjusted his glasses as he looked over Mike. "I'm looking for my wife. And who are you?"

"My name is Mike Williams, sir. I work here at the club. I'm out here replacing the toilets. Someone's in the men's room. It might be your wife."

The old man was insulted. He leaned over and looked Mike in the eyes. "I beg your pardon, young man. My wife would never go in a men's room." He was staring at Mike's rough appearance. "I can't believe the Shreveport Country Club would hire a person like you."

After a few seconds of impatiently looking for his wife around the outdoor restroom, he walked up and kicked open the men's room door, only to find his wife sitting on the urinal. Right when he was about to start chewing her out, he heard a voice yelling from a distance.

"Excuse me, Dr. Holley. Do you mind if we play through?"

Jim P. Sandras, D.D.S.

The old man turned to see two anxious golfers standing on the tee box next to his customized, purple and gold, LSU club cart.

"Go ahead," he regrettably replied while trying to control his temper. "I'm waiting for my wife."

"Thanks!" replied the out-of-shape young man as he teed up the ball. He took four practice swings, and then swung at the ball like he had a neurological disorder. He sliced it so badly it went two fairways over, into a pond. He banged his new Ping driver on the ground. His playing partner started laughing and teasing.

"Nice shot, Arnold Palmer."

The guy took a few deep breaths, wiped the mud and grass off his driver, and reached into his pocket. "I guess I'll take my mulligan." He then teed up a red striped range ball. Dr. Holley was so mad he was grinding his 28 porcelain crowns as he watched his high-class wife trying to dry herself with a wall mounted hand dryer.

"Now look what you've done, Joyce!" he yelled as she pulled up her skirt. "We'll never finish 18 holes today playing behind that group." He was still yelling as he walked back to his cart by himself. "I told you to quit taking those damn fluid pills."

The humiliated woman quickly walked out of the men's restroom and pointed at Mike. "This is all your fault, you hippie! You should've had these restrooms fixed by now!" She continued to scold Mike for several minutes before walking off to join her angry husband. Mike was totally insulted. He wanted nothing more than to punch the old couple, but he knew it would definitely cost him his job, not to mention months of legal problems. Like usual, he absorbed the criticism, thinking "I can't take much more of this".

Dental School Debacle

By 3:30 that afternoon he finally finished replacing the toilets, and was picking up his tools when his boss, Mr. Frank, pulled up in a golf cart and walked towards him. He didn't look happy.

"Where have you been, Williams?"

"I've been replacing these two toilets, just like you told me to."

"It took you all day just to change two toilets?"

"I told you, Mr. Frank, I've never done this before."

"Didn't you graduate from college?"

"Yes sir, but I majored in chemistry, not plumbing. Besides, the golfers kept interrupting me."

"What the heck are you going to do with a degree in chemistry? Check the ph of the club pool?" Mr. Frank spitefully chuckled.

"I want to be a dentist."

"Dentist? Ha! I wouldn't let you work on my dog's mouth."

"I didn't know you had a girlfriend, Mr. Frank."

"Real funny, Williams," replied the impatient man as he walked back to his golf cart. "Make sure you clean your mess. Then head to the clay courts. They need to be raked and watered down for tomorrow's tennis tournament."

Mike was stunned. "But Mr. Frank, that'll take me several hours. I'm supposed to get off at 4:00." He just ignored the pleas and drove away. Mike was furious. He threw the toolbox in the back of the John Deere work cart, making a loud crashing noise. Mike then heard someone else yell at him.

"HEY YOU, DUDE! DO YOU MIND?" Mike turned around and saw two bratty, teenage boys standing on a nearby green pointing at him. "WE'RE TRYING TO PUTT!" they yelled.

Mike finally lost it. He was tired of being treated like a peon,

Jim P. Sandras, D.D.S.

especially by someone younger than him. He hopped in the gas-powered work cart and headed straight for the two boys. At first, they didn't think Mike was serious. But after he drove up on the green and picked up the flag, the two boys took off running. Mike began chasing them while holding the flag like a medieval knight jousting. The boys quickly sprinted into the nearby woods. Mike yelled, threw the flag at the slower one, and then headed to the tennis courts. As he was riding down the cart path he was barking like a dog at every golfer, especially those about to hit a ball. When he approached the 16th hole tee box, he recognized two of his former high school classmates waiting to hit their balls. Mike hadn't seen them in years and decided to stop and say hello.

"Hey Peter! Eddie! What are you guys doing out here?" Mike asked as he approached them.

They didn't recognize him. "Do I know you?" asked Peter.

"You don't remember me? I'm Mike Williams. I graduated from high school with you." Mike got out of his work cart and walked over to shake their hands. He was glad to see his old friends, but they were acting like they were better than the lowly country club employee.

"Oh yeah, I recognize you now," said Eddie without smiling. "I see you decided to let your hair grow. You look like Greg Allman."

"Yeah, there's a long story behind that."

"How long have you been working here?" asked Peter, as if he cared.

"For three years."

"We just joined the country club," said Eddie, trying to sound

Dental School Debacle

important.

"Must be nice," replied Mike. "So, what do y'all do for a living?"

Peter stood up straight and conceitedly smiled. "I'm an attorney. I work for the law firm of Morris and Bart."

"That's awesome," replied Mike.

"I'm a chemical engineer at Monsanto," bragged Eddie.

Mike was happy for them. "That's fantastic! You guys really did well for yourselves."

"What happened to you, Mike?" Peter asked. "You used to be smart."

"I'm trying to get into dental school."

"Yeah, right," Eddie rudely replied.

"I heard you started doing drugs," said Peter.

"That's just a rumor," replied Mike. "I've never taken drugs in my life. People were saying that just because I let my hair grow long after I didn't get accepted in dental school the first time."

"First time? How many times have you tried?" asked Peter.

"Three."

"Three! What a loser," replied Eddie with a cocky smirk.

"If I were you, I'd dream of being something else," said Peter, "like maybe a hairdresser."

The two guys looked at one another and started laughing. This made Mike even angrier. If he weren't so afraid of going to jail, he would've taken a 5 iron and beat them.

"Come on, Peter," said Eddie, "the fairway's clear. Go ahead and hit. You have the honors."

Mike stepped behind their golf cart and graciously waited for them to hit their balls before taking off. He couldn't help but notice their expensive, name-brand, golf clubs. He kept thinking about how their clubs cost more than his truck, and started getting worked up. Not because of their success, but because of the way they were treating him. Suddenly he had an idea to get them back for their rudeness. While they were hitting, he quietly unhooked the two straps holding the rest of their clubs on the cart, unzipped the pockets, and slowly walked away. Both guys successfully hit their drives on the fairway, gave each other high-fives, and went back to their cart.

"That was two good shots," Mike complimented.

"Nothing to it," Eddie said.

"Well, it was nice to see you again," said Mike.

"Yeah, you too," Peter said without any emotions.

"Good luck with dental school," said Eddie, as he laughed out loud and sped off. Seconds later, both sets of their new, expensive golf bags fell onto the cart path and slid a few feet on the asphalt. When they heard the loud crashing noise, Eddie slammed on the brakes. The two guys quickly turned around to see their clubs, balls and tees scattered. Mike was just smiling and waving at the two.

"Hey guys!" yelled Mike as he drove off. "You forgot something!"

Peter jumped out of his cart and began shaking his fist and screaming at Mike. "I'll sue you for this, Williams!"

Mike was feeling a whole lot better as he drove away in the opposite direction. Finally, he came up to the 18th hole, where there were two serious looking older men on the tee box getting ready to hit their drives. Mike parked his cart behind theirs and waited for them to hit. The two men turned around and looked at

Dental School Debacle

Mike.

"Beautiful day, isn't it, sir?" asked Mike politely as he smiled. The two men turned their heads and ignored him. Mike had become accustomed to that type of treatment the past three years at the ritzy club. The first man was now ready to hit. He stood over his ball, took a fast back swing, and then hit the ball directly into a pine tree, causing it to bounce all the way back to the tee box. The angry man smashed his tee into the ground. Mike couldn't help but take advantage of the situation.

"You raised your head, sir."

The man became even more furious. "What do YOU know about golf? You with your girly hair."

Mike ignored the comment about his hair. "I know I can hit a ball better than that."

"I'd like to see you," challenged the man.

Mike got out of his cart and walked towards him. "I bet you $100 I can hit the ball down the middle of the fairway and over the pond—no practice swings."

The two men laughed. "I bet you don't have $100 to your name. Besides, that pond is 200 yards away. You'd have to hit it at least 250 yards in the air just to get it over."

"You're right," said Mike. "I don't have $100, but if I hit it in the water, I'll come to your house next Saturday and work all day."

The two men looked at one another and smiled. "You got a bet," said the man, and handed Mike his metal driver. The other man tossed him a brand-new Titleist and a tee. Mike first took a rubber band out of his pocket and put his hair in a ponytail. He spit on his hands and wiped them off on his dirty blue jeans.

Jim P. Sandras, D.D.S.

Then he pulled up some grass and tossed it in the air to determine the direction of the wind. He looked down the fairway, visualized his shot, teed up the ball and stood over it in perfect position. The two men were beginning to realize Mike knew what he was doing. He turned his head slightly to the right and stared at the ball with his left eye, just like Jack Nicklaus. He slowly started his back swing, still keeping his left eye on the ball and left arm stiff as a board. And with a nice smooth tempo he swung through perfectly like a tour pro. When Mike hit the ball, it sounded like the report of a rifle. The two men stood there with their mouths open as they watched the ball fly 20 yards past the pond. Mike walked over to the man, handed him his club, and smiled.

"I would prefer small bills," he said.

The two men shook their heads in disbelief. "You just hit that ball almost three hundred yards!"

"How 'bout that?" replied Mike, as he stuck out his hand waiting for the money. "Poor guys with girly hair can play golf, too."

The man pulled out his wallet and handed Mike $100. "Thank you very little," he said, grinning from ear to ear. Mike put the cash in his pocket and humbly walked away.

The two men just stood there in awe of Mike's ball on the other side of the pond in the center of the fairway. While they weren't looking, Mike couldn't resist unhooking the straps holding their clubs on the cart, since it worked so well the first time. He hopped in his work cart and took off, waving goodbye to his new friends. It was just a matter of minutes before he was at the clay tennis courts. As he pulled up, he noticed dozens of

Dental School Debacle

young attractive women in tennis attire standing around the courts with rackets in their hands. He got out of the cart and walked over to one of his only friends at the country club, Ryan, the tennis pro. He was sitting in the bleachers at center court, wearing his designer tennis outfit, and drinking a diet Sprite while making eyes at the nearby women.

"What's going on here, Ryan?" asked Mike, looking around at all the tennis skirts.

"Isn't this great, Mike?" he replied. "A bunch of local nurses are having a ladies tennis tournament tomorrow to raise money for charity."

"What charity?"

"I'm not sure," replied Ryan, "but I hope it's for free breast implants for all women in Louisiana." Ryan stopped talking for a few seconds so he could smile and say hello to three nurses walking by. "Most of them are here today to practice," he continued. "I can't remember the last time there were this many good-looking women around here."

Just then, Mr. Frank walked up to Mike and pulled him to the side of the building to talk to him in private.

"Williams, I was thinking about what you said earlier, you know, about being a dentist and everything. Do you really know anything about teeth?" Mike could not believe he was talking nicely to him.

"A little," replied Mike. "I haven't started dental school yet, but I do read a lot of articles and books about dentistry. And I subscribe to the *Journal of the American Dental Association*."

"Let me ask you a question, Mike. My gums are really red and swollen, and they bleed all the time. What should I do?"

Jim P. Sandras, D.D.S.

Mike realized he now had a chance to get his boss back for always treating him like dirt.

"Do your gums itch?" asked Mike professionally.

"Sometimes. Why?"

"I just read an article in last month's JADA about this condition. A year ago, the only treatment was to cut open the gums with a scalpel, then flap them back and scrape your roots and bone with a stainless-steel file and drill."

Mr. Frank was squirming at just the thought of it. "Sounds painful."

"Extremely. And very expensive." Mike had him believing every word. "But just recently a few graduate students at the University of Proctor and Gamble developed a new, less invasive treatment, and they're getting excellent results."

"Does it hurt?"

"Not at all," replied Mike. "And it's much cheaper."

"What do I need to do?"

"Brush your teeth and gums with Preparation-H three times a day."

Mr. Frank was confused. "Preparation-H? Isn't that for hemorrhoids?"

"It's not just for hemorrhoids anymore," Mike replied like a professional. "Studies show that it's useful for a lot of things, such as arthritis and mouth ulcers."

"Really?"

"Really. They always knew it relieved the swelling and itching of hemorrhoid tissue, now we know it does the same for the gums and joints."

"That's interesting."

Dental School Debacle

"I know. That's why I want to be a dentist."

"Hey, thanks a lot, Williams," said Mr. Frank as he patted Mike on the back. "I'll pick up a tube on the way home."

"Don't forget, you can also use it on your sore knees."

"I'll try it," said Mr. Frank as he walked away. "Don't forget the clay courts. They have to be finished by tonight."

"Yes sir," replied Mike. Then he walked back to the courts and sat next to Ryan.

"What did Mr. Frank want?" asked Ryan.

"He wanted some advice about his swollen gums."

"Swollen gums? You know about stuff like that?"

"No."

"What did you tell him?"

"I told him to brush with Preparation-H."

"Preparation-H? Did he believe you?"

"Every word. He'll probably be rubbing that stuff all over his body for the next few days. I can't wait to see what he smells like on Monday."

Ryan was laughing so hard he was in tears. "That's one of your better ones, Mike," he said in between laughs. "I'll have to remember to tell Mr. Frank how good his teeth look."

As the two were talking, an attractive, long-legged, middle-aged woman wearing a short tennis skirt walked up to Ryan.

"Hi, Debbie," said Ryan with a smile from ear to ear. "How's the tennis going?"

"Not too good, Ryan. My mixed doubles partner can't make it tomorrow. He has to go out of town. Will you be my partner?"

"I'd love to, Debbie, but I'm already playing with someone else. I'm sure Mike would love to play with you. He's really

Jim P. Sandras, D.D.S.

good."

Debbie glanced over at Mike and looked puzzled.

"Don't let his looks fool you," said Ryan. "He's an excellent player. He even beats me sometimes."

The lady was impressed and smiled at Mike. "He is cute."

Ryan introduced the two. "Debbie, I'd like you to meet Mike Williams. Mike, this is Debbie Mouton. She's the organizer of the tournament."

Mike stood up and graciously shook her hand. "The pleasure's all mine," he said. "I'd love to play with you, but I have to work tomorrow. Besides, I can't afford the entrance fee."

"Don't worry about the entrance fee," said Debbie. "I can have that waived."

"Can't you take off tomorrow?" asked Ryan.

"I'll ask Mr. Frank, but I doubt it. He really needs me here to keep the courts raked, and to clean up. Otherwise, he'll have to do everything himself."

"Just let me know," said Debbie. "Would you guys like to play a set now? I could sure use the practice."

"I'd love to," replied Ryan. "I'll get a partner and we'll play you and Mike in doubles."

Ryan ran off to find a partner, leaving Mike and Debbie alone.

"So, Mike. How long have you been working here?"

"Three years."

"Do you like it?"

"It's alright, but I really want to be a dentist."

Debbie raised her perfectly shaped eyebrows. "A dentist? I hate going to the dentist! I don't see how anyone could stick their hands in people's mouths all day long."

Dental School Debacle

"I know it's not as glamorous as being a nurse," Mike replied. "I mean, bathing half dead, senile people, changing bed pans and giving enemas to screaming women in labor has to be a blast. But at least I'll be making six figures a year, and I'll be my own boss."

"You made your point."

Minutes later, Ryan came walking back with a tall auburn-haired girl ready to play. "We need to go to the end courts," said Ryan. "We're getting ready to rake the center ones for tomorrow." He handed Mike a racket.

"I don't know about this, Ryan. I'm supposed to be working."

"I thought you got off at 4:00."

"I'm supposed to, but Mr. Frank told me I had to rake and water the courts before I left."

"Don't worry about Mr. Frank. I'll help you with the courts when we finish."

The four players walked to the back court and started hitting balls. The girls were more impressed with Mike than Ryan because he had on old jeans and worn-out tennis shoes, but was playing just as well. They were not expecting him to hit the ball like a pro. Mike was beginning to relax and get into his rhythm when Mr. Frank walked up.

"What are you doing out here, Williams? You're supposed to be working! If you want to keep your job, you'd better get over to the center courts and start raking, now!"

Mike was more embarrassed than mad. If he didn't need the job so badly, he would have quit right then. The worst part was being humiliated in front of the two ladies. He hung his head down like a punished dog and humbly handed Ryan his racket.

"Thanks anyway," said Mike.

Jim P. Sandras, D.D.S.

"I don't know why you put up with it, Mike. You graduated from college three years ago. You could be head greens-keeper by now, or even my boss. What's the deal?"

"I don't want to work for a country club all my life," he replied. "I want to be an actual member someday."

After two hours of hard, continuous, manual labor, Mike finished the courts and was ready to go home. He was exhausted, physically and mentally. He punched his timecard, slowly walked to the parking lot, and got in his hand-me-down Ford pickup truck. He turned the key, but nothing happened. Mike banged on the dashboard. Totally frustrated with his life, he put his head on the steering wheel and started tearing up.

"Why me?" he mumbled to himself. "I can't wait for this day to be over." He regained his composure and walked back to the club house to call his dad from the phone in the men's locker room.

"Hello, dad, the truck won't start, again. What did you say? You have some good news for me? Sure, tell me now. I could use some good news. What was in the certified letter? I WHAT? You're not joking, huh Dad? ALRIGHT! I'VE BEEN ACCEPTED INTO DENTAL SCHOOL!" Mike hung up with his dad and jumped up and down in the locker room. He ran straight to Mr. Frank's office and barged in without knocking.

"Mr. Frank, are you busy?" Mike had sparkles in his eyes.

"Yes. What do you want, Williams?"

"I won't be able to work tomorrow."

He now had Mr. Frank's full attention. "And why not?"

"I'm playing in the tournament."

Mr. Frank stood up and looked Mike in the eyes. "What kind of joke is this? I need you here tomorrow to help with the

Dental School Debacle

tournament. Who's going to rake the courts, and pick up the trash? If you're not here at 7:00 in the morning, you're fired!"

Mike had been waiting for this moment for a long time. "You can't fire me, because I quit. I just got accepted into dental school. I'm moving to New Orleans! And tomorrow, you'll be picking up trash behind ME."

Mike slammed the door and ran to the parking lot to wait for his dad.

Freshman Year

Tennis Anyone?

The alarm clock went off at 6:30 a.m. Monday morning, July 17, 1980-something. Destin instinctively hit the snooze button. He had been sleeping until lunch the past two months and was not ready to get up. The day after graduating from college he moved his "luxury" mobile home from Lafayette to a trailer park in New Orleans on Chef Menteur Highway, only 20 minutes from the dental school and five minutes from Lake Pontchartrain. Since then, he had been doing nothing except playing hard and sleeping late. His trailer looked like an airplane crashed into a sporting goods store. There were clothes, golf balls, deep sea fishing poles, water skis, tennis rackets, and empty wine bottles scattered everywhere. And it smelled like a combination of an old bar and a live bait shop. He even started dating his old high school sweetheart, Heather.

Fifteen minutes later the alarm went off again. This time he accidently turned it off. It was a new clock-radio his Aunt Mattie had just given him as a graduation gift and he was not used to

Jim P. Sandras, D.D.S.

working it yet. He rolled over and adjusted his pillow.

"I'll get up in two minutes," he mumbled to himself, and then fell back asleep. An hour later he rolled over and looked at the clock.

"Oh God!" he yelled as he jumped up. He had 15 minutes to get to class. He rushed to the medicine cabinet, brushed his teeth, washed his face, and tried to comb his hair, but he couldn't. He had just cut it shorter than it was when he started kindergarten. Destin was ready to straighten up and begin a new conservative life as a disciplined dental student. But here it was the very first day and he was running horrifically late. He put on his shoes, got in his pants, grabbed the first shirt he found, and ran out the door—all in that order. He quickly pulled out of the trailer park and found bumper to bumper traffic. He had not yet been up this early and wasn't expecting it.

"I can't believe this," said Destin in frustration while holding his brake and clutch peddles depressed. It was only the first day and he was already in trouble. "If I make it through these next four years without antipsychotic drugs it'll be a freakin' miracle."

The traffic finally started to move, but not fast enough. It took him over 20 minutes just to go one mile. Finally, he made it over the interstate high rise where he was able to speed up to 90 m.p.h. Minutes later he was pulling up to the main building of the LSU School of Dentistry. Without hesitation he pulled into a handicapped parking spot and limped out of the car, into the building, straight to the crowded elevators. He got off on the fourth floor and went to Auditorium 'A', just like the orientation letter instructed. He opened the large wooden door and rushed in. To his surprise he was standing in front of the auditorium—

Dental School Debacle

right next to the podium where the dean of the dental school was giving his annual freshman orientation speech. The packed room instantly came to a silence and all eyes were on Destin, standing there looking like he just woke up. The dean stopped talking and looked at him, glancing at his gold wristwatch, and then stared him down.

"What is your name, young man?" asked the tall, middle-aged man. His posture and crew-cut made him look like a Marine drill sergeant in a white clinic jacket.

"D-D-D-Destin, sir. D-Destin Dufrene."

"I'm so glad you decided to come to class, Mr. Dufrene."

Destin apologized. "I'm sorry I'm late, sir. I got caught in traffic."

The dean folded his arms. "Young man, it's almost 9:00. Class started at 8:00. I distinctly remember when I started Dental School. I went a week early, studied the blueprints of the buildings, and memorized the names of my professors. And the first day, I arrived at 6:00 a.m. just to make sure I wouldn't be late. You're in Dental School now, Mr. Dufrene. It's time to start acting like a professional, and that means being punctual, whatever it takes. Now have a seat and try to make a friend so they can tell you what you've missed."

"Yes sir. Thank you, sir." Destin humbly walked up the aisle looking for the first available seat. He quickly found one on the end next to a guy who had a haircut almost as bad as his. Destin nodded hello to his new classmate and sat down. The dean continued with his speech.

"As I was saying, you represent the top 1 percent of all college students. You knew what you wanted to do in life and worked

Jim P. Sandras, D.D.S.

hard to get here. Most students give up and settle for something less. If you make it through the next four years, you will be more educated than 99 percent of the people on earth. I know you thought that getting accepted into dental school was the hardest part. True, we only accepted 75 students out of the 600 qualified applicants. But for the next four years you will be working harder than you ever dreamed possible. You will eat, drink, and sleep dentistry. As of right now, most of you probably don't realize that dentistry is very hard work. It is a complex mixture of physics, biology, psychology, and art. In order to be a good dentist, not only must you master the basic sciences of chemistry, pharmacology, and pathology, but you must also be able to get along with all types of people, and at the same time earn their respect and trust. If you don't feel as if you can do this, you might as well quit now, because you'll never be successful."

"This guy's making me depressed," whispered the guy next to Destin.

"Yeah, I know what you mean," he replied quietly. "I'm about to cry."

The dean paced back and forth on the stage while he eyed each individual student.

"You're becoming professionals," continued the dean. His black shoes were so shiny that he could almost make a whole row of students squint.

"Everything you do from now on will reflect you. Patients won't trust a dentist with a high-speed drill in their mouths if they see them smashed at parties. And you should always dress appropriately, especially at the dental school. We do not allow short pants, muscle shirts, or sandals in this building, ever."

Dental School Debacle

The student next to Destin grunted. "That's all I own!"

"Out of 80 different professions," continued the dean, "dentists are ranked number three in order of respect by the public, and we intend to keep it that way."

"I wonder who's number one and two?" whispered Destin.

"That's easy," replied the guy next to him. "A golf pro, then a hockey referee."

"When we're finished here," said the dean, "you are to go to the second floor to take your ID pictures. For security reasons you are to always wear this picture when you are in this building. Anyone without theirs will be escorted out. Is that understood?"

"Yes sir!" replied several students, like they were in boot camp.

The dean neatly stacked his notes, put them in his folder and looked over the freshman class one more time.

"Again, I would like to welcome you to the LSU School of Dentistry, but more importantly, into dentistry—one of the most lucrative and satisfying professions in the world. Study hard, don't get behind in your work, and don't forget your P.M.A." The class stood up and applauded the dean as he walked off the stage. The students were extremely excited to be there. Little did they know what was in store.

Destin turned and looked at the guy next to him. "What's P.M.A.? Sounds like something my girlfriend gets every month."

"P.M.A. stands for Positive Mental Attitude," he replied. "That's all Sergeant Carter talked about before you got here. Believe me, you didn't miss a thing."

"The glare from his shoes was making my eyes water," said Destin.

"If he would've said the word "professional" one more time I

Jim P. Sandras, D.D.S.

would've gone into convulsions," said his classmate. "He made me feel like I was training to be a Jehovah's Witness."

"God forbid," replied Destin.

"Maybe this dental school thing was a bad idea," said the guy.

"Anything's better than working."

"I guess I could always teach high school science," replied the guy.

"I think that's called a job," said Destin, "and I don't want any part of it."

The guy smiled and held out his hand. "I'm Mike...Mike Williams." The two shook hands.

"I'm..."

"I know. You're Destin Dufrene. Remember, you announced it to the whole class?"

Destin smiled. "Yeah, I guess I did make a heck of a first impression."

"Ahh, don't worry about it," said Mike. "Anybody with hair like yours can't be that bad. It's sticking up in five different directions."

"I woke up late and didn't have a chance to wash it," Destin replied, and then looked at Mike's hair. "If I were you, I wouldn't talk about haircuts. What did you cut yours with, a weed eater?"

"I just had mine cut Saturday for the first time in three years."

"Three years?"

"Yeah, it was halfway down my back, and I had a goatee. I made the mistake of going to my dad's barber. He thought I was a hippy and hacked me up good. I think he used a butter knife."

"Why did you let it grow so long?"

"I told my mom I wouldn't cut it until I started dental school.

Dental School Debacle

At first, I was joking, but when I got turned down the first time, I decided to keep growing it."

"I bet you looked real professional," said Destin with a smirk.

"Yeah," replied Mike as he looked down at Destin's rumpled clothes. "Just like you do now."

They looked around and noticed they were the only ones left in the auditorium. Everyone else had gone to the second floor for ID pictures. The two rushed to the elevators. The dental school accepted students from the entire country, so very few of the freshman students knew any of their new classmates. It was like starting first grade. Mike and Destin were talking so much that they ended up being the last ones in line for their pictures.

"So, Mike, you used to work at the Shreveport Country Club?"

"For three years."

"I've played golf there," replied Destin. "It's a beautiful course, and I love those clay tennis courts. Do you play tennis?"

"Yeah, my friend Ryan and I used to play some."

Destin got excited. "I didn't think I would find anyone in our class who played tennis. Hey, what ya say we play this afternoon? The weather's beautiful."

"Sure," replied Mike. "All we're doing this afternoon is getting our supplies and locker assignments. We should be finished by 3:00."

"Great!" replied Destin. "Let's meet at the Timberlane Country Club at 4:00."

"That's the real nice place on the Westbank, isn't it?"

"I like it," replied Destin.

Mike frowned. "I can't afford to play there. After buying my books this afternoon, I'll be broke."

Jim P. Sandras, D.D.S.

"Don't worry, my brother's a member there. We can play for free, anytime."

"Cool, I'll be there."

***

The flowers were in full bloom at the exclusive club in Gretna. There were breathtakingly beautiful floral designs scattered throughout the extensive landscaping. Destin pulled up to the tennis area and sat there for a few minutes with the top down on his convertible, jamming to *Reelin' In the Years*. He was enjoying both the majestic view and having the afternoon free. He couldn't wait to beat his new friend in tennis. As he was getting out of his car, he was startled by several loud pops that sounded like a pistol. He turned around and saw Mike driving up in an old, dark yellow pick-up truck. He pulled up next to Destin. As soon as he turned off the loud engine, it backfired. Mike rolled his window down and opened the door from the outside handle.

"Your truck scared me to death," said Destin. "I thought I was in the middle of a drive-by shooting."

"It's my dad's truck. The timing chain needs to be adjusted."

Destin gave him a friendly smile. "It's nice. I bet the chicks love it."

He kicked opened the door and got out. Destin couldn't help but notice Mike's attire. He was barefoot and wearing old, faded blue jean cutoffs, a skintight, black, muscle shirt with "LED ZEPPELIN 1977 Tour" etched in red letters, and a red bandana around his head. He was holding a pair of worn-out shoes stuffed with socks in one hand, and a Jimmy Conners Aluminum T2000 racket in the other.

Destin was amused. "Where are you going? I said let's play

Dental School Debacle

tennis, not go to a rock concert."

"This happens to be what we wear where I'm from."

"Oh, I'm sorry," said Destin, "I didn't know you were from Tijuana."

Mike smiled while noticing Destin's $150 Sergio Tacchini tennis outfit. "That's real funny, Mr. Hoity Toity. I just hope you're a better tennis player than you are a comedian, 'cause if you're not, I'm going to run your butt off the court."

"We'll just have to see about that, doc."

He then reached in the back of his convertible and grabbed his custom bag with six Prince graphite rackets, two new cans of Penn balls, and an ice chest filled with Perrier bottled water. The two students strutted over to the courts like gladiators ready to fight to the death.

"We're on court number two," said Destin. "I called at lunch and reserved it." They walked to opposite sides of the court and began stretching and loosening up. Then Mike put on his worn-out shoes. Destin just knew he was going to blow this guy away. He figured there was no way a guy who dressed like that and played with an outdated, aluminum racket could be any good. Besides, tennis was Destin's favorite sport and he had been playing since he was six. He opened both cans of balls and walked over to the baseline.

"Are you ready?"

Mike was bouncing around on the tips of his toes. "Ready," he replied.

They started off right away hitting the ball as hard as they could with no warm-up shots. After 15 minutes they stopped for a breather. Both guys were impressed with the other's ability.

Jim P. Sandras, D.D.S.

They seemed to be evenly matched. Mike put down his racket and walked up to the net.

"Hey Destin, can I try one of your graphite rackets?"

"Sure," he replied. "Just don't scratch it. They're brand new."

They rallied a few more balls. Now Mike was playing even better. Destin wanted to take his racket back.

"Are you ready to play a set?" asked Destin, trying to catch his breath.

"Sure," replied Mike. "You serve first."

After a few practice serves they began playing as if it were the Wimbledon finals. Early in the match Destin was winning four games to three. Mike served a beautiful slice to Destin's back hand, and ran to the net ready to volley, but Destin hit an even better return shot down the line for a winner. In a mad rage Mike smashed Destin's racket into the net post. Hundreds of pieces of graphite flew all over the court. Mike looked up at Destin standing there with his mouth open.

"Nice shot, Destin," he said calmly. "Uhh, do you think I can borrow another one of your rackets? That graphite is sweet."

After staring at the fragments of his former racket for a few seconds, Destin spoke up. "That's a $300 racket."

"Not anymore," replied Mike. "Hey look, I'm sorry. I get carried away sometimes. When I get to be a rich and famous dentist, I'll buy you another one."

Destin looked at Mike and shook his head. "You're crazier than me. Remind me to never let you work on my teeth." Destin walked to the side of the court, took the cover off one of his new rackets and tossed it to him.

Mike was pumped up. He made a comeback and was serving

Dental School Debacle

to take the lead. He hit an easy spin serve to Destin's forehand, which he tried to kill for a winner, but instead hit it in the net. Destin was furious. He yelled so loudly they could hear him inside the club house.

"WHAT A STUPID SHOT!" Without looking, he took his racket and threw it over the fence, hitting a woman on a moped. She lost control and swerved into the pond in front of the 9th hole green. The two dental students started laughing so hard they had to sit down.

Mike tried to talk but was still laughing and had to mumble. "Did you see the splash she made?"

"Yeah," said Destin, wiping the tears from his eyes. "For a second there I thought I was at Sea World."

While they were sitting on the bench watching four good Samaritans pull the woman out of the pond, two beautiful young girls in designer tennis skirts walked onto court one and started playing.

Destin smiled at Mike. "Let me show you how to meet rich women."

The two walked back onto the court and started playing, but this time very poorly. They were more worried about impressing the girls than hitting the good shots. While they were hitting, they were talking loudly so the girls could hear them.

"Yeah Mike, dental school is going to be tough."

"That's why they only accept the top students in the country," replied Mike loudly as he adjusted his strings.

"Just think about all the money we'll be making," said Destin after hitting the ball out.

"Yeah, and we'll be our own bosses."

Jim P. Sandras, D.D.S.

The two girls could clearly hear the guys bragging but were not at all impressed. They rolled their eyes at each other and then just ignored them. Realizing they were getting nowhere, the two guys decided to continue with the serious match.

"Are you ready to finish the set?" asked Mike.

"Yes, and it's your serve."

The two briefly forgot about the girls and continued with their all-important set. They knew they would be friends for at least the next four years and this set would give the winner bragging rights. After playing several tight points, Mike was serving to win. Destin was so intense that he wasn't blinking as he bounced around the base line waiting. Just as Mike tossed the ball in the air to serve, a large dragon fly flew in Destin's face distracting him. Mike's serve blew past him for an ace.

"I WON! I WON!" shouted Mike, as he jumped up and down with the thrill of victory.

Destin didn't like to lose, but was happy he had just met a friend who played tennis.

"Good game," said Destin. As he was walking to the net to shake Mike's hand, the dragonfly flew back in his face. In a made rage, Destin swung as hard as he could at the flying insect, but his racket slipped out of his sweaty hand.

They heard a deep thud, followed by a girl screaming.

Destin turned and saw the girl on the court next to him bent over, holding her neck and grasping for air, and his graphite tennis racket was on the ground next to her. She also had one of the large insect wings stuck to the side of her face.

The girl's playing partner ran over and helped her friend catch her breath. Destin and Mike didn't know whether to help the girl

Dental School Debacle

or flee the scene.

"You stupid ass dental student!" yelled the girl's friend, kicking Destin's racket across the court. Destin walked towards the girls, but the injured one motioned for him to stay away. He could only stand there feeling like a jerk as the two girls walked to the locker room.

Mike laughed. "So, Destin, this is your technique for meeting rich girls? I'd hate to see what you do to meet poor ones!"

"I think it's time to go," he said. He ran and picked up his racket and quickly jumped into his convertible.

"Where are you going in such a hurry?" asked Mike. "I thought the loser was supposed to buy dinner."

Destin started his car and put it in reverse. "Meet me at the Tavern by the school."

Mike squinted. "That hole in the wall? What do they serve, roach subways?"

"Their po boys are awesome," said Destin as he shifted into first gear. "I'll meet you there."

***

The Tavern was an old turn-of-the-century, French-style home across the street from City Park. Years ago, it had been gutted and turned into a restaurant/pool hall/bar. It was dark and smoky inside, but always crowded. It had become a popular hangout for both the dental and medical students since it was so close to school. When Destin and Mike walked in, there were no tables available, so they sat at the end of the bar and ordered oyster po-boys and beers. The new friends began talking about everything from ex-girlfriends to politics, to the antichrist, to Fred Couples, but mostly about John McEnroe, whom they both

Jim P. Sandras, D.D.S.

agreed was their favorite tennis player of all time.

Mike took a sip of his cold beer. "I'll tell you, Destin, I've only been in New Orleans for two weeks, but I love it here."

"There's no place like it," replied Destin. "Except for maybe Rio de Janeiro."

"The food is amazing. Everyone is so friendly. Plus, you can go to any corner gas station on a Sunday morning and buy a fifth of rum. And I keep seeing these drive-through daiquiri places everywhere. What a concept!"

"That was the archbishop's idea," said Destin. "Wait til you go to a Saints game, Mike. My brother, Benedict, has six season tickets, but he never goes. I'll take you. Everyone at the game gets so drunk they have to read the Times Picayune the next morning to see how bad they lost."

"So, Destin, I'm curious about something. If your family has so much money, why are you going to dental school?"

"My daddy would put me to work if I wasn't in school," he replied.

"God forbid," replied Mike sarcastically.

"They wake up way too early for me. I can't handle getting up before dark. There should be a law against it. Besides, ever since I was in the sixth grade, I wanted to be a dentist. I want to do something for myself, not ride on my dad's coat tails. But most importantly, if you're in college you can get away with being irresponsible. That's what I enjoy the most."

As they were talking, a scary looking guy with a lip full of Copenhagen walked out of the kitchen with their po-boys, placed them on the bar, and then pointed at Destin.

"I know you," he said. "You're Destin Dufrene."

Dental School Debacle

Destin was worried. "You're not an Orleans cop, are you?"

'No, I'm in dental school, in your class," he laughed. "You introduced yourself to the entire class this morning, remember?" He stuck his hand out and introduced himself. "My name is Bobby, Bobby Clinton."

Bobby looked more like an Italian hit man than a dental student. He was well built, although slightly overweight; with thick, black, curly hair. And he talked loud and rough, like most people who grew up in New Orleans. The first thing anyone noticed about Bobby was his blue eyes and white teeth. They were so white and perfect they almost looked fake, even with a mouth full of smokeless tobacco, and he didn't hesitate to flash them at every girl who walked by.

Destin shook his hand. "Clinton? Any relation to the governor of Arkansas, Bill Clinton?"

"He's my uncle," replied Bobby, without hesitating. "I'm trying to talk him into running for President."

"Good luck with that," answered Destin. Then he turned to his new friend. "Bobby, this is Mike Williams. He's a dental student, also."

Mike shook his hand. "Nice to meet you, Bobby. So, how long have you been working here?"

"Almost four years," he replied. "I was born and raised here in Nawlins, well, really the 9th Ward. My cousin owns this dump, but don't tell anyone. He lets me hang out here whenever I need money, which is most of the time. It's a cool part-time job. I eat and drink for free, get to meet a lot of girls, and all I have to do is help in the kitchen, and break up fights." He then reached under the counter and grabbed his half full plastic cup and proceeded to

Jim P. Sandras, D.D.S.

spit into it. Then he wiped his lips and continued the conversation.

As Bobby was talking, he heard someone banging on the jukebox. He started yelling at the guy from across the noisy room, but he didn't hear him. Bobby reached behind the bar, grabbed a lemon, and threw it, hitting the guy in the back and getting his attention.

"HEY DUDE!" Bobby yelled, "HIT THAT THING ONE MORE TIME AND I'LL COME OVER THERE AND BEAT THE CRAP OUT OF YOU!" Bobby grabbed a bat from behind the bar and quickly walked over to the jukebox to convince the guy to behave.

Destin looked at Mike perplexed. "This guy's a dental student?"

Bobby finally got the situation under control. He came back, sat down at the bar, spit into his cup again and smiled at Destin and Mike.

"So, you guys want to be dentists?" asked Bobby, making conversation. The whole time he was sitting there he was constantly smiling and talking to other people walking by.

"Well, really, I want to be an orthodontist," said Mike.

"I might go into oral surgery," replied Destin.

Bobby motioned to the bartender to bring three beers. "My goal is to discover a whole new field of dentistry," he said. Then he stood still and stared seriously at the two. "I want to be the first ever Gynodontist."

They weren't expecting an answer like that.

"Gynodontist?" asked Destin. "What the heck is that?"

Bobby gave them a big white smile. "It's a dentist who only

works on females. No men. No exceptions. Period. It's a good idea, don't you think?"

Destin and Mike didn't know if Bobby was serious, or not, so they both just nodded.

"Hey, you know tomorrow we're starting Gross Anatomy," continued Bobby, "and they're putting us in groups of four to dissect the cadavers. What ya' say, y'all want to be partners? It'll be fun. Just think, we might get a woman."

Neither Destin nor Mike knew what to make of Bobby. But for the sake of not being rude, they agreed to be his partners. They had no idea what they were getting into.

Happy Birthday Benedict

The next morning Destin woke up at 6:00 and jumped out of bed. He made sure he wasn't late today. He met Mike and Bobby outside the auditorium, and then quietly walked in and sat together in the second to last row. All the students seemed so serious this morning. They were starting Gross Anatomy, the class that freshmen feared the most. Not because of the amount of material they had to learn, or the dead bodies they would be working on for six months, but because of the professor who taught it: Dr. Hicoff. The students had heard nothing but horror stories about her from the upper classmen. Hicoff trained in East Germany where her father was a Gestapo commander in World War II. She was from the old school—do everything the longest and hardest way possible. There was only one way to do things in this class, and that was her way. She enjoyed cramming copious amounts of material down students' throats to the point where they were regurgitating Latin anatomical terms. Ninety percent of students who failed out of

Jim P. Sandras, D.D.S.

dental school did so because of her. Every student was in the auditorium early, nervously waiting for class to begin. At exactly 8:00 Dr. Hicoff walked in, followed by three male professors wearing long, white clinic jackets. She was carrying four large textbooks under her right arm, and a mug of steaming coffee in her left hand. The class was staring at the woman, trying to figure her out. She looked like a large, muscular land amphibian, and wore her gray hair pulled back over her large ears into a tightly knitted bun on the apex of her head. Cosmetics were obviously not on her shopping list. If it wouldn't have been for her large breasts and her hair bun, she could have passed for a man. She walked up to the podium, put her books and coffee down, snapped the microphone to her collar, and examined the class.

"Before we get started, I'd like to welcome you to dental school, and to Gross Anatomy, the science of the human body. By the end of this course, you will know every bone, muscle, nerve and blood vessel from head to toe: that's if you pass." Hicoff smiled sadistically at the other three professors, who responded in the same manner.

"My name is Dr. Hicoff. I am the course director and will be lecturing to you on the development and anatomy of the human body." She was talking so loudly that the screws holding the speakers to the wall were vibrating. She had all the students squinting or covering their ears. Bobby looked around and noticed that some had rolled-up pieces of paper stuck in their ears. He couldn't take it anymore.

Bobby raised his hand and interrupted her. "Uh, excuse me, Dr. Hicoff," shocking the students and the professors. Hicoff stopped talking, folded her arms and looked Bobby in the eyes.

Dental School Debacle

She was rarely interrupted by a student, and never 10 minutes into the first class.

"Yes, what can I do for you?" she asked.

"Do you really think you need that microphone?" Bobby replied. Everyone thought Bobby was really bold, really dumb, or both. "You're about to blow out either the woofers or our ear drums, whichever goes first."

Hicoff was stunned. "What is your name?" she asked abruptly.

"Bobby, Bobby Kennedy."

Hicoff smiled. "Any relation to 'The Kennedy's'?" she asked.

"Distant relatives," he replied.

Destin and Mike were confused. They looked at one another and simultaneously shrugged their shoulders. They were both wondering what type of crazy, lying, schizophrenic freak they had just met, and was now their lab partner.

Hicoff looked at the students. "Am I too loud?"

The entire class reluctantly nodded their heads. Hicoff unhooked her microphone and continued lecturing, but was still loud enough to be heard outside the auditorium. Both the assistant professors and the students couldn't believe what had just transpired. In just one morning a freshman student had tamed Dr. Hicoff. There was something about Bobby's blue eyes and white teeth that had this effect on people.

Destin elbowed Bobby in the side. "You told us your last name was Clinton."

Mike leaned over and looked at Bobby. "You don't have a girlfriend named Sybil, do you?"

"Shhhh," replied Bobby with his index finger over his lips. "I'll explain later."

Jim P. Sandras, D.D.S.

Destin was still making a confused face at Bobby as Dr. Hicoff continued lecturing. "This afternoon you will be assigned into groups of four for each cadaver," she said while pacing back and forth on the stage. "Each cadaver is in its own tank submerged in a liquid mixture of formaldehyde, gluteraldehyde and several preserving chemicals. We in the department call it Dead Juice."

She looked at the other professors and winked, then stopped pacing and put her hands on her hips. "You are to treat these cadavers with the utmost respect. There is to be no unnecessary cutting, mutilating or playing with the bodies. And absolutely no cameras or video recorders are allowed in the anatomy lab, ever. I know everybody wants to take pictures with their cadaver to show their family and friends. But remember, these bodies are someone's relatives. Treat them like they were your own grandparents. Also, I shouldn't have to say this, but unfortunately it happens every year. There are to be no body parts, organs or glands taken from the lab. This is a federal offense and will result in immediate expulsion. I will randomly assign you to the groups, unless you know someone. If you do, write your name on a piece of paper along with the students you'd like to work with and hand it to me after class."

Dr. Hicoff paused, finished her coffee, and then picked up her notes and began lecturing. "Today we will begin by studying the chest and pectoral muscles. In the lab this afternoon we will perform the dissections." She continued lecturing about the human chest all the way through lunch without a break. The students had cramps in their fingers from trying to keep up with Dr. Hicoff. She closed her notebook. "Are there any questions?" No one dared say a word.

Dental School Debacle

"Then I'll see you this afternoon on the ninth floor."

Destin ripped a page out of his notebook and wrote down his name, Mike Williams, Bobby Kennedy and a blank, and turned it in to Hicoff. As soon as he walked out of the auditorium, he and Mike cornered Bobby.

"What's your problem, dude?" asked Mike. "Why did you lie to us?"

"Yeah," said Destin, "you don't lie to friends; you lie to girls."

Bobby wasn't the least bit embarrassed. "Lying about my last name is a habit." Bobby stopped and looked around to make sure no one was listening. Then he lowered his voice. "You see, my real name is Bobby Pubix, like crotch hair."

"Pubix!" replied Mike loudly.

"Keep your voice down," said Bobby. "Ever since I was in grammar school, I've been making up last names. At first it was to keep from being picked on, but now it's an adventure. I like to see how long I can get away with it. I've ordered eight name tags to wear around school, all with different last names."

Destin could not believe what he was hearing. "Are you sure you're a student here?"

Bobby smiled with his white teeth. "I scored second highest in the history of the school on the admission exam."

Mike shook his head in disbelief. "Where do you think you are, dude? This is the LSU dental school, not a bar. Hicoff is going to kill you when she finds out you lied to her in front of the class."

"I'll cross that bridge when I get to it," he said. "The element of uncertainty is what I enjoy."

"This I have to see," replied Destin. "I've been around some crazy people before, Bobby, but you top them all."

Jim P. Sandras, D.D.S.

"Thank you," he said. "Now that we have that out of the way, let's grab lunch."

The three went down to the snack bar on the first floor, bought cold sandwiches out of a machine, and sat down and talked for an hour. Mike and Destin were extremely concerned about their association with Bobby at first, but the more they talked to him the more they realized he was fairly normal, and very intelligent. He graduated with a 4.0 GPA from The University of New Orleans, which had a reputation of being a very tough school. Bobby was just your typical crazy New Orleans boy who loved to have fun and enjoyed lying, especially about his name.

"So, who do you think our fourth lab partner will be?" asked Destin.

"I don't care," replied Mike, "just as long as it's not that plump, red haired girl."

"Her name is Kate," said Bobby. "I met her yesterday."

"Can you imagine going to a dentist office with a toothache and have her walk in?" asked Destin.

"If I was in the woods hunting and saw her walk out, I might shoot it," replied Mike. "Don't look now, Destin, but she's staring at you."

Destin turned and saw the overweight student two tables down eating a bologna sandwich. She stopped chewing when she noticed Destin looking at her, and then swallowed a large bolus of food, wiped the mayonnaise off her lips, and smiled at him.

"I just lost my appetite," said Destin as he pushed his food away.

"Let's call her Trog," said Bobby.

Dental School Debacle

"Trog? What are you talking about?" asked Mike.

"That's short for tree-frog," replied Bobby. "That's what she reminds me of."

They agreed. "Trog it is." Destin looked at her and smiled back. "This is going to be fun," he said without moving his lips.

"What kind of people end up as cadavers?" asked Mike.

"Probably old winos they find dead on Bourbon Street," replied Destin.

"I just hope we don't get a fat person," said Bobby. "I sure don't feel like digging through years of gumbo and bread pudding just to find a muscle."

Mike tensed his face. "I think I'm getting sick."

The three threw their trash away and then went up to the ninth floor. As soon as they got off the elevators, they could smell the stench from the anatomy lab. There were already several students gathered around the door reading the list of lab partners. Mike walked over and looked for his group.

"Who's our partner?" asked Destin.

"Sherry Custard, whoever that is?" he replied.

"I bet that's the girl who always sits in the first row with the thick glasses," said Destin. "She's kinda cute."

"That's her," replied Bobby. "I tried to introduce myself to her this morning, but she wouldn't put her notes down long enough to talk. Very rude. Definitely a Gunner."

"What's a Gunner?" asked Mike.

Bobby got serious. "Gunners are students that only care about THEIR grades and would chew the ears off another student if that's what it took to make a better grade. Sherry seems like the type of person who would walk barefoot through glass for an

Jim P. Sandras, D.D.S.

'A'."

"I guess we'll find out, because here she comes," said Destin. Sherry was neatly dressed in a skirt, and carried several notebooks in one hand and an extra-large purse in the other. She was thin and walked and talked like she was in a hurry.

Mike introduced himself. "You must be Sherry Custard. I'm Mike Williams."

She forced a smile. "Hi," she said, and then looked at Bobby. "I thought you told me your last name was Onassis. Didn't you tell Dr. Hicoff you were a Kennedy?"

Bobby smiled. "Onassis is my middle name," he explained. "My mother gave it to me to keep the Greek tradition."

Sherry was confused but seemed to believe him. Seconds later Hicoff, followed by the three professors, walked into the lab.

"We better get in," said Mike. "The list said we're at tank 18." Everyone walked in and gathered around the stainless-steel tanks. They looked just like a raised coffin, except they had two overlapping doors instead of one. And on the ends were two large levers hooked to cables under the tank which were used to raise the bodies.

"Carefully open the tanks," said Hicoff. She was casually walking around the foul-smelling lab sipping coffee out of her large liter sized cup. "Then push down on the levers, lock them in the 'up' position, and remove the sheets from the cadavers."

There was an atmosphere of both anticipation and fear in the lab. The students were anxious to see what type of person was lying dead in their tank, but at the same time were not sure if they could handle it. One by one you could hear the metal tops opening. The smell was becoming so strong that everyone's eyes

Dental School Debacle

were burning, except for Hicoff who was standing in the middle of the room inhaling and enjoying the moment. Sherry was the only student prepared for the situation. She put on a surgical mask, chain-saw goggles, and rubber gloves, took out a jar of Vaseline, and rubbed it all over her arms.

"Would you like me to get your back?" joked Bobby.

"No thank you," she replied. "I'm only putting it on the parts that might touch the cadaver."

Destin's curiosity was getting the best of him. "Why? You plan on giving it a massage?"

"It prevents the embalming fluid from penetrating my epidermis, so I won't stink all night."

Mike smiled. "My type of woman."

Bobby and Destin walked to opposite ends of the tank and began pushing down the levers. They were both surprised by how much force it took to raise the cadaver. Finally, after a small struggle, the body was raised. They locked the levers and stood there staring at this wet, stained, white sheet covering a dead human laying there ready to be exposed. All they could hear was the Dead Juice dripping to the bottom of the tank. The nauseating stench was really getting to them now.

Mike broke the silence. "Alright, who wants the honor of uncovering our new friend?"

"I'll do it," said Destin. "I like this kind of stuff." He was joking around and acting like a magician as he grabbed the corners of the sheet and with a quick tug, pulled it off. Destin didn't realize the sheet had been soaking in Dead Juice for two weeks. The embalming fluid splashed the students at the nearby tanks. They jumped back in shock, now in wet, stinky clothes,

Jim P. Sandras, D.D.S.

and made evil faces at Destin.

"That was brilliant, dude!"

"How did YOU get into dental school?"

"You idiot!"

"You must be on drugs!"

Destin just smiled and made apologetic jesters. "It was an accident," he said.

"You'll be getting my cleaning bill," said one girl.

Mike looked at Destin and giggled. "Man, you really know how to make friends."

Bobby wasn't paying attention to anything that was going on. His full attention was on the cadaver. "I don't believe it," he said. "It's a woman, and look at those flabby breasts. They hang to her navel. Look, she even has a flower tattoo on the right one."

Destin turned his attention to the cadaver. There laid a dark-haired, middle-aged woman, completely naked, with her eyes open. Her wet skin had a grim, shark-colored grey tint with no color contrast throughout her whole body, except for the flower tattoo. She looked more like a block of Spam than a human. There were no visible signs of trauma, only a large hysterectomy scar. They stood there wondering what kind of person she was and how she died.

"She probably O.D.'d at a Grateful Dead concert," said Destin.

"Let's call her Rose," said Bobby. He then grabbed her breasts and slapped them together, making sounds like a large seal applauding with its fins.

Sherry was appalled. She dropped her textbook and backed away from the tank. "You pervert!" she yelled, while pointing at Bobby. "You sinner! You abused her!" She took off in a rage and

Dental School Debacle

ran toward Hicoff.

"Why did you do that, Bobby?" asked Mike in disbelief.

"It's a habit."

"You're sick," said Destin shaking his head. "I can't believe you did something like that in front of Sherry."

"I didn't think she'd get that upset."

"Don't look now," said Destin. "Here comes Hicoff, and she doesn't look too happy."

"What are you going to tell her?" asked Mike.

"I'll think of something," replied Bobby nonchalantly. "I always do."

Destin shook his head. "Bobby, you should've gone to law school."

Hicoff walked up to the tank, followed closely by Sherry, put her hands on her hips, and looked at Bobby. "Mr. Kennedy," she said sternly. "Miss Custard says that you grossly abused the cadaver, already, and we haven't been in lab five minutes! Dental students are supposed to be professional." Hicoff's loud voice easily carried throughout the lab. The noisy room came to a silence.

Bobby smiled at Hicoff. "No ma'am," he said. "I did no such thing. This female cadaver obviously falls into the highest category for breast cancer. I was just checking for lumps. We're getting ready to dissect through her breast to find the pectoral muscles, and I want to know what I'm getting into."

Destin and Mike could not believe that Hicoff was buying his lie. She angrily turned and looked at Sherry.

"You better not be lying to me young lady," said Hicoff, "because if there is one thing I detest…it's a liar."

Jim P. Sandras, D.D.S.

Sherry started crying, and for the first time Bobby was getting nervous about lying. His countenance changed.

Hicoff looked at Destin's name tag. "What did you see, Mr. Dufrene?"

"I didn't see anything," he replied. "I was too busy admiring your hair."

Hicoff ignored Destin and looked at Mike. "Did you see what happened?"

"No ma'am," he replied politely. "She blinded me with science."

Hicoff squinted. "I don't know what's going on here," she said. "But I don't like it, and I will get to the bottom of this. I have way too much work to do to mess around with child's play like this. I'm arranging a meeting for you two to see the dean tomorrow. He gets paid to handle crap like this." Bobby's and Sherry's hearts both dropped. "In the meantime, I'm swapping Miss Custard with someone else. It's obvious this group is mismatched."

Hicoff looked at Sherry. "Grab your books and follow me." Hicoff looked over at Bobby and paused. "I have a strange feeling about you, Kennedy," she said, and then walked away with Sherry following.

"What are you going to do now, Bobby?" asked Mike.

"I'm not scared of Hicoff," he said. "She looks too much like Rodney Dangerfield to be taken seriously."

Destin shook his head. "Bobby, you must have some huge testicles."

"But what are you going to tell the dean?" asked Mike.

"I'll just do what I do best," said Bobby, "lie."

Dental School Debacle

"Oh no," said Destin. "Here comes our new partner."

"It's that redneck dude who looks like Opie Taylor," said Mike. "I guess we get a red head after all."

This tall, skinny, country boy with short red hair walked up to their tank and introduced himself without smiling.

"I'm Sam Adams," he said with his emotionless freckled face. He had a very strong country-twang accent. "Dr. Hicoff assigned me to this tank. She said she made a mistake."

"Yeah," said Bobby, "she used to be a man."

Mike and Destin started laughing, but Sam didn't even crack a smile. He stood there looking at the three students like they were kids. "Are you ready to start dissecting?" asked Sam in a monotone voice. "We have a lot of work to do."

"Yeah, we sure do," said Destin. "We have to remove this woman's boobs, which could be messy. But at least I finally get to see what's inside them suckers." Sam didn't find Destin too amusing. He ignored the comment and started dissecting while the other three watched. This guy was way too serious for them.

Mike watched Sam initiate the dissection. They were still apprehensive about touching a dead person. As they cut through the skin, they were surprised there was no blood: only the dreaded Dead Juice oozing out of the tissue. "I can see this class is going to be more fun than humans should be allowed to have."

The other three finally got serious and finished their work by 5:00, along with most of the class. When Destin finished, he went to the library and waited for everyone to leave the Gross Anatomy lab. Today was his brother Benedict's birthday, and he had been so busy that he forgot to buy him something, although he did have a great idea for a gift. Destin's brother was a few years older, married with two children, and lived on the Westbank of New Orleans where he managed a branch of the family business. As soon as Destin was sure that everyone was gone, he went back up to the lab and stopped at the closest tank by the door. He took out his surgical blade and meticulously removed the scalp from the cadaver and put it in his gym bag. When he got in his car, he put the smelly object in a shoe box and went to the nearest K&B Drug Store to buy gift wrapping paper. When he arrived at his brother's house in Timberlane Country Club in Gretna, the party was in full swing. There were hundreds of balloons and "Happy Birthday" signs all over the large, white Acadian style home. Destin walked in and noticed that everyone was formally dressed, unlike him. He made his way into the crowded living room where he found his snobby, big-mouth, out-of-shape sister-in-law. They didn't get along too well. Destin nicknamed her 'Baby Fat', and she hated it.

"Destin, I'm so glad you could make it," she said from across the room, trying to be nice in front of her high-class friends. She walked over and gave Destin a fake hug. Immediately her eyes crossed. She pushed Destin away and grabbed her nose.

"My God, Destin! You stink! What have you been doing? You didn't kill another cow, did you? Your brother told me all about it." She started shaking her head and pointing her finger at him like a child. "I cannot believe you killed a cow with a hammer! And you want to be a dentist! I would never send my kids to you."

She always knew how to aggravate Destin. He looked around the room at all her uppity friends dressed in their expensive formal wear, and then looked back at Baby Fat sipping her

Dental School Debacle

champagne. He began talking as loud as he could so that everyone in the large living room could hear him.

"NO, I DIDN'T SACRIFICE ANY HUMANS TODAY!" The room instantly became silent. They all turned and looked at Destin in his old, soiled clothes. "I'VE BEEN HACKING ON A WOMAN'S BREAST ALL AFTERNOON. BUT DON'T WORRY, SHE WAS DEAD ALREADY. I CAME STRAIGHT HERE AFTER I REACHED HER HEART. I DIDN'T WANT TO MISS A THING!"

The guests were petrified. They assumed Destin was a devil worshipper and began leaving the room to warn the others. His sister-in-law grabbed him by the arm and pulled him aside. "Benedict is in the den," she said. "Why don't you go back there. He's about to open his gifts."

"Here, I have one for him," he said, and handed her the package. But she pushed it away.

"Don't touch me with that thing," she said. "There's no telling what's in it. I know how you are, Destin. I still can't believe you gave my daughter a dead nutria wrapped in a doll box for Christmas. She still has nightmares about it."

"It wasn't dead when I put it in there," he said. "Besides, I was young and foolish then."

"That was last year!"

"Wow, time really flies when you're on drugs."

She got behind Destin and started pushing him towards the den. "Why don't you give it to Benedict yourself. He'd appreciate it more. And please, Destin, walk far around the guests. We wouldn't want to gross out our friends with your body odor, would we?"

Jim P. Sandras, D.D.S.

"No, we wouldn't, BABY FAT. By the way, I like your parachute pants. How many did it take to cover your butt, two or three?" Destin walked away leaving his sister-in-law speechless. He entered the den where his brother was opening gifts with all his upper-class friends. Destin and Benedict were very close and used to do a lot of things together and play practical jokes on one another, until he married Baby Fat. She claimed that Destin was a bad influence on him. Benedict was very proud of his younger brother, especially now that he was in dental school. When he saw Destin walk in the room, Benedict was so excited that he didn't notice everyone making faces at him and talking about how bad he smelled. He ran over and embraced his little brother. Seconds later he jumped back.

"Man, Destin! You smell like a morgue," he said while fanning his nose with his hand.

"Good guess, Benedict. You're exactly right." Destin went on to explain to everyone why he smelled like toxic meat. After a few minutes of talking about dental school, Destin handed Benedict his gift.

"I hope you like it."

Benedict eagerly reached for his gift. Destin always gave him something funny. He removed the K&B purple wrapping, opened the shoe box, paused, and then made a puzzled face as he held up the unknown wet object.

"What is it?"

"It's a human scalp," he replied proudly. "I got it just for you. But don't tell anyone. The federal government frowns on this."

Benedict turned green, threw the scalp on the floor, and ran outside for fresh air—along with the other guests. They were all

Dental School Debacle

bent over gagging, and those with the weaker stomachs were throwing up their bite size party snacks they had just ingested. Destin grabbed a glass of champagne, walked out on the porch, and watched his brother and his rich friends barfing on their tuxedos. He raised his glass and toasted his brother.

"Happy birthday, Benedict."

He looked over at Destin from the corner of his eye and grunted. Destin knew that grunt all too well. He put his glass down and quickly rushed out the front door.

A Gross Night at the Hyatt

It was 8:55 the next morning. Bobby and Sherry had been silently waiting outside the dean's office since 8:30, not saying a word to each other. Bobby admitted to Destin earlier that he was a little nervous. He was dressed in a suit and tie for the occasion. On the other hand, Sherry was so nervous she was catatonic. She had already chewed her fingernails to the skin and was now working on the cuticles. Bobby could tell she wasn't accustomed to situations like this and wished she would have simply turned her head instead of crying to Hicoff. The only thing keeping Bobby calm was the ingenious ploy he devised the night before that he was certain would get him out of this mess. At 9:00 the door opened. Hicoff walked out and looked at the two students.

"You can come in now," she said, without moving her teeth.

As Bobby walked past Hicoff he gave her one of his famous smiles, but she only grunted. "Good luck, Mr. Pubix," she said. "I told you I detest liars. If I have my way, you'll be selling Lucky

Jim P. Sandras, D.D.S.

Dogs on Bourbon Street the rest of your life."

Bobby felt a cold flash shoot through his body. His knees were shaking as he walked into the dean's office. It was a huge, well-organized office with cherry and oak cabinetry, Early American furniture, and a brass wet bar in the corner. The desk was pushed all the way to the back of the room against a large window that overlooked the picturesque campus and had an unobstructed view of downtown New Orleans. The dean was sitting in his leather chair looking out the window with his back to them.

"Have a seat," he said. Bobby and Sherry anxiously sat in the two small chairs in front of his desk. The dean turned around and stared down the two students.

"Dr. Hicoff and I have been discussing this matter all morning, and I must say this is a first. I've been the dean here for seven years, and this is the first time I've had to meet with freshman students for discipline reasons, and it's only the third day! You're supposed to be too busy for shenanigans like this." The dean leaned forward and looked Bobby in the eyes.

"Mr. Pubix, Miss Custard alleges that you abused your cadaver yesterday afternoon. Dr. Hicoff and I spent half the morning looking through our records for a Bobby Kennedy and couldn't find one. Finally, we went through the admissions records and found your picture, Bobby Pubix." The dean leaned back in his chair and folded his arms. "You are an embarrassment to this institution. What do you have to say for yourself, son?"

Bobby gave the dean the most innocent looking, puppy dog face he could. "It's not what you think, sir," replied Bobby with a very sincere voice. "First of all, sir, I'm a very strict, practicing Catholic. I've attended Catholic schools all my life and very

Dental School Debacle

strongly support the faith." (Bobby got the idea for this story yesterday afternoon when he saw the dean ride by in his Cadillac, with a pair of rosary beads hanging from the rear-view mirror and a Knights of Columbus sticker on the bumper.) "I've been wearing ties since I was six and say the rosary every night." The dean was impressed and smiled for the first time. "My parents taught me to have respect for the dead, sir. In fact, we prepare months ahead for All Saints Day. It's almost like Christmas around our house. To me, assaulting a dead person would be like shooting the Easter Bunny." By this time, he even had Sherry believing him. "And as far as my last name, sir, my godfather used to call me Bobby Kennedy when I was a boy. He said I looked like him. Ever since then my family and friends called me that as a nickname. It's special to me, sir, especially since he was such a fine Catholic man." Bobby leaned forward and whispered to the dean. "Sir, wouldn't you use a nickname if your last name meant crotch hair?"

The dean smiled at Bobby and nodded his head. "You should change it," he replied.

Bobby was finally able to relax and leaned back in his chair. "I'm working on it now, sir," he replied. "I've already applied for a student loan for the legal fees."

"So, tell me, son, where do you attend mass?" asked the dean.

Bobby was not prepared for this. It had been years since he had been to church and couldn't remember the name of any off hand. But being the liar he was, he had no problem coming up with something. "I attend mass at Our Lady of Perpetual Poverty."

The dean curled his eyebrows. "Perpetual Poverty? Never

Jim P. Sandras, D.D.S.

heard of it."

"It's a small church in the lower 9th Ward," replied Bobby. "It keeps me humble."

"You're a good man, Mr. Pubix," said the dean. He had already concluded that Bobby was innocent. He then switched his attention to Sherry, who was quietly sitting there staring blankly.

"So, what do you have to say for yourself, young lady?"

"Uh, excuse me, dean," interrupted Bobby. "I believe I can explain why Miss Custard thought she saw what she did." Bobby stood up and walked over to the desk. Sherry didn't know what to think or say. She just sat there in awe. Bobby turned and looked at her and shook his head.

"I hate to do this to you, Sherry, but the entire class wants what's best for you." Bobby reached into his pocket, pulled out a hand full of blue and clear capsules, and tossed them on the dean's desk. "This fell out of her purse yesterday in the locker room." Sherry was too stunned to speak. She couldn't believe someone would make up a lie like this. Bobby focused on the dean. "I didn't know what kind of pills they were," he continued, "so, I went to the library and looked them up in the P.D.R. It's phenylpropanolamine, otherwise known as "speed". We believe she's hooked on them, sir. That explains her visual disturbances and euphoric actions. Sir, you ought to see her run around this building."

The dean was admiring Bobby's beautiful white teeth as he listened to him talk. "Is this true, Miss Custard?"

Sherry stood up and forced out some words. "No sir," she replied. "I've never seen those pills before in my life." She was so upset she began shaking.

Dental School Debacle

"Sir," interrupted Bobby, "look at her shaking. That's one of the side effects I read about. She's probably on mega doses right now."

"That's not true!" shouted Sherry.

The dean stood. "I've already come to a decision on this matter. Miss Custard, you will be put on disciplinary probation for a year and will undergo random urinalysis. Any more trouble from you and you're gone. Now, you two go to class and I don't want to see you again until next year at Sophomore orientation." The dean smiled at Bobby and shook his hand.

"Don't worry, sir," said Bobby, "I'll keep an eye on her. I know she would do the same for me."

"This world needs more people like you, Bobby," replied the dean. "I might see you one Sunday at Perpetual Poverty. I'm anxious to see what it's like."

Bobby swallowed. "Thank you, sir," he said as he followed Sherry out of the room. As soon as the door closed, Sherry grabbed Bobby by the arm and looked him dead in the eyes. She was so mad she was squinting. "How can you lie like that?"

"Practice," he replied, and pulled his arm away. "I've only known you for three days, Sherry, and I can tell already you don't care about anybody except yourself. Most of the class can't stand you." She made an ugly face, stuck out her tongue like a child and walked away.

"This is going to be a fun four years," he thought.

The two walked into histology class, which was already in progress, and sat down as if nothing happened. The entire class knew what was going on and focused in on Bobby waiting for some type of response. He looked around and then gave a

Jim P. Sandras, D.D.S.

thumbs up. This put everyone at ease. Already everyone had taken a liking to Bobby, even though he lied all the time. There was just something about him that made him loveable. On the other hand, Sherry was getting a reputation for being rude and academically egocentric.

***

The next few months were relatively uneventful—just tons of homework on the basic sciences. However, they were finally starting to learn some things about teeth. They were learning the difference between and upper and lower molars, the embryonic development of a tooth, how to take an impression, how to get impression material out of their hair and clothes, how to carve objects that looked like teeth out of blocks of wax, how to get brain damage by inhaling liquid resin and mercury vapors, how to take criticism, and how to use an over-priced, confusing contraption called an articulator. And the weirdest of all was some strange concept called centric relation, which the instructors said was three dimensional, relative to space and time, the gravitational pull of the earth, the frame of mind of the practitioner and the degree of viscosity of the synovial fluid in the meniscus capsule. They were also getting used to hearing a lot of new words that could only be heard around a dental school, or maybe a prison. Words like line angles, malocclusion, carious lesion, cusp of Carabelli, saliva queen, open-face burrito, plaque index, protein transfer, sticky wax, gingiva, deep probing, deep scaling, palatal bruise, tartar baby, inlay, onlay, shelay, transverse ridge, oblique grove, high velocity suction, saliva ejector, Wall's carver, curve of Spee, Joe Dandy disc, Lucy bend over, powder/water ratio, amalgam plug, enamel pearl, remediate,

Dental School Debacle

lubricate, palpate, gum massage, soft reline, lip cream, vibrator speed, tongue thrust, hum job, slick 'em, yank 'em, prime it, calculus bridge, face bow, cheek spreader, finger diddle, puss pocket, TMJ, MOD, PCP, M-Q lube, rear delivery, overhead mount, and hundreds of other dental terms they were now using and understanding. But still they couldn't figure out what all of this had to do with filling and pulling teeth. They had so much more to learn.

***

It was two weeks before Christmas, but more importantly, it was the night before the Gross Anatomy final. The first semester was only one day from being over, and then they would have three weeks off for the holidays. The anatomy lab was about a third full of last-minute crammers reviewing test material before the big exam tomorrow. Destin, Mike, Bobby and Sam had been diligently studying the last few months and had become very serious about school. They stopped goofing off...at least temporarily. Not only did they get to know one another extremely well and were now the best of friends, they had developed a sense of respect for each other. They were with one another at least 12 hours a day and on weekends, which was more time than they spent with their families and non-dental student friends, and were beginning to feel like brothers who could uniquely relate to each other through their shared experiences. They had very little time to do anything except study. However, all work and no play were getting the best of them. Cabin fever was setting in. One student brought a large portable stereo to the lab to break the "dead" silence they had become accustomed to working in. The radio was set on WRNO, a local rock station.

Jim P. Sandras, D.D.S.

The up-tempo music helped the students to relax a little. The freshmen had been so intense lately that no one was joking around. They only talked about anatomy and the other courses they were taking. Everyone in the lab could sense an atmosphere of impending insanity on the verge of busting loose. Destin was carving Heather's name in the cadaver's liver. A student across the lab was acting like he was drinking Dead Juice out of the top of a skull. Mike was chewing on the cadaver's fingernails. Bobby had a mouth full of Red Man tobacco and was spitting on the cadavers. The students at tank 4 sat their cadaver up and put a Nike headband on it, which was the only thing holding the head together since they had cut it in half with an electric saw. Bobby walked over and put one of his Swisher Sweet cigars in its mouth and lit it.

Mike looked at Destin. "I'll be right back," he said, and then ran out of the lab. A few minutes later he walked back in with a brown paper bag.

"What's in there?" asked Destin.

Mike pulled out an unopened fifth of tequila. "I bought it for tomorrow after the test," he said, "but I have a feeling we need it now."

Bobby spotted the bottle from across the lab. He ran over, pulled it out of Mike's hand, took several swallows, and then squinted and punched a cadaver in the neck. He took another swallow and then held the bottle in the air. "Party time!" he yelled, giving the bottle back to Mike. They all started yelling and cheering as they passed the bottle around. Surprisingly, Kate was first in line for it. She took one big swig, and then went to her napsack and took out a pair of large pink underwear and a bra.

Dental School Debacle

She walked over to her tank and tried to put the underwear on her male cadaver but was having a hard time. Bobby, who was watching Kate closely, walked over and gave her a hand. Seconds later the pink underwear was on the dead man.

Bobby smiled at Kate and gave her a high five. "Good job, Trog. I didn't know you had it in you."

"I've been dying to do that," she said. "By the way, Bobby, why do y'all call me Trog?"

"In the Bohemian theology, Trog is the Milk Goddess, Empress of all Dairy products. And since you have beautiful, milky white skin we thought it was fitting."

"Sweet," she said, and then left to look for the bottle. As she was drinking, Sam walked over and pulled the bottle and the bra out of her hands. The room instantly got quiet. At first everyone thought he was upset with their behavior, but then Sam wiped off the neck of the bottle with his shirt sleeve and proceeded to guzzle the tequila, pushing Trog to the side. They were all dumbfounded. No one had ever seen Sam do anything that even resembled craziness. Now he was walking over to Sherry's tank with the bra and the tequila, and a crazed look in his eyes. Out of the silence Destin started cheering him on. "Go, Sam, go. Go, Sam, go." Everyone else joined. "Go, Sam, go. Go, Sam, go." He put the bottle down, opened Sherry's tank, and in no time had the bra on her cadaver. He picked up the bottle, took a swig, and jumped up and down with his hands in the air like he had just won an Olympic gold medal. Mike grabbed his scalpel and scissors and went to each tank messing up the dissections to aggravate Hicoff. When he finished, he removed an ear and threw it at Bobby as hard as he could, hitting him in the chest.

Jim P. Sandras, D.D.S.

Then Destin heard Bruce Springsteen's song, "Dancing in the Dark" come on the radio. He loved Bruce Springsteen, especially that song. He ran to the podium where Hicoff lectured, turned on her microphone, and put it up to the stereo so the music could be heard throughout the large lab. He then went to Hicoff's box of disarticulated bones, grabbed a humerus, ran back to the stage, and started lip synching the song, using the bone as a microphone. Destin was dancing and singing just like the music video. He had it memorized.

"This gun is for hire, even if we're dancing in the dark...Hey Baby!"

Destin pulled Kate onto the stage like Bruce did to Courtney Cox and began singing to her. The students loved it. Sarah Wilson, the only black girl in the class, removed a lung from her cadaver, and unexpectedly slammed it against the wall. She was extremely beautiful, and everyone respected her. Sarah's athletic body, even partially hidden in a long clinic jacket, drove all the guys crazy. She put her way through college on a combined track and scholastic scholarship. Now she was ripping a lung out of a dead person. Gross Anatomy does funny things to students. Mike walked over to her wearing a female cadaver scalp on his head.

"What are you doing, Sarah?" asked Mike as he pushed the wet, dead hair out of his eyes.

"This lung feels just like a Nurf Football," she replied. "It even bounces. Do you want to go out for a pass?"

"Absolutely," he said. "This is something I can tell my grandchildren when I get old."

Dental School Debacle

Sam walked over to Sarah carrying a human rib in one hand and the bottle of tequila in the other. "Can I play?" he asked.

"Sure," she replied. When the other students saw Sarah, Mike and Sam throwing around the lung they all started saying the same thing: "Pass it to me!"

By this point in the song every student in the lab was either throwing, banging on, or playing with the cadavers. The dean would have been proud of his selection of freshmen. One student snuck a Polaroid Instamatic camera in the lab and took pictures of students with their mutilated cadavers, just like Hicoff warned them not to do.

***

The next day was not a delightful one for the students. The test started at 8:00 and ended at 4:00. In the morning they took the written part, which consisted of 26 pages of multiple flex type questions, diagrams to be filled in and several essay questions. In the afternoon they took the practical part in the lab, where they had to identify the labeled tissues on the dissected cadavers. As they walked into the auditorium on this cold December morning there was a young, nerdy looking graduate student with black framed glasses and short, greased back hair.

"Only sit at a desk that has a manila folder on it," he kept repeating as he waited for everyone to take their seats. Before Destin sat down, he signaled to Mike and Bobby to meet him at the third-floor clinic after the test. As soon as everyone was quiet, the graduate student continued with the instructions.

"Dr. Hicoff and the other professors are up in the lab labeling the cadavers for the test this afternoon," he said, "so they asked me to give you the written test." He pulled out handwritten

Jim P. Sandras, D.D.S.

instructions and read them to the class. "Open the manila folder on your desk and remove the test packet. Count to make sure you have all 26 pages. We wouldn't want to cut anyone short. Also sign your name at the top of every page. If any of you finish early, which I doubt, put the test back into the folder and hand it to me on your way out. Any talking or looking around from this point on will result in immediate failure. And don't forget that the lab part starts at 1:00 this afternoon. We will lock the doors at exactly that time, so I suggest you get there early." The graduate student paused for a few seconds and looked around at the anxious students, trying to smile, but his teeth wouldn't come together for some reason. "OK, you can begin," he said, and then laughed to himself. "Have a great morning." A few of the students were tempted to run over and slap the nerd, but they had too much work to do. They all picked up their #2 pencils and started reading and writing like the room was on fire. Some broke out in a sweat from stress and writing so fast. Four hours and 26 pages later the graduate student walked back to the podium.

"Time's up," he said abruptly. "All pencils down, now!" He looked around the room with a hawk's eye making sure no one was still writing. "Now put your test back in the manila folder and hand them to me on the way out." The whole class stood up, stretched, grabbed their folders and walked to the front of the auditorium. Most were complaining about finger cramps from writing so much, so fast.

"I hope you have as much fun this afternoon as you did this morning," chuckled the graduate student as they exited the auditorium.

"That little cretin," said Destin as he walked up to Mike. "He

Dental School Debacle

thinks he's cute."

"I feel like punching him out," replied Mike, "but my fingers hurt too badly."

Destin looked around at the exiting students. "Where's Bobby?"

"You didn't see him leave?"

"No," replied Destin, "I was too busy having fun with the essay questions."

"He finished an hour ago," said Mike. "You know Bobby, he's always the first one to finish a test. He's probably on the third floor in the clinic waiting for us."

They walked down to the third floor where they found Bobby in the clinic lying face down, sound asleep, in a dental chair. He had lowered the back of the chair all the way down and was using his rolled-up jacket for a pillow.

Destin looked at Mike. "This dude never ceases to amaze me."

"I don't know how he does it," said Mike, and then he kicked the bottom of the dental chair. A few seconds later Bobby turned his head to the side. He had fallen asleep with a wad of chewing tobacco in his mouth.

"What's the matter, Bobby?" asked Destin. "Hicoff's test too hard for the little boy?"

Bobby cleared his throat several times and then sat up. As usual, he spit a huge, brown, oyster looking phlegm in the spittoon and then turned the water on to wash it down. He looked at Destin and Mike and grinned.

"I swear, when I get out of dental school, the first thing I'm going to do is have one of these spittoons installed on the side of my bed." He ran his fingers through his curly hair and yawned.

Jim P. Sandras, D.D.S.

"Man, I couldn't get to sleep last night, even after the Captain Crunch."

"What about the Nyquil?" asked Destin.

"I was out. I tossed and turned until about 3:00. Then I got up and went back to the anatomy lab by myself to go over everything one more time. I didn't get back to my apartment until 6:30 this morning. I had just enough time to take a shower and guzzle a quart of coffee. Right now, I feel like an old douche bag at a retirement home."

"Well, how do you think you did on the test?" asked Destin.

"Pretty good," answered Bobby, "I used the Italian, scientific method my dad taught me. It never fails."

"Italian scientific method?"

"I can't wait to hear this," said Mike.

"I hold my pencil six inches over the test," explained Bobby. "Close my eyes, make three circles over the question, pray to Saint Anthony, then put the pencil on the page and open my eyes. Whatever answer I'm closest to, that's the one I use. I believe in biorhythmic religion."

"Yea, right," said Destin, "knowing you, you probably made an 'A'."

"All I know is I'm starving," said Mike. "Let's get something to eat."

"Where do you want to go?" asked Destin. "We have less than an hour."

Bobby stood. "We can go to the Tavern," he said. " I can get extra fast service. Besides, I need a break from this building."

They agreed, got in Bobby's Cutlass and were there in five minutes. They sat at the only available table. They weren't there

Dental School Debacle

20 seconds when Bobby reached over and pinched the waitress on the butt. She rolled up her fist and turned around ready to punch out the culprit, but when she realized it was Bobby she smiled.

"I should've known it was you," she said, and then gave Bobby a kiss on his cheek. "What are you doing here, Bobby? I thought you had a big test today?"

"We're in the middle of it," he replied. "We have to get back to school as soon as possible. Tell Chris to put our sandwiches first in line."

"I'll try," she said, "but Chris got in a big fight with his wife last night, again, and started drinking early this morning. He already got several orders mixed up and is having to remake a lot of sandwiches."

Bobby shook his head in disgust. "I'm going to have a long talk with him someday."

"By the way, Bobby," said the waitress, "did you talk to your uncle about getting me that job on TV? You remember, you promised me you would when I was at your apartment the other night."

"Not yet," he replied. "I've been really busy lately studying for this anatomy test. I'll try to call him tonight. I promise."

"Thank you so much," she said, smiling from ear to ear.

Destin was confused and looked at Bobby. "What do you mean, get her a job on TV?"

Bobby kicked Destin in the leg under the table.

"You mean you don't know who this is?"

"I think so," replied Destin, "but tell me anyway."

"This is Bobby Turner," she said as if she was extremely proud to know him. "Ted Turner's nephew. You know, Ted Turner, the man who practically owns all of cable TV."

Mike and Destin struggled not to laugh. "Oh yeah, that's right," said Mike. "He did mention something about it. But you know Bobby, he's so humble."

Bobby put his arm around the girl as he ordered. "I'll take a large roast beef po-boy, dressed, and with lots of mayonnaise and extra onions."

"I'll have the same," replied Mike.

The waitress looked at Destin, ready to write on her pad. "And what will you have?"

Destin made a serious face. "I'll take a large after birth po-boy with extra umbilical sauce."

The waitress backed away from the table making a nauseated face. She had to put her hand over her mouth to keep from vomiting. That even grossed out Mike and Bobby.

"That is the most disgusting thing I ever heard in my life," she said.

The waitress looked at Bobby. "Where did you find this derelict?"

"We just met," he said. "Just give him the same."

"Anything to drink?" she asked, trying not to look at Destin.

"Get us three Barq's root beers, stat!" said Mike. "We're in a hurry, remember?"

A few minutes later the waitress walked out with their drinks and placed them on the table, still not looking at Destin. "Your order might be a little longer," explained the girl. "Chris is drunk now and got more orders mixed up."

Bobby leaned forward. "You tell Chris that Bobby Turner said

Dental School Debacle

if he doesn't have our sandwiches ready in 10 minutes, he'll never get that tryout for the Atlanta Braves like I promised."

"I'll tell him," she said, and then went back into the kitchen.

Destin looked at Bobby and laughed. "I hate to say this, Bobby, but I'm starting to see the humor in your lying."

"Yeah," said Mike. "I've never seen anyone lie as good as you."

"Thank you."

The three were finishing their root beers and talking about the test when the waitress walked back without sandwiches. "Chris just put your po-boys on the grill. It'll only be a few more minutes."

"Uh, excuse me, Miss," said Destin politely. She turned around. "Not only are we in a hurry to take a test, but I'm so hungry I could eat the maggots out of a dead armadillo. Please bring me something to eat, even if it's just dead flies from the windowsill."

The waitress tensed her face. "You are the most disgusting person I've ever met." She rushed back into the kitchen. Five minutes later there was still no sign of the waitress.

Mike was getting restless. "Destin, what time do you have?"

He looked down at his Tag Heuer and immediately jumped up. "Crap! It's quarter to one! Let's get out of here!"

As soon as they took off running the waitress came out with their sandwiches and yelled at Bobby. He ran over, snatched them off her tray, kissed her on the lips and continued running. He hesitated at the doorway, then turned around and looked at her. "Put this on my tab," he said. "And I'll call you tonight."

The three jumped into Bobby's Cutlass and made it back to school in record time, scarfing down their sandwiches on the

Jim P. Sandras, D.D.S.

way. Bobby threw his car in park while it was still moving, causing it to jerk back and forth. They entered the building and sprinted down the crowded hall running between people and even shoving some to the side. At this time of the day the lobby was crammed with doctors, students and patients going to 1:00 appointments. As soon as the three racing students turned the corner, they saw the crowd standing by the elevators, but were unable to stop on the thickly coated waxed floors. They slid right into the mass of people, knocking down at least two dozen innocent bystanders. As Destin was getting up, he could hear patients moaning, doctors cursing, and some kid crying. Just then one of the four elevator doors opened. Bobby, Mike and Destin were the only ones in position to catch it. They jumped in and Mike started banging on the 'Door Close' button. They all took a deep sigh of relief as the elevator started moving, until they noticed there were three janitors riding with them who were coming from the basement, and that they had already pressed five different floor buttons. Mike was getting anxious.

"Destin, what time is it?" he asked.

He quickly looked at his watch. "12:57."

"We'll make it," said Bobby, trying to keep cool.

By the time they reached the eighth floor there was just one janitor left in the elevator. He kept smiling to himself, staring at the buttons and picking his teeth with a toothpick. When the elevator doors opened on the eighth floor, they could see the clock on the wall. It read 12:59. They kept waiting for the janitor to get out, but he never did. Mike banged on the 'Door Close' button, again. As the elevator doors were closing the janitor noticed a female janitor walking down the hall. He quickly stuck

Dental School Debacle

his hand in the opening and pushed the doors back open, and then leaned out, howling down the hall.

"Hey baby, you lookin' good," he said. "Where was ya' for lunch? I was lookin' for ya'."

She slowly turned around. "I told you to leave me alone. I'm married."

The janitor leaned further out of the elevator and gave her a big smile showing his two gold teeth. "Come on, baby. You is too fine for one man."

The three students could not believe what was happening. Here they were running extremely late for one of the most important events in their lives while some old, frisky janitor was making passes at a married woman. Mike couldn't take it any longer.

"Forget about her, buddy," he said, and then reached over with his foot and pushed the janitor out of the elevator. The old man fell flat on his stomach. This time Destin started banging on the 'Door Close' button.

"Don't ever mess with a married woman," yelled Bobby as the doors were closing. As soon as the elevator doors finally opened on the ninth floor they started running. Mike looked up at the clock at the end of the hall and it was 1:00. "I sure hope that's fast," he said as they headed for the anatomy lab. As they turned the last corner, they could see the doors closing. They picked up the pace and busted through the doors knocking down the nerdy graduate student. The keys he was holding to lock the doors flew in the air and landed at Hicoff's feet. She looked down at the keys, slowly lifted her head, looked at the three students and clinched her fist. Bobby was smiling at Hicoff as he helped up the

Jim P. Sandras, D.D.S.

graduate student. This made her even more upset.

"Ten more seconds and you three would've been repeating the year," she said. Hicoff walked up to Bobby. "I'm already in a bad mood, Pubix. Kicking you out would make me feel a hell of a lot better." Now they knew she was upset—they never heard her use words like that before. "You have exactly five seconds to get to your tank." Not wasting a second, the three rushed to their positions. Hicoff picked up the keys and threw them to the graduate student to lock the doors. She walked to the podium, put her microphone on and started berating the entire class.

"I'm so mad I could easily fail this whole class and feel good about it." She was spitting as she talked.

"Never in my 34 years of teaching at this Medical Center have I witnessed such an immature and vulgar display of vandalism as what I saw this morning when I walked into this lab. It looked like the Civil War was fought here last night. There were human parts scattered from wall to wall. And it took me, three professors and four janitors over two hours to clean and mop up Dead Juice. It was disgusting. One of the janitors had to leave for religious reasons. We found a cadaver sitting against the wall with an empty bottle of tequila in its hand. Three cadavers were wearing clinic jackets and two were wearing women's underwear. There was one sitting up in the tank with a sweat band on its head and a cigar in its mouth."

She paused, took a few deep breaths, and tried to regain her composure. "This shows a complete lack of professionalism. But the worst part," she said, "is that one of the cadavers is missing. I told you at the beginning of this course that removing any body part was a federal offense, but I never dreamed that someone

Dental School Debacle

would be stupid enough to remove a whole body. Every dental school and medical school in this country is going to hear about this! It makes both me and the university look bad."

Hicoff paused again. Her entire face was dark red, and her temples were bulging from the intensity. "I've already notified the city, the state, and the FBI about the missing cadaver. At first, they thought I was a student playing a practical joke, but after the dean called them, they knew we were serious. The FBI told me they would conduct a full-scale investigation." Destin and Mike looked over at Bobby. He grinned and winked at them. Now they were sure Bobby had something to do with it.

"This type of behavior is totally uncalled for," continued Hicoff, again looking at Bobby. "And I promise, if it's the last thing I do, I WILL find out who stole that cadaver. I was in a good mood this morning as I drove to school. I was going to make the test easy. But some of the cadavers are so mutilated that it's hard to tell which end is up. Some tanks look like they're full of chili. The professors and I had a hard time finding anything to label, so now the test will be three times harder."

Everyone's hearts skipped a beat. The two-thirds of the students who had nothing to do with the massacre last night were extremely upset.

"I know the whole class is not responsible for what happened here," said Hicoff, looking at Bobby. "But unfortunately, the good apples have to suffer for the bad ones. Although, I know how dental students are— everyone knows when one student has diarrhea, and I'll bet my Ph.D. that in just a few days everyone will know who's responsible. That'll give the other students three and a half years to get even with the bad apples."

Jim P. Sandras, D.D.S.

Mike glanced over at the guys standing at the tank next to them and noticed they were angrily staring back, especially James Bonnin, whose nickname was Brick. Brick played defensive end for LSU, and then for the Green Bay Packers for three years until he suffered a career-ending knee injury that never completely healed. He still walked with a slight limp. Brick was easily the largest guy in the school, maybe even in New Orleans. Everywhere he went people stared at his enormous size and huge muscles. His high school coach gave him the nickname Brick, and James insisted that everyone call him that. Everyone did. Brick worked on the same cadaver as Terrance Swilley, and they had become good friends. Terrance was a typical New Orleans native—loud, funny, outgoing and very likable. He was easily elected as the class President. Neither Brick nor Terrance was at the lab party last night and were gritting their teeth at Mike, Bobby and Destin because they knew the three had something to do with it. Now the test was going to be much harder.

Mike whispered to Destin. "I think Brick's upset with us."

"How do you know?"

"He just broke the pencil behind his ear just by tensing his temporal muscles."

Hicoff took out the instructions for the lab test and read them loudly to the class. As she was reading, the professors passed around clip boards with three sheets of paper numbered to 180.

Hicoff finished reading the instructions and put her notes down. "Are there any questions?" she asked. No one made a sound. "Remember, you only have one minute at each station. When I blow my whistle, you must stop writing and immediately move to the next station. Ready, go."

Dental School Debacle

Most had a hard time not laughing as they walked from tank-to-tank trying to identify the labeled body parts. The professors had removed most of the clinic jackets and underwear from the cadavers, but Sherry personally removed the bra from hers. She had become fond of her cadaver and couldn't bear the sight of seeing the old man with a bra. Three hours and 180 blows of the whistle later, they finished. The exhausted students handed their tests to the professor as they left the lab.

Bobby walked up to Mike. "I'll be hearing that dumb whistle in my sleep tonight," he said.

"I'll be dreaming about shoving it down Hicoff's throat," replied Mike. "I felt like I was in boot camp."

"But just think, Mike," said Bobby. "We're finished with anatomy, and Hicoff."

Destin ran and caught up with his two friends as they walked down the hall toward the elevators.

"Everybody's upset with us," said Destin. "I overheard several people, and they're not too happy about that test being so hard. They're blaming it on us, even calling us names. Terrance wouldn't look at me."

"I noticed that, too," said Bobby. "Every time I looked at Brick during the test, he clinched his fist at me."

"What are we going to do?" asked Mike. "We can't spend the rest of our lives with our classmates hating our guts."

"I have an idea," said Destin.

The whole class was quietly waiting for the elevators, so Destin seized the moment. He rushed to the front by the elevator door and made an announcement.

"Uh, excuse me everybody," he said. They all gave him their

attention, curiously waiting to see what he had to say. "I believe I speak for all the bad apples who were involved with the massacre in the lab last night. We're sorry for making the test harder for everyone—we got carried away. Trog started drinking tequila and took her clothes off. Everyone went crazy after that."

Terrance looked at Kate and pointed at her. "I knew you had something to do with this, Trog," he said. "You're the only one in this class who could've fit in the underwear on that cadaver."

Kate nervously looked around with a guilty look on her face. "I wasn't the only one. There were at least two dozen people in the lab last night, and I didn't take my clothes off!"

"I believe everyone here is stressed out," continued Destin. "What we all need is a good party to chill us out, and to celebrate the end of Gross Anatomy."

"Yeah!" interrupted Sam. "No more Dr. Hicoff!"

And then it hit them—the first semester was over. They had been so uptight all day that it was just becoming reality.

Destin continued with his speech. "Let's forget about the test and celebrate no more Hicoff. I have an idea. Let's have a Dead Juice party tonight. I'll rent us a large suite at the Hyatt Regency next to the Superdome. We'll supply all the food and drinks. When you get to the hotel just ask the information desk for the room number of Dr. Hasel Hicoff. That's where the party will be."

Only a few of the students looked interested. Destin started pleading with the class. "Please come, it'll be a lot of fun."

Bobby put his arm around Destin's shoulder and smiled at his classmates. "I have a surprise for tonight," he said. "If you miss it, you'll be sorry." He had everyone curious, especially Destin and

Dental School Debacle

Mike.

Terrance stepped forward. "We have been under a lot of stress lately. A good party is just what we need. We'll be there."

***

Destin, Mike and Kate held a meeting in the freshman locker room to make a game plan for the Dead Juice party. Kate was delegated to take care of the food, Mike was responsible for the Dead Juice, while Destin went to the hotel to rent the largest suite they had. No one knew where Bobby went. As soon as he got off the elevator he went straight to his Cutlass and left, although they could tell by the look in his eyes that he was up to something illegal. Several students said they were going to the party just to see what Bobby had for his surprise.

Mike went straight to an old Texaco station by his apartment, where he had seen a discarded, 25-gallon, plastic oil container with a nozzle on the bottom. When no one was looking, he snuck in the back gate, grabbed the plastic drum, threw it in the back of his truck and went straight to a car wash to clean it out. After he was sure there were no remnants of hydrocarbons in the container, Mike went to a liquor store and went nuts with Destin's Visa card. He bought four gallons of rum, four gallons of tequila, four gallons of scotch, four gallons of vodka, four fifths of Everclear whisky, 10 liters of Bailey's Irish Cream, and a case of Moose Head beer. After Mike poured them all together in the plastic drum, he wasn't satisfied with the appearance of the Dead Juice. So, on his way to the Hyatt, he stopped at a grocery store and purchased three large cans of V-8 juice and 10 cans of potted meat, stirring it into the volatile mixture. When he pulled into the parking lot of the exclusive hotel he couldn't stop

Jim P. Sandras, D.D.S.

laughing.

"Wait until they taste this brew," he kept saying to himself. He parked next to the building and went inside to the information desk to ask for the room number of Dr. Hasel Hicoff. The girl said, "1207". Mike grabbed the largest luggage cart he could find and asked a bellhop for assistance. Mike kept waiting for the bellhop to ask what was in the extremely heavy plastic container, but he didn't seem to care. When they walked into the large, Presidential suite on the 12th floor they found Destin by himself reclined in a beautiful, plush, lounge chair smoking a cigar, drinking a Heineken and watching The Three Stooges. Destin jumped up and walked over to the large plastic drum and started rubbing his hands together.

"So, this is the Dead Juice."

They slowly lifted it off the cart and placed it on the wet bar next to the sink. Destin could sense the bellhop was uncomfortable listening to them talk about Dead Juice. He tipped him $5, and he was quickly gone. Destin took a puff of his cigar, then looked at Mike seriously.

"What's in it?"

"You don't want to know."

"How much did it cost?"

"You don't want to know."

"What does it taste like?"

"Jet fuel. I'd put out the cigar if I were you."

"Is it legal?"

"Barely."

"Is it dangerous?"

"Extremely.

Dental School Debacle

"Would you let you mother drink it?"

"No way."

"Good. Then I'll drink it."

Destin turned on the spout and filled his glass. He intended on drinking the entire thing, but after two swallows he had to stop. He immediately put down the glass, took a deep breath, stuck his face in the bar sink and turned on the cold water. After several seconds of washing his face and tongue, Destin dried off and smiled.

"Good job, Mike," he said. "You're right. I should put out the cigar."

A few minutes later the door swung open. Kate walked in with the same bellhop and a luggage cart full of food. Mike and Destin helped the bellhop unload. Kate had prepared various types of finger sandwiches and assorted snacks. Among the food was a large, five-gallon aluminum pot covered with foil.

"What's in here, Trog?" asked Destin as he lifted the heavy pot onto the table.

"I call it Cadaver Chili," she said. This made the bellhop even more nervous. He unloaded the cart as fast as he could.

"I got the idea from Hicoff," continued Kate. "Remember how she said that some of the bodies were so mutilated they looked like chili? I tried really hard to duplicate it. I even added large sections of sliced meat to the chili to make it look like actual human tissue."

They heard a plate drop and the door slam shut and noticed that the bellhop had run out of the room.

Kate shook her head. "He must be a vegetarian."

Shortly afterwards, students started arriving. In no time the room was half full. They were all standing around the wet bar cautiously examining the large plastic container. Destin took a permanent marker and wrote on it:

"<u>CAUTION</u>: DEAD JUICE-
MAY BE HAZARDOUS TO YOUR CAREER"

Finally, a few brave souls tried the mixture. They could only take one swallow at a time. After each taste they would grab ahold of the furniture and start hyperventilating. But the more they drank, the more they liked it. Mike could always tell when someone finished a glass. The person would start acting like a junk yard dog, barking and biting randomly—both signs of central nervous system malfunction. Everyone was complimenting Mike on his brew, and how it was the same color and consistency as the real Dead Juice. Sam walked up to Mike and patted him on the back.

"Hicoff would be proud of you," said Sam. "You should save her some—mail it to her for Christmas. She'd enjoy it." Mike agreed.

By the time Brick and Terrance arrived, everyone had been drinking the Dead Juice for over an hour. They walked in to find a tag team wrestling match taking place on the king size bed while the others bet on the outcome. Destin was standing in the middle of the bed shirtless, sweating profusely, when he saw the two walk in. He jumped down and went over to greet them.

"I've been waiting for you guys," said Destin breathing heavily. "The Dead Juice is in the back room on the wet bar, and there's plenty of food on the table. Make yourself at home. I have to get

Dental School Debacle

back to the wrestling match—I'm the referee. I'll talk to you later." Destin ran back and jumped on the bed, knocking one of his classmates onto the nightstand, breaking the lamp. As the two walked to the wet bar they couldn't believe how loud and rowdy all the students were. They had never seen them act this way before.

"It must be the Dead Juice," said Terrance. "I wonder what's in it?"

"I don't know," replied Brick, "but it must be good. Everyone's drinking it."

They filled their glasses and started daring one another to guzzle the entire glass without stopping. A few students who were standing by the wet bar heard Brick and Terrance daring each other, and were now daring them, too. Both guys had big egos and always tried to act like macho-men. They agreed to try it now that people were watching.

"Are you ready?" asked Brick.

"Ready," replied Terrance. "One, two, three, GO!"

The two students began drinking the volatile mixture as fast as they could, having no idea what was in it. Halfway through, Terrance stopped and grabbed his throat and starting gasping for air, while Brick continued drinking. Seconds later, Brick slammed his empty glass down. He stood there for a second, gazing off into space. Brick instantly turned a light green color. He ripped off his shirt and started flexing his muscles like the Hulk. He poured another glass and drank the whole thing as if it was water, and then ran to the bed and began challenging his classmates to wrestle. No one took his offer. He angrily ran to the large potted plant in the corner and smashed it against the wall. Porcelain and

Jim P. Sandras, D.D.S.

mud flew everywhere. He then jumped on the bed and started grunting and flexing his muscles, again.

"Come on," he said like a man possessed, waving them on. "I'll take on all of you, at the same time."

Then, out of nowhere, Terrance came diving through the air like Superman, knocking Brick on his back. Over a dozen students standing close by, including girls, jumped on Brick and began wrestling with him with limited success. Brick was in such good shape that in no time he threw everyone off. Amongst all the loud commotion, a loud whistle started blowing at the entrance to the suite. Everyone stopped what they were doing and looked in the direction of the whistle. There stood Bobby in the doorway pushing a wheelchair with some unknown person wearing a white clinic jacket and sunglasses sitting in it. Bobby put the whistle in the person's mouth and closed the door.

"Dr. Hazel Hicoff has arrived!" he yelled. No one knew what to think at first. As he pushed the wheelchair into the room, they could smell the funk that came along with it. They instantly knew by the smell that it was a cadaver. Bobby had worked hard to make it look like Hicoff. He had the hair down to a tee. He found an old wig with a bun on top and stapled it to the head. Destin, followed by several others, threw their drinks on it to cover up the smell they had learned to hate so much. He rolled the wheelchair to the middle of the room and held up a large freezer bag full of darts. The crowd went nuts.

"Whoever sticks it in her nose, wins," he said. Bobby emptied the darts on the floor and went to the wet bar. The students were fighting over the darts, throwing them at Hicoff as fast as they could pick them up. Brick punched the cadaver in the chest so

Dental School Debacle

hard that it blew the whistle. As Bobby poured a glass of Dead Juice, Terrance walked up to him shaking his head.

"I knew it was you who stole the cadaver," Terrance said.

"How did you know?"

"You're the only one in the class crazy enough to do it, yet smart enough to get away with it."

"Why thank you, Terrance," said Bobby. He took several large swallows of the Dead Juice without blinking an eye.

"How did you get it out of the school without anyone seeing you?" asked Terrance. "There's always a security guard at every entrance."

"It was easy," replied Bobby. "I went back to the lab at 4:00 this morning and picked out one of the few intact bodies. Then I dragged it by the feet up the stairs onto the roof and pushed it over the side into some shrubs by the parking lot."

Terrance was stunned. "You threw the cadaver off the roof?"

"I figured, what could go wrong? It's only 90 feet. Besides, it was dead already, although I think I heard it moan after it hit the ground. I rushed down to the parking lot, and I swear, it was sitting up with its eyes open. It gave me goose bumps. I had to put my sunglasses on it to keep it from staring at me. I wrapped it in a sheet and put it in my trunk."

"What about the wheelchair?"

"I took it from the front desk in the main lobby."

"No one saw you bring it into the hotel?"

Bobby smiled. "Only a few people in the elevator said anything. I just told them it was my grandmother. One lady whispered in my ear that I should give my grandmother a bath, and that she smelled like she had been dead for over a year. I had to laugh. As I was getting out of the elevator, I told the lady that my grandmother had been dead for only a few months, not a year. You should've seen her face, Terrance. I think she threw up."

Just then, Brick came running over, now only wearing his black, Speedo underwear. He put his entire mouth over the spout and turned it on. After 10 seconds of continual drinking, he turned it off and began yelling and banging on his chest like King Kong. Brick spit on the wall, and then wiped off his face and looked at Bobby.

"This is the best party I've been to in years," he said. Then Brick turned around and noticed that Sarah was standing next to the bed with a drink in her hand. He took off running and knocked her off her feet onto the bed and started wrestling with her. Sarah was not at all intimidated by Brick's large size and quickly thought out her strategy. It only took her a few moves to pin down the ex-professional football player. Sarah impressed everyone, especially Brick, who was now looking at her like he was in love. He had a newfound admiration and respect for her.

The party was a huge success. Almost everyone in the class showed up, except for a certain few, including Sherry. The students who caused the test to be harder were totally forgiven. They agreed that this would be the first of many class parties. Bobby urged everyone to sleep in the room, but he called taxis for those who had to leave. He radically opposed drinking and driving but would not explain why.

Early the next morning Bobby and Mike snuck the cadaver to his Cutlass, threw it in the trunk and rode around the city looking for a place to dispose of it. After making several wrong turns,

Dental School Debacle

they ended up in the middle of the dreaded Desire housing project. While frantically trying to find their way out of the dangerous area, Mike spotted a 1976 two tone, lime green Cadillac with white wall tires, a TV antenna, and open hood. They both agreed that anyone who owned a car like that would be much better at getting rid of a dead body than they were. Bobby pulled alongside the Cadillac and popped open his trunk. They picked up the body and leaned it against the front fender with the head and arms laying on the engine, making it look as if the cadaver was working on the alternator. Seconds later they were out of the projects and on their way to a Christmas vacation.

The Love Boat

The students had to be back at school by 8:00 Monday morning, January 3rd. They were nervously looking forward to starting a new class—Operative Dentistry, where they would drill and fill their first tooth, an extracted tooth, that is. No real patients, yet. Included with their acceptance letters into dental school was a separate letter instructing the future students to take quart jars containing 1% formalin solution to various dentists and oral surgeons in their community and ask them to put all their extracted teeth in them. Right before moving to New Orleans, they gathered up their jars and examined the teeth for hours, wondering what type of person they belonged to only weeks earlier. They wondered why the teeth were extracted, and if the patients even miss their former partners of mastication? The budding students were proud of their jars full of decayed, rejected, neglected, bombed out, sorted out, rotted out, knocked out, filling-filled, cracked, chipped, broken, stained, crowned, endodontically treated, tartar covered teeth. They showed their family and friends the jars of teeth, only

Jim P. Sandras, D.D.S.

to get the standard negative reaction.

On this first morning back, after a delightful three-week Christmas break, they had to sort out the teeth. They looked for ones in the best possible condition to put in a mannequin to work on like a real patient. This was the first time they opened the jars since picking them up seven months earlier. Some didn't follow the instructions properly and tried a less expensive preserving medium instead of the 1% formalin solution, which didn't work. It was easy to spot these students—they were walking around with jars containing black water and black teeth with a dark vapor accumulating inside. The instructors told them to be careful opening their jars because of the possibility of gas pressure building up from the decomposition of organic matter, which could cause a small explosion and stink up the entire nine story building. As they removed the lids, the stench quickly filled the lab. It was as bad as the smell of the cadavers, maybe worse. Although it was a different kind of bad. It had a strong chemical odor, but at the same time smelled like an old hobo's breath in the morning, or a dead goat that died from drinking a gallon of liquid paper. The instructors left the room before the students opened the jars and said they would return at 11:00 to check the teeth.

By 9:00 half the class was either gagging and choking or had left the room. A few students tried wearing masks, but the smell of the extracted teeth, along with the formalin, was too much for them. Most were having a hard time selecting good specimens. Some jars were full of nothing but broken pieces, usually given by the Oral Surgeons. Most of the teeth were decayed, had trashy fillings, or were covered with tartar. Some even had bone and

Dental School Debacle

tissue still hanging on them, which had to be cleaned off in order to tell if they were useable. One tooth had part of someone's jaw still connected to it.

The students were hurrying to finish when suddenly they heard a loud crash in the back of the lab. Everyone turned around only to realize that Sam had knocked his jar off the bench onto the floor. The vapor that filled the room was toxic and was giving everyone a head rush.

Brick yelled from across the room, "You dumb redneck! How can you be so stupid? What are you trying to do, KILL US?" Brick was in a mischievous mood this morning and felt like messing with someone. He saw how upset Sam was about his broken jar and his hundreds of teeth on the floor, and decided he was a prime candidate.

"You're probably used to this kind of smell, huh Sam?" yelled Brick from across the room. "I bet this is what your mama's house smells like." Sam was not in a joking mood. He tried to ignored Brick while he gathered up the teeth and wiped up the mess. But Brick wasn't going to let Sam get off that easy.

"Hey, Sam! How many of those teeth are from your sisters?"

This put Sam over the edge. Besides, his eyes were burning, he had a headache from the fumes, and his legs were cramping from crawling on the teeth-covered floor. "That's it!" yelled Sam. "I love my sisters too much to take that type of abuse." He threw a molar at Brick so hard that it made a humming noise flying through the air. Brick jumped out of the way, causing it to hit Terrance on side of his head.

"OWWW!" yelled Terrance, as he rubbed his head. "Who threw that?" Brick pointed to Sam. In a mad rage, Terrance reached over to his lab desk, grabbed a hand full of teeth, and threw them at Sam, hitting everyone nearby except him. The assaulted students were looking around the lab trying to find out who threw the hard, wet objects. Then Brick stood up and yelled:

"TOOTH FIGHT!!!"

He threw a hand full of teeth at Terrance, hitting him, Mike and six other students. Before they knew it, a war was in progress. Decayed teeth were flying everywhere. Bobby, who was in the middle of everything, saw Sherry trying to sneak out of the room to avoid the crossfire. He couldn't let her get away unscathed. Right when she was walking out the door, Bobby threw a wisdom tooth with a side arm shot, hitting Sherry on the ear. She let out a high-pitched scream that sounded like someone had stabbed Minnie Mouse. She covered her head and ran down the hall. The tooth fight went on for a while, until everyone was either injured or had run out of teeth. There were now hundreds of extracted teeth scattered all over the lab floor.

At 11:00 the instructors walked back into the lab wearing masks and rubber gloves, ready to work, only to find the students crawling on the floor searching for teeth. They could not believe their eyes. They were crushing teeth with every step. One of the instructors walked over to Destin, who was under a desk examining a central incisor.

"What the HELL happened here?" he yelled.

"We had a tooth fight, sir," Destin replied casually. "You should have been here. It was great! It's ten times more fun than a food fight. Did you know you can put a knot on someone's

Dental School Debacle

head with a direct hit from an upper molar?"

The professors were outraged by the childish behavior of the class. The head of the department walked to the podium, slipping on teeth on the way, and scolded the class for their lack of professionalism. They were only halfway through the first year and were already sick of hearing that word—*professionalism*.

***

The second half of the freshman year was mostly book work. Nothing exciting would happen until they began examining patients. Gradually, they were learning a little more about dentistry, but it wasn't fun stuff, like pulling teeth. The students learned about this thing call Preventive Dentistry, which they all agreed should be stopped. They wanted to start their own course—Induced Dentistry. Now they realized why most dentists were not happy about fluoridated water and sugarless candy. And they finally learned what those rubber points on the handles of toothbrushes were for. Most of their time was spent in auditoriums listening to Ph.D.'s lecture on boring topics like embryology and physiology. All they wanted to learn about was teeth and how to make money, not about the oxidative decarboxylation of pyruvate into acetyl CoA during the citric acid cycle. Terrance organized a group of note takers. These five students took turns bringing a tape recorder to class and recording the lectures. Afterwards, they would take the tapes home, type up the notes, and include every professor's word, graph and illustration. For a small fee, any student could buy them, and most did. It was far better than the notes they were used to studying with. The best part was they didn't have to go to the lectures unless they were one of the note takers, like Mike

Jim P. Sandras, D.D.S.

and Bobby. It was a great way to make sure they studied, and pick up a few extra dollars on the side. On the other hand, Destin was rarely seen around school, unless it was raining. While his friends were in class taking notes, Destin was busy with something he felt was far more important: trying to improve his tennis serve-and-volley technique and lowering his golf handicap. On the way back to his trailer each day he stopped at school to pick up the notes from the previous day and took them home to review with a bottle of his favorite red wine – MD 20/20 Plum Supreme.

The further the semester went along, the more the students detested Sherry. She was quickly developing a reputation for being selfish and rude to students, and for schmoozing the instructors. If Sherry knew an instructor would be grading her, she would make them a cheesecake and go out of her way to compliment them. On the other hand, if she knew an instructor wouldn't be grading her, she didn't even look at them. And even worse, she never associated with her classmates. She acted as if they were on opposing teams. Bobby's locker was right next to Sherry's. It took him months of sneakily looking out the corner of his eyes to figure out the combination to her lock. Once a week he would go back to school late at night and rearrange everything in her locker just to mess with her head. Then Terrance got the note takers together and declared war on Sherry. They made a separate set of notes just for her. It took up a lot of their free time, but they felt it would be worth it if they could make her fail just one test. Up to this point she made straight A's and was the number one student in the class. They all vowed they would not let this happen any longer. They said they would rather have Scooby Doo as their valedictorian. But somehow,

Dental School Debacle

Sherry kept making the grades, even with notes laced with errors and made-up facts. They even tried a few other things, like stealing her books and ripping pages out of her notes, but she still made A's. She must be sleeping with the instructors, they thought. The note takers were getting discouraged, but they knew Sherry's time was coming.

***

It was getting close to the end of the freshman year. They had already finished most of their lecture courses, such as radiology, neurology, human behavior, and medical emergencies. They had just one more course, Oral Diagnosis, before they were off for a month. In Oral Diagnosis students would see their first real patients. They were excited, even though they would simply take x-rays, record medical history and chart teeth. They also had to perform an oral cancer examination on every patient, which made the students feel like real doctors for the first time.

It was the last lecture of the course. Two days from now they would be in clinic with their patients. After this, the freshman year was over. Dr. Loin, the head of the Oral Diagnosis Department, was giving the lecture.

"We will give each of you an envelope containing a patient's name and phone number. You are to call them tonight and make an appointment for this Friday afternoon at 1:00. If there are any problems getting the patient in at this time, come see me in my office on the fifth floor. When you get your patient on Friday, the first thing you will do is take a set of full mouth x-rays, which consists of 20 separate radiographs. Next, fill out a chart on them, carefully going over their medical history, checking for any allergies, and finding out if they take any type of medications. If

Jim P. Sandras, D.D.S.

they do, you are to look up that drug in the P.D.R., write a summary on it, and hand it to the instructor before he grades you. And don't forget to palpate their face and neck, checking for swollen lymph nodes. Also make sure you examine the whole oropharyngeal region for anything that resembles oral cancer. Can anyone tell me what you should be looking for when screening for oral cancer?"

Breaking the silence, Sherry stood up and excitedly stated, "One should examine the floor of the mouth, lateral borders of the tongue and the soft palate for any leukoplakia or erythroplakia, sir."

"Very good, Miss Custard," said Dr. Loin. "Although, I suggest you lay off the caffeine." The class started laughing because Sherry always had a large cup of coffee on her desk.

"What Miss Custard stated was correct," he said. "Always examine the high-risk areas for any type of red or white lesions. Remember, around 15 percent of all white lesions turn into cancer, but an alarming 90 percent of all red lesions are premalignant and have a very low survival rate. These kinds of lesions are very easy to spot and too serious to miss. You should get into the habit of checking for this on every patient that walks into your office, especially if you plan to practice in the southern part of the United States where tobacco use is much more prevalent. Now, if there aren't any questions, I'll pass out the envelopes and see you Friday afternoon." Dr. Loin stepped off the stage and went down the aisle passing out the envelopes.

Destin turned and looked at Mike and Bobby. "Y'all want to come to my trailer tonight and call our patients? We can make a party out of it."

Dental School Debacle

Mike and Bobby agreed.

***

Later that evening, they met at Destin's trailer and dared one another to go first. They had never done anything like this before and had no idea what to expect. They were more nervous than calling a girl to ask for a date.

"OK, who wants to be the first to call his patient?" asked Bobby.

"I'll go first," said Destin. "I'd just as soon get it over with. These patients can't be that bad. They wouldn't give us any difficult cases—we're only neophyte freshmen."

Destin got on the phone and started dialing. The only information they had was their name, age, sex, and phone number.

"Hello, may I please speak with Mr. David Terrebone? Hi, Mr. Terrebone. My name is Destin Dufrene. I'm a student at the Dental School. I'm calling to make an appointment with you to take some x-rays and see what kind of dental work you need. Excuse me, what did you say?"

Destin sat there in silence for several minutes listening to the man talk. Then Destin mumbled something over the phone and quickly hung up. He made a face like he had just found a dead rat in his refrigerator.

"What's the matter, Destin?" asked Bobby. "Did you fart again?"

"I wish," replied Destin. "I asked my patient if he could come this Friday, and he said, sure, but wanted to know if I could pull all 12 of his teeth."

Mike squinted. "All 12 teeth? You've got to be joking!"

Jim P. Sandras, D.D.S.

"No, and it gets better. He said they're abscessed, and that the puss is running down his throat and into his stomach, making him sick."

"You're getting *me* sick."

"He said he hasn't been to work in two weeks," continued Destin. "His teeth are making him that sick."

"Oh gross!" said Bobby. "I thought you said these would be easy cases. Are you going to call him back?"

"Hell no!" he replied. "There's no way! I'm not putting my hands in that nasty mouth! I'd probably get some weird disease, like Ebola. I'm going to Dr. Loin's office tomorrow, telling him Mr. Terrebone moved to Phoenix, and asking him for a new patient." Destin picked up the phone and grinned. "So, who wants to go next?"

The other two sat there passing the phone back and forth. Now they didn't know what to expect. "I'll go, what the heck," said Mike. "There's no way mine could be as bad as Destin's. I have a 21-year-old girl named Jonquil." Mike picked up the phone and started dialing.

"Can I speak to Jonquil Hendricks?" he asked. "This is Jonquil? You sound a lot older than 21. My name is Mike Williams. I'm calling from the Dental School to make an appointment with you. No, I'm only a student. How old am I? I'm 26, and you're 21, right? Good, that means you're legal. No, I said I have an opening this Friday afternoon at 1:00. Can you make it? Great, just go to the fourth floor waiting room and I'll call your name. Ok? Then I'll see you Friday. Have a good night." Mike hung up the phone and looked at the other two.

"Man, did she sound sexy! I love a woman with a deep voice. I

Dental School Debacle

can't WAIT to put my phalanges in her mouth."

"Calm down, boy," said Destin. "Remember, they told us we're not supposed to fool around with our patients."

"You don't believe that do you Destin?" asked Mike.

"I wouldn't be in dentistry if I did."

"OK, Bobby, it's your turn," said Mike as he handed him the phone. "You see how easy this is."

"Yeah, this could be interesting," he said. "My patient's 40 years old and divorced." He picked up the phone and started dialing. "Hello, can I please speak to Ms. Picateen Garrison...Picateen Garrison! That's real nice, young man, now please leave the dog alone and go get your mama for me. Hi, Ms. Garrison, what a pretty name. No Ma'am, your son wasn't rude. No, Ms. Garrison, don't hit him again." Bobby held the phone away from his ears until the screaming subsided. "My name is Bobby, Bobby Coitus. I'm a student at the Dental School. I'm calling to make an appointment with you for this Friday afternoon at 1:00. Oh, that sounds painful. When did it happen? I'm sorry to hear that. No problem. A hu...A hu...A hu, look, we can talk about all of this later." Bobby held the phone away from his ear, again, and then interrupted the woman. "I'll see you this Friday on the fourth floor, goodbye." He hung up the phone, took a deep breath, and started looking for something to drink.

"That broad has problems," he said. Mike and Destin were intently listening. "To start off with, last week a ceiling fan fell on her head. She was also in a car wreck and has to wear a neck brace. Then she tells me her ankles swell every time she goes to the dentist, and yesterday her new tattoo got infected. Then she started listing all the drugs she's taking—she sounded like a pharmacist taking inventory. Now I have to write summaries on each one of them stupid drugs. But worst of all, she had one of those annoying, squeaky voices—the kind that makes you wanna slap your grandma."

"I like your new last name Bobby... Coitus," said Mike. "That's an original."

"Yep, I just made it up."

Destin began shaking his head in disbelief. "You better quit lying about your name, Bobby. It was funny at first, but now you're getting out of hand. Suppose she calls you Mr. Coitus in front of the instructor?"

"That'll never happen," he said with confidence. "And if it does, I'll come up with something. I always do."

Destin walked to the kitchen. "Well, now that we have that over with," he said, "it's time to play Love Boat!"

They looked at him strangely. "Play Love Boat? What's the matter with you, Destin? You're not one of them swingers, are you?"

"Have you ever watched that program, The Love Boat?"

"Never," replied Mike.

"Only when I have the flu," answered Bobby.

"To be honest with you," explained Destin, "I didn't watch it either, until I moved to Lafayette. You see, my first semester I got kicked out of the dorms, and then out of a trailer park."

"You got kicked out of the dorms, and a trailer park in one semester?"

"Yep."

"How did you manage that?"

"It was easy. Me and Fred, my roommate, got caught with

Dental School Debacle

some illegal explosives. We accidently blew up half the 4th floor bathroom of Voorhies dorm. So, they kicked us out and put us on disciplinary probation."

"But how did you get kicked out of a *trailer park*?" asked Mike.

"I'm not really sure," he explained. "After I got kicked out of the dorms my dad bought me a new mobile home. Then me and Fred moved it to a trailer park close to campus. One morning, two weeks later, a policeman showed up at our door with a stack of papers saying we had a week to move out—something about loud music and a missing Virgin Mary statue. I can't really remember. That first semester is a little blurry. Then we moved the trailer to a park way out in the country, about 10 miles from campus. I needed some peace and quiet. But we were so far out in the woods, we couldn't get cable TV. The only station we could get played The Love Boat reruns late at night. At first, we thought it was stupid, until Fred and I invented this game. Then we never missed it. Now I think it's one of the best shows ever made, except for *The Three Stooges*."

Bobby was curious. "So, tell me, Destin, how do you play The Love Boat?"

"It's easy," he replied. "All you need is a six pack of 7-Up and a bottle of tequila—both of which I keep in stock."

"Then what?" asked Mike.

"At the beginning of each program they show the celebrities who are on the cruise. Each player is randomly assigned a passenger. Since there are only three of us, we'll each get two passengers. Each time one of your assigned passengers gets kissed, invited to dinner, lied to, or finds a lost relative, you fill a glass with half seven up and half tequila, cover the glass with your hand, bang it on the table, and shoot it down. But, if your passenger achieves the ultimate cruise objective—to have dinner at the captain's table, you fill the entire glass with tequila, no 7-Up."

"This could be fun," said Bobby, "even though I hate the show. I keep hoping the Love Boat drifts off into Communist waters."

"You just don't appreciate good acting," replied Destin.

The three anxiously sat around for almost an hour waiting for The Love boat reruns. Finally, at 11:00, the program came on. Destin ran to the television and turned it all the way up. It was so loud that the small speaker was rattling. Destin stood up and began dancing.

"I love this song," he said, as he started singing along:

"The Love Boat...soon we'll be making another run...The Love Boat...promises something for everyone..."

Mike and Bobby couldn't believe how much Destin was enjoying it. Before they realized it, they were singing, too. This episode started off slowly, but the last 20 minutes were steamy. They were banging drinks on the coffee table as fast as they could pour. After the program
ended, Mike and Bobby complimented Destin on his game, and said they wanted to play it more often. That night they all slept at Destin's trailer since Bobby would not let anyone drive after drinking.

The Forgotten Tomato

Friday couldn't have come quickly enough for the students. It was now 12:45 p.m. on the last day of the freshman year.

They were anxiously hoping their patients would show up. If they didn't, they would receive an 'Incomplete' grade. Then they would have to stay in school over summer vacation and complete two patient exams instead of one. Today they would see their first real patients, even though they were not doing any work. They were still afraid they wouldn't know how to act and maybe say the wrong thing. Sure, they had a class on Human Behavior which taught them to be kind, gentle, and sympathetic: but this was real life. The budding professionals were standing behind swinging metal doors that led to the waiting room. No one wanted to be first to walk out and call their patient's name. After taking a few deep breaths, Mike bravely stepped forward.

"I can't wait any longer," he said. "I've got to see what Jonquil looks like." Mike walked into the waiting room, followed by the rest of the students.

"Ms. Jonquil Hendricks," announced Mike.

"Over here," said the deep voice from the corner chair. To his

Jim P. Sandras, D.D.S.

surprise, this tall, thin, and very beautiful black girl stood up and walked towards him. Mike thought she looked like Whitney Houston.

"Hi, I'm Jonquil," she said with a big smile. "You must be Mr. Williams."

"Call me Mike, please." The two shook hands. "I have to warn you," he said, "I love a woman with a deep voice."

Jonquil continued smiling. "I wasn't expecting a student as handsome as you."

Mike was flattered. He grabbed her by the arm and escorted her into the x-ray room and sat her in the chair.

***

Meanwhile, Terrance was in the waiting room calling his patient. "Mrs. Blanchard."

"That's me," said this large woman wearing a pink night gown and dirty slippers, struggling to stand up.

Terrance walked over and gave her a hand. "How are you doing today, Mrs. Blanchard?"

"So, so," said the woman breathing heavily. "I'm a little tired."

"I can understand why," he said. "I know being pregnant must take a lot out of a woman, but look how big you are. You must be carrying twins!"

The woman stepped up to Terrance and angrily looked him in the eyes. "I'm not pregnant."

Terrance's heart dropped. "What a way to start off a three-hour appointment," he thought to himself. He apologized to the woman and blamed it on her pink robe, saying it distorted her figure.

The rest of the students took turns calling their patients. By

Dental School Debacle

1:20 p.m. everyone had a patient in the chair except for three students, including Destin and Bobby.

"I can't believe that nut isn't here yet," complained Bobby. "She must've stopped off at the drug store."

"Mine should've been here, too," said Destin. "Dr. Loin gave me a new patient yesterday. I talked to him last night on the phone and he said he would be on time."

Just then the sedate music in the clinic stopped. That only meant one thing—someone was about to make an announcement.

"Mr. Coitus, Mr. Bobby Coitus," said the receptionist over the loudspeaker. "Your patient is here."

Bobby freaked out. All the students, faculty, and assistants looked at him. He turned three shades of red and hung his head.

"I told you," said Destin.

Bobby hurried towards the waiting room, still holding his head down. As he walked through the doors, the first thing he saw was a middle-aged, flabby woman wearing a neck brace and a head bandage, leaning against the wall, with a cane in one hand and a cigarette in the other. When he saw the infected tattoo on her bicep, Bobby knew it was his patient.

"You must be Picateen Garrison," he said.

"Yeah, that's me," said the woman, as she took one last drag. Then she dropped the cigarette on the floor and put it out with her cane.

"I'm Bobby, nice to meet you."

"What da hell kind of name is Coitus?" she asked.

"It's French. So how are you feeling today?" asked Bobby, trying to change the subject.

Jim P. Sandras, D.D.S.

"I'm not doing too good," she said. "My head still hurts from the ceiling fan, my neck is killing me from the car wreck last month, my back is sore, my allergies are acting up, I have arthritis in my knees..." The lady continued lamenting to Bobby about her ailments as he escorted her into the clinic. "My nose started bleeding, my hysterectomy scar itches, my ankles are swollen—just like I told you they would, my toes are chapped, my mouth's dry, my gums hurt, my teeth are loose..." Bobby sat her in the chair and put a napkin around her neck. "Hey, how 'bout them Atlanta Braves," he said trying to make conversation. "Did you see the game last night?"

The woman looked at Bobby as if he had a birth defect, and then went into a coughing fit that lasted several minutes. When she finished, she took the napkin from around her neck and wiped a huge wad of phlegm off her tongue. Bobby thought he was going to lose his lunch. He had to get the woman a new napkin before he continued. He couldn't look at that one any longer.

***

In the meantime, Destin was the only student whose patient hadn't shown up. He was pacing up and down the clinic, becoming extremely agitated. Destin was always in a hurry to get things over with and hated to run late. But more importantly, he didn't want to spend his summer break at school looking in degenerates' mouths, which is what would happen if he didn't finish. He anxiously walked over to the receptionist. "Can you please page Mr. Emile Wilson? He was supposed to be here an hour ago."

"Mr. Wilson has been here since this morning," she said. "He

Dental School Debacle

was here before I was. That's him over there." She pointed at this old, skinny black man who was sound asleep in a chair in the back of the waiting room. Destin quietly walked up to the man, who was snoring lightly with his mouth open. The gold crown on his front tooth had a crescent-shaped moon engraved on it. Destin gently shook him and called out his name, again. The old man closed his mouth, slowly sat up and barely opened his eyes.

"No, no, honey, I'm not sleeping. What? Who are you? Where am I?"

"You're on the fourth floor of the Dental School. My name is Destin Dufrene. You remember? I talked to you on the phone last night."

"Oh yeah, that's right," said the man, slowly regaining his senses. He yawned and rubbed his eyes as he looked around the room. "I've got an appointment with the dentist at 1:00. What time is it?"

"It's almost 2:00. How long have you been sleeping?"

"All I remember is that I got here this morning when the security guards were opening the doors. I came here instead of going home. I didn't feel like hearing my ol' lady nag."

"I've been calling your name for an hour," said Destin. "I was getting ready to blow you off and go home."

"Man, I'm sorry I fell asleep. After I talked to you last night I went out with a buddy of mine, and we drank Old Charter until 6:30 this morning. Then he dropped me off here on his way to work."

"Your friend went to work after drinking whiskey all night?"

"He works for the State. They can do stuff like that."

"That's nice," said Destin. He helped the man up and directed

Jim P. Sandras, D.D.S.

him into the clinic. "We have a lot to do this afternoon and we're already late, so let's get moving. First we need to take x-rays."

Destin rushed the man over to the x-ray room, pushed him into the dental chair and threw a large lead apron on the skinny old man, knocking the wind out of him.

We have to take 20 x-rays, so we have to hurry," said Destin as he quickly put on a pair of gloves. He had already decided that he was going to set a freshman record for taking a full mouth set of x-rays. "Before we get started let me take a quick look in your mouth."

When the old man opened his mouth, a green, vapor-like mustard gas surrounded Destin's head. Destin backed up, waving his hand in front of his nose. He wasn't expecting anything that foul. "Holy crap! When was the last time you brushed your teeth?"

"I used to brush them about every two weeks, whether they needed it or not. But when I did, it pulled the food out of the holes and they started hurting, again. So I quit brushing."

"That's very interesting," said Destin, trying not to breathe through his nose. "We can discuss your hygiene later. But right now, we have to get started with these x-rays if we want to finish today."

Destin took all 20 x-rays in less than 15 minutes, extremely fast for a freshman. On his way to the darkroom, he walked by Mike who was still taking x-rays on Jonquil. He should've been finished a long time ago. Destin stopped and watched. Mike had his whole hand in Jonquil's mouth, causing her to gag badly and make awful noises. He finally took his hand out, angrily threw the x-ray and Rhen instrument against the wall and walked over

Dental School Debacle

to Destin.

"What are you trying to do the poor girl?" asked Destin. "Palpate her vocal cords?"

"You're a lot of help," said Mike, wiping the sweat off his forehead. "I'm having a hard time getting a good x-ray of her wisdom teeth. Every time I put the film back there, she starts gagging, and then the film moves. I've already taken 34 x-rays on just her uppers. If I don't get it soon, she's going to crystallize from all the radiation. I can already detect a change in her voice. Just look at her. She's starting to glow."

"I know a trick," said Destin. "Go to the dispensary window and ask the lady for a can of xylocaine spray. Then spray it in her mouth and down her throat. That'll numb her whole pharynx. She won't gag for hours, I promise."

Mike took Destin's advice. He sprayed Jonquil's mouth for over two minutes. She was so numb she couldn't talk or swallow, and was even losing control of her eye movements. Mike then took the x-rays of her wisdom teeth with no problem, getting them each on the first try. The numbness was starting to wear off when he returned with the developed film.

"Where can I buy some of that spray?" she asked.

"Why? What do you want xylocaine for?" asked Mike curiously.

"I've always had problems with gagging."

All kinds of things were now running through Mike's head. "The only way you can get xylocaine is with a DEA number... unless you know a dental student." Mike looked around the clinic, and then put the rest of the can in her purse. "We can work out something later," he said.

Jim P. Sandras, D.D.S.

"Thank you very much," said Jonquil, rubbing her palate with her tongue while eyeing him suggestively.

"We need to get busy if we're going to finish." They were the last ones to take x-rays, and the only empty dental chair was across from Sherry. Nobody wanted to sit next to her. Having no other choice, Mike sat Jonquil there and began reviewing her medical history.

"Have you ever been hospitalized?"

"Yes, about six months ago I had an operation," she said.

"What for?"

"It was for reproductive reasons. That's all I can say."

"Sure, OK, whatever you say," said Mike, writing in the chart. "Are you on any type of medication?"

"I take 500 mg. of progesterone every day."

"So, in other words, you're on the Pill."

"I guess you can say that" she said. "I definitely can't get pregnant."

"OK, next question. Do you have any type of oral habits?" asked Mike, giving the girl a dirty look.

"What are you talking about?" she asked.

"Oh...like...chewing your fingernails, using toothpicks, sucking on poultry, things like that."

She started laughing. "You're pretty funny for a white boy. To answer your question, I like to scratch my palate."

"You mean like this?" Mike put his finger in her mouth and started tickling her palate. She started squirming in the chair.

"Ah...Ah...Ah!"

Mike couldn't believe she liked it. Neither could Sherry, who was just across the aisle looking into the mouth of a little old lady

Dental School Debacle

with purple hair. Sherry was irritated with Jonquil's noises. Trying to be considerate, Mike stopped and got back to work. As he was going down the list of questions, he was constantly interrupted by Sherry's loud squeaky voice and fake laughs. While he was taking Jonquil's blood pressure, Sherry was taking pictures with her patient.

"That girl is making me sick," Mike said to Jonquil. "She doesn't care about her patient. She's making sure the woman tells the instructor how nice she was so that she can make an 'A'. What a jerk." Mike thought of a vindictive ploy. "I have an idea," he said to Jonquil. "This'll teach her a lesson. But I'm going to need your help."

"I'll do anything for you, Mike."

"As I take your blood pressure, I want you to start groaning like I'm inflicting pain on you...loudly. And make it sound real." He put on his stethoscope.

"Sure," she said. "This sounds like fun."

As Mike was pumping the sphygmomanometer, Jonquil was letting out a groan with every pump, each one getting a little louder. Then, to Mike's surprise, she changed her tone from a painful groan to a sexy moan. She seemed to be good at it, Mike thought. Her voice carried easily through the clinic. Sherry, who had just resumed working again, stopped and put her instruments down to cover her ears.

Sherry looked at her patient with sweat forming on her upper lip. She took her thick glasses off and wiped her face with a brown paper towel. "I don't believe this," said Sherry to her patient. "I have to apologize for my classmate. I can't believe he's doing this."

Jim P. Sandras, D.D.S.

"That's terrible," said Sherry's patient. "I thought dental students were respectable people."

"Most are," she replied. "But not in this class. These guys are possessed with demons. Only Satan himself could be responsible for putting so many heathens in one school." As they were talking, Jonquil started screaming.

"I can't take this anymore!" said Sherry. She stood up and stomped through the clinic towards Dr. Loin while purposely avoiding looking at Mike.

"That girl has a lot to learn," said Mike, as he watched Sherry rush away. Suddenly, he had an idea. He quietly walked across the aisle and picked up her patient's chart. In a matter of minutes, he had changed all the information and her charting of teeth. He charted cavities on her crowns, put down gum disease where she didn't have teeth, and randomly crossed out teeth for extractions. Then he wrote that Sherry recommended dentures for the patient.

"Dr. Loin, Dr. Loin! Come see, hurry up!" yelled Sherry, running through the clinic.

"What's the matter?" asked Dr. Loin, relaxed in his chair, reading the ADA Journal.

"Mike Williams is taking advantage of his patient in the dental chair, sir."

"You've got to be joking. No one is that stupid."

"His patient has been moaning ever since they sat down," she said. "I think he's been fondling her, sir."

"She could just be in pain," he replied.

"It's not a pain moan, sir."

"This better not be a joke, young lady." Dr. Loin and Sherry

Dental School Debacle

walked across the clinic where they found Mike taking Jonquil's pulse like a real professional. Dr. Loin made Sherry wait in her cubical while he went to talk to Mike.

"How is everything going, Mr. Williams?"

"Great sir, why?"

"Miss Custard says she's been hearing strange noises coming from this cubical. Do you know what she's talking about?"

"No sir, but it's funny you mention it," said Mike, with a straight face. Jonquil looked up at the instructor and shook her head no. "Earlier this week Sherry kept asking everyone where the bats were coming from. And just this morning she asked me if I could hear the microwaves flying through the building. I think she's losing it, sir. I bet she's back on those stupid amphetamines." Mike started shaking his head.

"I heard she has to take random urine tests," said Dr. Loin, "but I didn't know why."

"She does speed, every day," said Mike. "How do you think she keeps making all those A's. I thought you knew that."

"That explains the hallucinations," said Dr. Loin. "I'll have a talk with her. So, how are you coming along with your work, Mr. Williams?"

"Fantastic! All I have to do is my charting of teeth, and then I'm finished for the year."

"Good job, young man. Let me know when you're ready to get checked off."

The instructor then walked over to Sherry and looked down at her. "I think you were hearing things, Miss Custard. Mr. Williams was not fooling around with his patient, even she told me that. In fact, he's almost finished with his work."

Jim P. Sandras, D.D.S.

"Well, I am finished," bragged Sherry.

He was impressed. "You're ready for a grade?"

"Yes sir." He washed his hands and sat in the chair next to Sherry's patient.

"How are you doing today, Mrs..."

"Cuevas," said the woman.

"Hi, Mrs. Cuevas, my name is Dr. Loin. I'm Miss Custard's instructor and will be giving her a grade for her work today."

"I think she's doing a real good job, myself," said Mrs. Cuevas. Sherry smiled and patted herself on the back.

"That's nice, but I still need to check your mouth. Open please." The woman opened wide. Dr. Loin began checking Sherry's charting of teeth and immediately found everything incorrect. He picked up the chart and examined it closely. "This is all wrong, young lady!" he said. "You have teeth marked as missing, and they're obviously still there. And how can she possibly have a cavity on a porcelain crown? And there are no signs of gum disease, like you say here."

"What are you talking about, sir?" asked Sherry, puzzled.

"For your treatment plan you have written down: Patient is an old swamp rat with poor oral and body hygiene. She doesn't own a toothbrush, nor cares to, and thinks dental floss is for fishing. I recommend we slick her gums and give her some plastic teeth with purple gums to match her hair!"

Mrs. Cuevas, who was listening intensely, was extremely insulted.

"A swamp rat with gum disease? Young lady, how dare you!" She sat up and tried to hit Sherry, but Dr. Loin wrestled her back down and started explaining.

Dental School Debacle

"I'm sorry, Mrs. Cuevas, but we have a little issue here and I feel obligated to tell you. You see, Miss Custard has a drug problem—they give her energy." Sherry was stunned. She couldn't believe she was hearing the same lie again, and this time from an instructor. "These pills can cause a person to see and hear things that really aren't there," he explained. "We thought she was off them, but obviously she's not. I believe it's in everyone's best interest that I dismiss you. And if she's better in two weeks we can try this again."

"But sir, that's not true; it's just a rumor! I've never done drugs in my life!"

"We know, Miss Custard, we know. Just meet me in my office at 5:00 this afternoon, and we can discuss it further."

Mike and Jonquil had to bite the insides of their cheeks not to laugh as Dr. Loin helped Mrs. Cuevas out of the chair and escorted her out of the clinic. Nearby students couldn't believe what was going on. When Dr. Loin walked back to Sherry, she was distraught as she picked up her instruments.

"I'm really surprised at your behavior, Miss Custard. Never take anything that can hinder your performance in clinic, even if it's just cough syrup. And as far as the swamp rat with plastic teeth, never talk about your patients like that. Don't ever write any personal thoughts on a chart, no matter how much you hate them. There's a good chance the patient will find out and take you to court for slander."

"But sir, I didn't write that on there!"

Dr. Loin ignored her pleas and started walking away. "Just meet me in my office at 5:00; we'll talk about it more. I hope you don't have anything planned for the summer."

Jim P. Sandras, D.D.S.

Sherry was practically in tears. She didn't know what to do. She grabbed her instruments and walked away like a punished child.

Mike turned and looked at Jonquil. "Hey, thanks a lot," he said, giving her one of his easy looks with his soft brown eyes. "I've never dated a black woman before, but I would be honored if you'd come with me to our first annual End-of-the-Year Party. It starts this afternoon and goes until Sunday. We're having it at this mansion on the Gulf of Mexico in Mississippi. It ought to be a blowout—everyone's talking about it."

She smiled. "I'd love to."

"Great, it'll be fun," said Mike, leaning her chair back and pointing the light on her face. "First, let's get this dental stuff over with."

***

On the other side of the clinic, far from Sherry, Destin was examining his patient's radiographs. He noticed a large dark area on the x-ray around the man's upper right canine. This usually indicated a lesion or an infection inside the jaw, eating the bone away. Destin showed the film to the patient and tried to explain the situation.

"We have a problem right here, Mr. Wilson. This dark spot around your root is an infection. Hey, I'm only a freshman, but by the look of this radiograph I'm willing to bet my sister that we won't be able to save it. I think it's a goner."

"Which tooth are you talking about?" asked the hung-over man.

Destin gave the man a mirror and pointed to his upper right canine and said, "Yeah, I think this one's history."

Dental School Debacle

"You mean you have to pull it?"

"That's right. We'll put some cold steel to it and pop it right out. Then you can take it home and put it under your pillow."

The man slapped his leg in frustration. "Man, and I just glued that thing in there good."

"What are you talking about?" asked Destin.

"Well, ya' see, that same tooth fell out a year ago and I stuck it back in with crazy glue, but it didn't work too good. Every few weeks it'd fall out. Then a few months ago I got this glue from a friend of mine who works for Dow Chemical. I glued it in with that stuff and it's been staying in there really good ever since."

"Excuse me for a second," said Destin, biting his lip. "I have to bleed my bladder. I'll be right back." He ran into the bathroom so the man couldn't hear him laugh. He was laughing so hard his sides were cramping. One of the patients in the bathroom thought Destin was having intestinal problems when he locked himself in a stall and started crying. When he finally got his laughter under control, he hurried around the clinic telling his friends.

"Hey, my patient glued his tooth in with a Dow chemical that's eating his skull away!"

Destin walked back to his chair, shaking his head and thinking to himself. "And this is only my first patient! Well, really, my first patient is still home sick to his stomach from swallowing puss, waiting for me to call him back. I can hardly wait to see what happens next."

***

It was now 3:30, and Bobby had finally finished taking the medical history of his patient. A normal 20-minute procedure

Jim P. Sandras, D.D.S.

had taken him two hours. If she didn't have every disease known to modern medicine, she knew someone who did. She had been hospitalized so many times that she had a permanent white ring around her wrist from wearing name bracelets. She was hospitalized for everything from motorbike wrecks, to ovarian cysts, to infected tattoos. She also had a kid every nine and a half months for 11 straight years, until she had a hysterectomy, which also got infected. To make matters worse, she was allergic to seven types of animals, two races of humans, cotton material (she could only wear polyester), all cosmetics, and 13 different kinds of drugs. And she was presently taking eight medications, each of which he had to look up and write a paragraph about. He also had to stop four times to let her take her pills. By the time he finished, he felt like he had written a biography on the woman.

"OK, now that I know how many times you urinate a day, let's begin the oral exam."

"This isn't going to hurt, huh?" asked the woman, scratching her infected tattoo. "Last time I went to a dentist he pulled a tooth without using Novocaine. And let me tell ya', that was worse than when I had twins at a KISS concert at the Warehouse."

"It shouldn't hurt," said Bobby, growing impatient. "Unless I don't finish this afternoon, and then I can't promise anything. The only thing I'm going to put in your mouth is this little mirror and an explorer, which is nothing more than a tiny metal pick that I use to feel your teeth." He showed her the instruments. "All I'm going to do is check your teeth with these. But before we do that, I have to give you a head and neck examination."

"Anything you say, as long as it don't hurt...or cost me extra

Dental School Debacle

money."

Bobby removed her neck brace and began palpating her neck. As soon as he touched the woman, she jumped up and slapped him in the face. "What the heck ya' think ya' doing, dude?"

"I - I - I was examining your neck for swollen lymph nodes."

"No dentist has ever done that to me before, and you're not going to start now! And give me back my neck brace before someone sees me."

"Well, I guess the head and neck exam is over. Everything looks just fine." Then he checked 'negative' on all the questions. "Now, let's check your teeth."

"It's about time," she said restlessly. "I've been here for almost three hours, and you haven't even looked in my mouth! Every time I went to the dentist before they never messed around with all these stupid questions, like, how many times I pee a day. A real dentist would've went straight to my mouth and pulled a tooth, no questions asked."

"Believe me, I wouldn't be asking you all this crap if I didn't have to," said Bobby, mumbling under his breath, "you overweight medicine cabinet."

"What did you say, dude?" she asked.

"Open wide please." Bobby immediately put both of his hands in the woman's mouth to make sure she wouldn't start talking again. But she went into another coughing fit and sat up to spit what looked like small pieces of lung tissue into the spittoon. Trying not to gross out, he calmly took the air and water syringe, aimed it at the foreign object in the spittoon, and sprayed it down the drain. After he was sure she had mellowed and cleared her throat, he began the oral exam. He started off by examining

Jim P. Sandras, D.D.S.

under and around her tongue, and then checked her cheek gums. Unexpectedly, he noticed a large red lesion above her gums next to her upper right molars. Bobby panicked—he found cancer! His heart rate jumped. How could he tell this woman that she was about to lose the side of her face? He tried to be as calm as possible, but frank with her.

"Uh, Mrs. Garrison, I found something in your mouth that is abnormal."

"W-W-What are you talking about?" questioned the woman as she gripped the armrest tighter.

"On the side of your gums, by your cheek, you have this large red sore, which usually isn't a good sign. Generally speaking, 90 percent of all red sores turn into cancer."

"Oh my God! I got cancer! Aaaahhh!!" The woman began screaming. Then she jumped out of the chair and ran up and down the aisle crying. She was hysterical. "I got cancer! I got cancer!" she kept yelling.

Dr. Loin, who had just gotten comfortable in his chair, jumped up and ran towards the excitement. "What's going on here?" he asked.

"Dr. Loin," explained Bobby, "I just told this woman she had an erythrymic vestibule."

"Oh my God!" screamed the woman. "I got a rytic messystool, too— aahhhh!!" The woman fainted.

Dr. Loin grabbed the oxygen tank and began administering it to the woman. A few minutes later she came to, sat up, and began screaming again.

"Calm down, just calm down. Everything's going to be all right," said Dr. Loin, putting his hands on her shoulders. "He

Dental School Debacle

couldn't have hurt you that bad."

"He didn't hurt me. He told me I had cancer!" Then she screamed and passed out again.

"What is she talking about, Mr. Pubix?"

"I was just giving her a routine oral exam when I noticed this large red lesion in her upper right vestibule. Then I told her that 90 percent of these lesions turn into cancer."

Dr. Loin walked up to Bobby and looked him in the eyes. "How stupid! That's just as good as telling her she had cancer!" The instructor was extremely upset. "No doctor, especially a freshman dental student, is in a position to make a diagnosis like that without a biopsy report!" Bobby felt dumber than a turkey caught in a mouse trap. "Young man, you could get sued for something like this. Give me a hand with this lady and let's put her back in the chair."

Bobby, Dr. Loin, and two other students struggled for 20 minutes to get her back into the dental chair. Then they administered her more oxygen until she came to.

"Give me that mirror and explorer," said the still upset Dr. Loin as he sat in the chair next to her. "Let me look at this red sore. Open your mouth for me, please. I just want to look." Dr. Loin took the mirror and examined the woman's mouth. After only a few seconds of observation, he looked at Bobby, shook his head, picked up the explorer, and pulled out a large red object.

"With a little more careful observation, Mr. Pubix, you would have noticed that this was not a red sore. This is nothing but a piece of tomato—look at the seeds in it. It was wedged between her teeth."

Jim P. Sandras, D.D.S.

"Oh yeah," said the relieved woman. "I had a salad for lunch."

Then the woman grabbed the piece of tomato from the explorer, tossed it in her mouth and finished eating it. "I love Creole tomatoes," she said while chewing.

Bobby grabbed his side and started gagging. Dr. Loin looked at him and laughed. "You haven't seen anything yet, son."

First Annual End-of-the-Year Party

The last day of freshman year, most of the class headed 60 miles east to Destin's family summer home in Pass Christian, Mississippi. It was a three story, six-bedroom, contemporary style home located on a picturesque two-acre lot overlooking Bay St. Louis and the Gulf of Mexico. It had its own private beach and 200-foot-long pier. The class nominated Terrance to take complete responsibility of organizing the three-day extravaganza. He had organized several parties throughout the year and had done a superb job, and he loved doing it. First, he sent all hygiene and dental assistant students handwritten invitations and maps to the party. Then, the day before the party, he and Destin drove to the house and posted large signs all along I-10 and various points along the route to make sure no one got lost. Terrance assembled a few of the musically inclined students together and formed a band called Synthetic Saliva.

Each student chipped in $45 to pay for the food, drinks, boat gas, fireworks, life insurance, and all the beer they could drink in a weekend. It was a real bargain. Students started showing up

Jim P. Sandras, D.D.S.

around 6:00 Friday afternoon. Terrance pulled up in a truck with 10 kegs of beer, just enough for a weekend with 50 thirsty ex-freshmen and their dates, 20 hygienists, and a few brave dental assistants. Most went straight to the pier and eventually set up a keg at the end. Destin borrowed his brother's 22-foot Cigarette speed boat and was taking everyone water skiing. Most didn't know how. They put on a ski vest, jumped in the water and hung on to the rope. Sooner or later, they were bound to come out of the water on the skis.

Later that afternoon, Synthetic Saliva started playing on the beach. Most partygoers gathered around the band and began slam dancing.

Around 10:00 that night, Bobby, and a few others drove off and came back with three large bags of fireworks. All the guys went crazy when they saw them and demanded more, lots more. They knew three bags wouldn't last long. Soon there were two carloads of students with pockets full of money on their way to the fireworks stand. It was just a matter of time before the small beach in front of the house sounded like a war zone. There were so many explosions that the students inside were having a hard time hearing each other speak. They had all types of fireworks, from Roman Candles to large rockets. But the most popular were the bottle rockets. They were small enough to throw at each other and aim with pinpoint accuracy, and yet take off with enough velocity to reach 100 feet, or put someone's eye out, depending on where it's aimed.

At 3:00 a.m. a few exhausted students tried to get some sleep, but every few minutes a particular crazed drunken student would throw a firecracker on the balconies outside the bedrooms,

Dental School Debacle

scaring everyone inside. Sleeping was impossible. The same reckless student shot a bottle rocket towards the house. It got caught in the screen door and started a fire. Luckily someone was there to put it out before there was too much damage. A hygienist finally wrestled the crazed student to the ground and took the firecrackers away. Soon afterwards most fell asleep, with several sharing each bedroom. Some also slept on the pier, or in tents, and a few even crashed out in hammocks. Sarah made the mistake of falling asleep in a hammock while Brick was still awake drinking. He walked up to the sleeping beauty and grunted.

"My sweet Sarah." He went to his car, took out some rope and an unopened bottle of Seagram's V.O. Canadian Whiskey and then sat on the porch next to Destin, who was gazing up at the Big Dipper with only one eye open. Brick opened the V.O. and started drinking copious amounts straight from the bottle.

"What are you doing with rope, Brick?" questioned Destin.

Do you have a ladder?" he asked.

"Why? You're going to hang someone?"

"Yep, and you can give me a hand." Brick took a few more big gulps of the whisky and handed Destin the bottle. "Let's wait for her to go into a deeper sleep. I think they call it REM."

The two took a few more shots, and then got the ladder. Brick walked up to Sarah, who was now sound asleep, grabbed both sides of the hammock, pulled them together over her, and then wrapped the rope around it, closing her in like a burrito. Then they untied both ends from the pine trees, carried her to an oak tree next to the porch, and tied just one end to a large branch. She hung there sleeping like a worm in a cocoon. Brick looked at her and started laughing, and then gave her a little push. She swung back and forth through the air like a tire swing, sleeping through it all.

The two went back to the porch where there were a few troopers still awake drinking. They were talking on the porch when the sun came up. By this time, the V.O. had helped them figure out the meaning of life and develop a new and better way to run the government. Destin and Brick were hooking up a fresh keg when they heard a loud scream. One of the hygienists sleeping in a tent outside, came running into the house scared to death.

"There's a bear outside!" she yelled. "There's a bear outside!" Then the rest of the girls came running in behind her saying the same thing.

"What's going on here?" questioned Destin. "There are no bears on the Mississippi Coast."

"Well, some type of large, ugly animal stuck its head in our tent and started making these weird noises," said the out of breath girl. "We all crawled out the back of the tent and ran for our lives."

"It's still out there!" said another girl.

"It looks like a hippopotamus with horns," said one of the girls.

Destin and Brick ran to the basement to grab a paddle and a pellet gun, and then went hunting for the unknown animal. By this time the two felt bullet proof and were ready for some action. They searched the sides of the house, in between the cars and around the tents, but didn't find anything except Kate, sleeping by herself in a van. Then they walked around the back

Dental School Debacle

of the house to the pier. When they turned the corner, they could see the rear end of an animal sticking out from behind a palm tree.

"It's Big Foot!" yelled Brick, as he took off running after it with the paddle. "We got you! We finally got a Big Foot. You ain't going nowhere! I'll be on the news."

"Stop it! I'm not a Big Foot!" said a voice from inside the animal. "I'm a cow!"

Brick freaked out and started beating on it harder. "Destin, come see! It's talking! It said it's a cow!"

"Stop hitting us! We're human!" yelled the cow as it took off running.

Destin ran after the animal, grabbed it by the horns, and wrestled it to the ground. When they hit the grass, the head fell off, and there was a familiar face.

"Fred!" yelled Destin, "I'm glad you made it. Man, I should've known you had something to do with this!" Destin gave his old friend a hug.

"Mais, wat 'bout me? I don't get a kiss?" asked the voice from the rear end of the cow suit as it was unzipping.

"Boulon! I can't believe it! Good to see you, bro." Destin turned and looked at Brick running over with the paddle getting ready to hit Boulon. "Brick, stop! It's alright. These are two good friends of mine dressed up in a cow outfit. Come meet them."

"Where did you get the cow suit?" asked Brick in between breaths.

Boulon was soaking with sweat from wearing the hot outfit. "My cou-san. It was left ova from Mardi Gras."

The three old friends stood up and started punching on one

Jim P. Sandras, D.D.S.

another like kids. After Destin introduced Fred and Boulon to everyone who was awake, they went to the porch and tapped a fresh keg. The remainder of the students finally woke up around noon. As they were sitting on the porch talking, Kate came walking out of the house toward the beach wearing an overly tight, one-piece bathing suit and carrying a portable radio and beach towel. Her matted hair was pulled up with a ribbon and her skin was ghostly white. The guys on the porch couldn't help but comment on her appearance.

"What the heck was that?" asked Fred, making a putrid face.

"That's Trog," said Destin. "She's cool, just don't stick your hand in front of her mouth."

Boulon gave her an evil eye. "Mais, I'd lik to hit ha wit my hamma".

"Don't make fun of the girl," said Brick. "She told me she has a glandular problem."

"Mais, looks like she got her a el-bow pra-blem to me."

"An elbow problem?" asked Destin. "What are you talking about?"

"Evera-time she done move her elbo, her mout opens up."

"So Destin, how's dental school going?" asked Fred.

"It's harder than I thought, but it still beats working for my dad. It's actually a lot of fun. When I started, I thought all my classmates would be a bunch of boring, straight-necks who only talk about teeth, but most of these guys are crazier than me! We've got some real characters in our class, especially this one guy named Bobby 'something'. He's a trip—one of a kind. He's around here somewhere."

Destin scanned the area for Bobby, who was nowhere to be

Dental School Debacle

found. "When I get out of school, I'm going to write a book about him. In fact, I'm already taking notes. Last week I overheard some of our instructors talking, and they agreed that our class has more lunatics than any other in history. And you ought to see the patients we have to work on, Fred. They're from a different world. I believe the dean recruits them from a psych ward on Rampart Street. Most only brush their teeth when there's a full moon."

Fred squinted. "Mmmm, I bet that smells good in the morning."

"Mais, I tink I would make dem rinse wit dat kerosine befo I look in a mout like dat," Boulon added.

"You have no idea what it smells like," said Destin, sipping on his morning beer. "So, Fred, how's school going for you? Are you still trying to set the world record for dropping the most classes while on the eight-year associate degree program?"

"Nope. I dropped the big one this time," he said, as he finished off his beer and threw the plastic cup off the balcony. "School."

Destin was shocked. "WHAT! You dropped out of college?"

"Yep," replied Fred humbly. "I wasn't sure what I wanted to do anyway. I've majored in everything at least twice. I have no earthly idea how many credit hours I have. And I've missed so many classes the local paper did an article on me. But after our cow expedition last year I finally realized my calling. Now I'm a butcher."

"A butcher!"

"That's me," said Fred. "Boulon's friend Ron Guidry got me a job at Veron's Meat Market after you moved the trailer. I started working part-time in packing, and then worked my way up to

Jim P. Sandras, D.D.S.

butcher, all in one year. Now I'm full time. And I have to say, Destin, every time I slaughter a cow, I think of you."

"I'm flattered."

While they were talking, a gun went off in the house. Everyone jumped and looked around to see what happened. Then they heard screaming and cursing coming from one of the bedrooms on the third floor. Seconds later, Jonquil came running out of the house half-dressed, right past Destin, sprinting down the pier and diving into the water. Then Mike came running out of the house in his underwear, carrying a large pistol in his hand.

"Where did it go? I'm going to kill it!" Mike said as he searched the porch.

Destin pointed to the water where the girl was now swimming away. Mike took three shots from the porch with his .38, just missing her.

"She was that good, huh?" joked Destin.

"What's going on, Mike?" asked Brick, ready to get in on the action.

"I made out with her all night," replied Mike as he checked to see how many bullets he had left in the chamber. "She even sprayed her mouth with xylocaine. When I caught a glimpse under the sheet this morning and saw that *she* was a *he*, I freaked out."

Mike paused and thought for a moment.

"That means I was kissing a guy all night. AHHH! I'm going to kill her, I mean him. Whatever it is, it's dead!" Mike took three more shots at Jonquil and yelled "You lied to me!" He ran inside to reload, and then ran to Destin who was now by the keg pouring beers for his two old friends.

Dental School Debacle

"Destin, can I use the boat, pleeease?"

"The keys are in the ignition. Just promise me you won't sink it. It's not mine. And don't hurt him too badly. Remember, you have three more years of school."

"Don't worry," said Mike. "I'm only going to turn her, I mean him, into crab bait."

He took another shot from the porch and purposely hit the water right in front of Jonquil. Mike started yelling violently and ran down the pier in his underwear, jumped in the boat and took off after her. All the commotion awakened Sarah, who was still hanging from the tree tied up in the hammock. When she first woke up, she was confused. When she realized where she was, she struggled to get loose, and her hammock started swinging.

"Help! Somebody get me out of here!" she pleaded. "I think I'm going to be sick. Help! Brick, if you had anything to do with this, you had better leave now cause I'm going to neuter you when I get down!" But everyone laughed, including Brick. "Come on y'all, get me down from here. I don't feel so good."

Still, no one moved. "You shouldn't have drunk so much," yelled Brick.

Sarah looked at him and threw up all over the hammock. Brick threw down his drink, ran over and quickly untied her. He then carried her to the side of the house where he hosed her off before bringing her inside and putting her to bed. As soon as he took her into the house, Mike came zooming by the pier dragging Jonquil by a ski rope. He was bouncing across the water, gasping for breaths of air. Mike was screaming and shooting his pistol in the air as he took off towards the Gulf of Mexico.

Fred shook his head and laughed. "Man, Destin, you always

Jim P. Sandras, D.D.S.

did throw the best parties. Do you think he's really going to kill him?"

"Nah...look now," Destin pointed. "He's cutting him loose by the pier next to Highway 90. He can hitchhike home."

Terrance finally rolled out of bed and went straight to the barbeque pit before brushing his teeth. By 10:00 they were eating boudin and drinking margaritas. Bobby kept the blender going and the frozen libations flowing. After lunch they set up a volleyball net on the beach and formed teams. The losers had to do the dishes and pick up trash around the house Sunday afternoon.

Later that day, after a few margaritas, Destin, Fred, Boulon and Brick went hunting in Kiln, a small country town about 20 miles north of the beach. All they took with them was a gaff, a hatchet, two hammers and a 9-iron. They came back several hours later with a dead goat.

Around 8:00 Bobby, Sam and two other students took out guitars and a harmonica and played Jimmy Buffett songs on the porch. They tried to get Jimmy himself, but he was busy that night. Everybody knew all the words by heart and sang along. By this time the blender was making a rough grinding noise and smoking—it had been running nonstop for over eight hours. After they finished playing, everyone gathered on the beach and started a large bon-fire.

Then the four hunters quietly snuck off from the crowd and came back to the beach wearing only towels around their waists and palm leaves on the heads, carrying the goat on a homemade stretcher, and placed it near the fire. The four spray-painted the goat purple, and shaved 'LSU' on its back. The whole class

Dental School Debacle

formed a circle around the campfire, and then Sarah came running out of the house dressed like a witch doctor. She danced over to the goat and sprinkled sand on it. It was obvious she was feeling better. The students stayed up all night roasting and eating the goat, while emptying the remaining kegs. They all woke up Sunday afternoon with Class V hangovers, i.e., loss of speech, blurred vision, dry heaves, severe dehydration, body pains, blood in the urine, fear of small animals, and any type of light.

Sam was the first one to get up, at 1:00 p.m. He went downstairs to the kitchen and grabbed an arm full of Cokes and a large bottle of Extra-Strength Tylenol and passed them around. Some were so sick they couldn't even swallow a pill. Eventually everyone got up and stumbled around. Kate was the last one up.

She was so sunburned she couldn't move. Terrence rubbed margarine all over her body thinking it would help. Thirty minutes later she looked like one big water blister and had to be driven home. No one was talking much because their throats were hurting from yelling all weekend. The losers of the volleyball match started doing dishes and picking up trash in the yard, while Destin walked around assessing the property damage. They eventually got the place cleaned. The students told one another bye and left for home to spend the remaining vacation days with their families. Mike, Bobby and Sam headed to Panama City to continue the party.

A fellow student, Bart Lucas, was looking for someone to travel on with him on his old, 20-foot, wooden sailboat. He asked several people, but most didn't know how to sail, or were afraid to. Finally, he asked Destin.

Jim P. Sandras, D.D.S.

"You know how to sail, don't you Destin?"

"It's been a long time. I used to have a 16-foot Hobie Cat. Why?"

"My uncle said I can use his sailboat all summer. He never uses it. I'd love to take it down to the Keys, but I don't want to go alone."

"When are you leaving?"

"Tomorrow."

"I'd love to, Bart, but I'm leaving Tuesday to go to Jamaica with my girlfriend."

"You have a girlfriend?"

"Yeah."

"Why didn't you bring her to the party?"

"This is no place to bring a lady."

"I understand," replied Bart. "Then I guess I'll see you in a few weeks at orientation. Thanks for the party, Destin. It was a classic." Destin, Fred and Boulon spent Sunday night at the house, reminiscing about the old times in the trailer park. The next morning Destin told his two friends good-bye, and then drove straight to his father's insurance agency to file a claim. He had to tell the agent the truth about what happened—that a group of Mexican drug warlords who were trying to illegally immigrate into our great country, landed on the beach, scared everyone away with guns, and then ransacked the mansion.

Sophomore Year

Microscopically Dead

The sophomore class was to meet in Auditorium B at 8:00 Tuesday morning, July 5th. The students were upset about starting school the day after Independence Day. Most of them would've called in sick if it weren't for the letter they received specifically saying NOT to miss the orientation Tuesday morning if they wanted to go on to the second year. The students were gathered outside the auditorium exchanging stories about what they did over the break as they waited for the dean. Most of the class was four shades darker than they were a month prior. The students without the tans were standing by the water fountains talking about this new thing called video games. Destin, Mike and Bobby were standing next to the ashtray by the elevators so Bobby could smoke his small, Swisher Sweet cigar.

"I had a blast in Jamaica," said Destin. "Heather and I went, but she left me there. Now we're not dating anymore."

Bobby nonchalantly blew out a ring of smoke. "Y'all broke up?" he asked. "What happened?"

"Our second day there Heather just wanted to hang out by the pool and tan, but I wanted to walk on the beach and explore. I was climbing these huge rocks when I met this native girl who looked just like the one in the island's commercials. I asked if that was her in the ad and she said no, but we kept talking. Then she lit up a cigarette that smelled just like chocolate. She called it ganja. She offered me some and I didn't want to be rude, so I took a puff. The next thing I knew I was underwater talking to the fish. The scary part was they were talking back. Then my mind went blank. I completely forgot about Heather. Later, she found me snorkeling with the girl. I couldn't remember who she was, until she started yelling. She ran back to the hotel room, packed her stuff, and flew back to Louisiana by herself. So, I just hung around with island girl the rest of the week, I think. I'm just starting to get my memory back."

Mike and Bobby were laughing at Destin's story. "So, it's definitely over? You're not even talking to Heather anymore?" asked Mike.

"Nope. I tried calling her to apologize, but both she and her parents kept hanging up on me. It's all for the best. She started talking marriage. Just the thought of marriage gives me diarrhea."

"Don't look now, guys," said Mike, "but guess who's walking this way?"

"Bob Hope," said Destin.

"Nope, but close. Darl Rose, the Yankee, and he has a new haircut."

"Yeah," said Bobby. "He kept trying to hang out with me at the End-of-the-Year Party."

"Didn't you cover him with Nair that Saturday night?" asked Mike.

"Yeah, and it looks like his hair is just starting to grow back, at

Dental School Debacle

least in some spots."

"Someone told me his stepmother spent a lot of money in bribes making sure he only got accepted into this dental school," said Destin. "She didn't want Darl within a 1000-mile radius of Boston, they say. Shh, here he comes."

"How goes it fellows?" asked Darl politely. The lack of hair on most of his head made him look as if he was undergoing treatment for leukemia.

"It goes great," said Bobby. "Now that I'm out on bail."

"Well, that's nice," said Darl. He didn't know what to say after that comment.

"Hey, nice haircut, Darl," said Destin. "Was it a mowing accident?"

"I know it's not too aesthetically pleasing, but it's comfortable," said Darl, making the best of it.

"Did you go back home for the break?" questioned Bobby.

"No, my stepmother wouldn't let me."

"Oh, how nice of her. I just love a close family," said Bobby. "So, what did you do on your vacation, Darl?"

He smiled. "I stayed around the school and worked on my project. I'm doing research on the hydrophilic and thermosetting expansion properties of dimethyl acrylate diisocycnate urethane methacrylate resins in Class II situations."

Destin facetiously banged on the wall. "Man, I was thinking about doing the same thing!"

The other two started laughing. As they continued talking, Terrance came running out of the auditorium.

"Come on, the dean's starting to lecture!" The whole class immediately ended their small talk and rushed into the auditorium.

"I hope I'm not interrupting anyone's little conversations out there," said the dean in an unpleasant tone while everyone hurried to get a seat. He waited for the room to come to a silence before he continued. "I can wait until everyone's finished talking about their vacation, if you'd like," he said. "I mean it's only ten after eight. You've only wasted 10 minutes of the sophomore year." The entire class was now staring at the dean in silence. "I thought I made it clear last year that I expect you to be punctual at all times, especially when I'm lecturing. We're not going to let this happen again, right?"

"No, sir!" answered the class in unison.

"Before we go on, I would like to congratulate you on making it through the first year of dental school, which is one of the hardest years in any school, except for maybe the junior year. I don't know if you've noticed, but this class is now six students smaller. Last year we started off with 75 students. Now it's down to 69. Four failed Gross Anatomy, one failed Biochemistry, and one student stole a sailboat from a marina on Lake Pontchartrain and sailed to Cuba, where he was picked up by the Cuban Navy. Now he's locked up in one of their schizophrenic wards. His parents called the Ambassador to try to get him out, but he sent word to his parents that he likes it there and wants to stay. I guess we won't be seeing Mr. Bart Lucas around here anymore."

"He told me the boat was his uncle's," whispered Destin. "And I almost went with him!"

"He did look a little tense," said Bobby. "I told him to start drinking more, but I guess he didn't listen."

Dental School Debacle

"He did listen," said Mike. "That's why he's in Cuba."

"Last year was 95 percent book work and 5 percent clinic," continued the dean. "This year will be 75 percent books and 25 percent clinic. Some of the lecture courses you will be taking are Physiology, Microbiology, General Pathology, Periodontics, and many others. In clinic you will learn how to make a complete set of dentures, clean teeth, and administer local anesthetic. This you will learn by giving injections on one another. It's always interesting." The dean smiled for the first time this morning.

"Then finally, clinical operative, the bread and butter of dentistry. This is where you learn to restore a decayed tooth. As you are aware, every day that you are in clinic you must wear a blue clinic jacket along with a tie. No white jackets are to be worn by students, as only the doctors wear white."

"I'm depressed," said Bobby. "You mean I'm not a doctor yet? And I've been going around introducing myself as Doctor Bobby."

"That's OK for you, Bobby," said Destin. "Cause that's probably the closest you're going to come to telling anyone your real name."

"Also, you must look like a professional at all times," said the dean with his perfectly starched jacket and shiny, black shoes. "That is, hair combed, daily shaving for you guys, short and clean fingernails, nostrils that are free of unknown objects, fresh breath, and a face that is void of white heads. And for God's sake, please use deodorant. Remember, your patients' heads spend most of their time under your arms. There's nothing that will run a patient out of an office like an unshaved, stinky, bad-breath dentist with grease under their nails."

Jim P. Sandras, D.D.S.

"Hey Mike, the dean's talking about you, again," joked Destin.

"Funny, Destin, you waterhead," replied Mike.

"And when you leave this building the clinic jackets are to come off," continued the dean. "We don't want you hanging out at places like, uh, what's the name of that hole-in-the-wall down the street where you students frequent?"

"The Tavern!" yelled out Bobby.

"That's it," said the dean.

Bobby took the opportunity to advertise. "Where it's happy hour every day from 5 to 7 p.m., and ladies' night every Wednesday, and..."

"That's enough, Mr. Pubix," interrupted the dean. "Like I was saying, no jacket bearing the dental school emblem is to be worn in any bar, lounge, tavern, or restaurant. We don't need that type of publicity. Students used to wear them out to bars. I guess they thought it would help them meet girls, but all it resulted in was dozens of phone calls to the school complaining about their vulgar behavior. Not only was it embarrassing to the school, but it was tying up the phone lines." The dean paused and shuffled through some papers on the podium. "Before I let you go, I would like to announce the names of the two students with the highest averages in the class last year. The number one student, finishing with a G.P.A. of 4.00 is Lewis Tripper." The whole class gave him a standing ovation. He just remained in his seat and calmly raised his index finger. "In second place," continued the dean," is a student who had all A's and one D, in Oral Diagnosis. With a G.P.A. of 3.90 is Miss Sherry Custard." She stood up and took a bow while the rest of the class remained in their seats. Only two people even attempted to clap. She turned

Dental School Debacle

red and quickly sat down.

"The classes you will be starting this week are Microbiology, which begins this afternoon, Pain Control, Oral Surgery, Removable Prosthodontics, and Occlusal Equilibration. As you finish one course, another one will be added. In just a few months you will be making your first set of dentures. By the end of the year, you will be drilling your first tooth on a patient and administering the anesthesia yourself. You can see that you have a lot to learn in a short amount of time, so don't get behind in your work. Are there any questions?" The room remained silent. They all had brains full of questions but were afraid to ask for fear of looking stupid. "Good," said the dean. The whole class got up and walked towards the elevators.

Bobby walked up to Mike and patted him on the back. "Good job, buddy," he said. "It looks like that little stunt you pulled on Sherry last year not only caused her to lose her summer vacation, but also cost her the first-place spot. I'm proud of you, my man. Just for that I'm going to tear up your tab at the Tavern for May, that you've been owing all summer."

"Hey, thanks a lot, Bobby. I know that bill must've been around $100."

"$342.75 to be exact."

"Wow, I must've been really thirsty that month."

***

After lunch, Mike and Bobby went up to the 6th floor Microbiology lab and sat in the back next to Brick and Sarah. A few minutes later the professor walked up to the podium, took one last puff on his cigarette, and threw the butt in a sink nearby. He then spent the next five minutes clearing his throat and adjusting the microphone. The students were grossed out by the loud hacking coughs. He was about 40 years old, thin, with long hair and a beard. He looked like the type that could have been arrested for selling LSD at Woodstock.

"First, I want to welcome you to the second year of Dental School," he said. "My name is Dr. Fagen, and this is Microbiology—the study of living things that are too small to see with the naked eye but will affect you every day as a practicing dentist. We're going to start off with a very easy, but practical exercise. I don't want any of you to brush your teeth for the next 24 hours, and tomorrow when you come in, you will take the plaque scrapings off your partner's teeth and fix them onto a glass slide to look at under a high-powered microscope. We will try to identify all microorganisms in the plaque smear. In the average human mouth one can identify over 400 different types of bacteria, which can change from day to day. You've all probably heard the saying, you're better off getting bit by a dog than a human. This is true. You will all be amazed at the number of different types of bugs you will see when you look in the scopes tomorrow. I've randomly assigned you partners. This will be your partner for the remainder of the course. I posted the pairings, along with desk and microscope numbers, on the side bulletin board. Go ahead and check the list, and then come to the front to pick up your assigned microscope. I have a lot of sample slides for you to look at today, so I suggest you get moving. And don't forget about the reading assignment on the blackboard."

The students rushed to the bulletin board to find out who their new partners would be. Among all the confusion, Destin, who

Dental School Debacle

was running late, snuck in the back door and walked up to Bobby standing at the back of the room.

"What's going on?" asked Destin.

"Dr. Fagen randomly paired us up. And get this, we can't brush our teeth until tomorrow afternoon."

"You mean I can't use my new cinnamon-flavored, extra-waxed dental floss?"

"Nope, not even mouthwash."

Mike looked happy as he walked back from checking the list. "Destin, you won't believe who your lab partner is for the next six months."

"Who?"

"Joseph Smith...the Mormon!"

Destin made a deep grunting noise, then punched Trog in the shoulder as she walked by.

"Why are you so upset?" asked Mike, "I heard he's pretty smart."

"Yeah, but he's about as much fun as watching Donny Osmond pick his nose. I bet he spends his Saturday nights sitting around watching PBS and drinking Tang. Some nights he probably gets crazy and puts an extra teaspoon of it in his glass. Ooh, what a party animal! I bet he wakes up in the morning with some type of anti-hangover."

Bobby gave one of his pretty smiles. "If you're lucky, Destin, he'll introduce you to his sister."

"Great! She probably looks like him, only fatter and with shorter hair, and probably not as fun."

"You're way off," said Bobby. "She's one of the best-looking women I've ever seen."

Jim P. Sandras, D.D.S.

"I don't know whether to believe you or not, Bobby."

"Hey look, I don't lie to friends, especially about something as serious as this. You've never seen her before? She comes to school sometimes with him. She has blond hair, big brown eyes, and is tall and thin. Believe me, she's HOT! Over the break I met someone at the Tavern who went to high school with her. He told me she was not the typical Mormon."

"It's true, Destin," said Mike. "I've seen her. She picks up Joseph from school. She's absolutely gorgeous! Playboy material."

Destin started thinking. "I don't believe I've ever said one word to Joseph. He probably doesn't even know who I am."

"Don't worry, Destin," said Bobby. "Everyone knows who you are. Ask him about his sister. You won't be sorry."

Bobby curiously looked at Mike. "Who's my partner?"

Mike grinned. "I'll give you a hint," he said. "Right now, he is trying to set a new trend in dental haircuts. That's right, you know him, you love him, and can't live without him, our good friend, Darl Rose. Have fun!"

Bobby just stood there gritting his teeth as he looked across the room at Darl, who was sitting at their desk waving at him.

"Look, Bobby, he's waiting for you," joked Mike.

"Now take it easy on him, Bobby," said Destin. "He likes you. Don't make him pay you to be your lab partner."

"I won't, I'll just get him to do all my lab reports. I wonder if he can do dishes?"

"Who's your partner, Mike?" asked Destin.

"Uh, nobody special. Just the number one student in the class, Lewis Tripper."

Dental School Debacle

"You lucky turd!" said Bobby.

"Thank you, thank you. I must be living right. I can get Lewis to show me all this micro-crap."

"Come on, let's get to work," said Destin. "I want to get out of here as soon as possible."

They walked to the front of the lab to pick up their microscopes, and then went to their desks to greet their new partners. Destin walked up to Joseph, who was already reading that night's assignment. "How's it going, Joseph? How was your summer break?"

"I know your type, Destin," he abruptly said. "Everyone in the school knows how you are, you and your two friends. Sometimes I'm ashamed to be in the same class with you three. You do a lot of things that I don't understand."

"Well, you see, Joseph, can I call you Joe?"

"No."

"Well, you see, Joey, it's like this. My girlfriend of seven years died the May before we started dental school. I really loved her. We were planning on getting married as soon as I graduated. Now I'm all alone. The only time I don't think about her is when I'm cutting up with Mike and Bobby. That's the only way I can handle it." Destin was straining to make his eyes water. "She was everything to me, Joey. I tried dating this one girl last year, but then she dumped me for a pharmacy student."

Joseph felt sorry for Destin—he believed him. "I'm sorry to hear about your girlfriend. The loss of a loved one is always difficult to handle, especially a future spouse. How did it happen?"

"She had the Hyperfytes," said Destin sadly.

Jim P. Sandras, D.D.S.

"Hyperfytes? I've never heard of it."

"It's a terrible disease," said Destin, tearing up. "Everything you eat turns to crap."

"Wow, that sounds awful."

"Yeah, and messy, too. What I need is to meet a nice, clean, pure girl, someone to talk to and trust. I'm afraid there's no one out there who will understand what I've been through. I've dated Catholic girls, but all they want to do is party and go shopping. And Protestant girls are no fun—they just want to make babies and eat. I need to go out with a different type of girl, like maybe... a Mormon, yeah, that's what I need. You Mormons are so gentle, so understanding, so, so...giving! You wouldn't happen to know of any single Mormonette that would go out with a lonely dental student? Like maybe a friend, cousin, or even your sister?"

"I have five sisters. Four are married."

"What about the fifth one?"

"I have a younger sister, but you wouldn't be interested in her," he said. "She's not an Orthodox Mormon like the rest of my family. She doesn't go to church regularly or sing in the choir. All she does is watch TV all night and sleep all day. I even think she drinks caffeine."

"Naaa, you're joking," said Destin, acting shocked.

"No. Sometimes I smell coffee on her breath. And besides, she's not as attractive as other Mormon women. She has dark skin and blonde hair, and she's not as healthy as the other girls at church—she's skinny. Perhaps I can fix you up with my cousin. She's nice and stout, fair-skinned, with beautiful, auburn, curly hair."

Dental School Debacle

"Mmmmm, my favorite kind," said Destin sarcastically.

"And she's also the lead singer of our choir. She has a beautiful voice. She would be perfect for you, Destin."

"Well, uh, you see my ears are really sensitive right now. Over the summer I had four beans removed from them. The doctor said I must've put them in there when I was two or three. He told me he sees it all the time. I didn't know they were there, until they showed up in a dental x-ray last year. Now everything seems so loud. There's no way I can handle a loud, overweight, red-headed Mormonette. Why don't you just fix me up with your skinny sister?"

"Well, my sister is going through some rough times right now. She said she's trying to find herself, whatever that means."

"Wow! I know exactly what that means! I have an associate degree in clinical psychology, and my final thesis paper was entitled: Finding Yourself. This is really weird, Joe."

"It's Joseph."

"Why don't you give me her phone number, Joey, and I'll give her a call. Maybe I can help. You know what they say: Do unto others!"

Joseph paused and thought for a minute. "OK, I'll give you her number. Maybe you can help. Call and talk to her, but that's all you better do, just talk. Remember, she's going through a rough stage."

"Don't worry, Joey, I'm a professional. Remember?"

"That's what I'm afraid of," he replied. He wrote down the number and handed it to Destin. "Her name is Candy. You can call her tonight."

***

Jim P. Sandras, D.D.S.

As soon as Bobby sat down next to Darl, he started making up rules for their desk.

"First of all, I'm the leader of this group," he said, looking Darl in the eyes. "Don't ever talk to me without me telling you to, unless you are either waking me up, or giving me an answer to a quiz."

"No problem, Bobby."

"I didn't tell you to talk."

"Sorry."

"You are to get up here every day at 12:45 and have everything set up by 1:00 when I arrive. You will also read the assignments carefully, highlighting the important parts for me. You wouldn't want me to read all the unnecessary crap, would you?"

"No, Bobby."

"And you will also be required to make two copies of all lab reports and turn one in for me with my name clearly written on it. Are you getting all of this, Karl?"

"It's Darl. Like Karl, but with a 'D'."

"Darl? What a strange name! What is it, short for Darling? Don't tell me your real name is Darling Rose."

"No, Bobby, I was named after my father, Darlton Rose. He died three years ago in a car accident. He was on his way home from the airport when it happened. I had just talked to him that morning on the phone. We were supposed to go to the Celtics game the following night." The more Darl talked, the worse Bobby felt. "He's the one who talked me into going to dental school. Now my stepmother acts as if my father didn't even exist. She collected millions on his life insurance. Now all she does is live off the interest and entertain men. Some guys stay for

Dental School Debacle

weeks at a time. I knew she didn't feel comfortable with me around the house. That's why she made sure I wasn't accepted into any dental school near Massachusetts. I came here because it has the best research facilities in the country, and I like to do research. My stepmother doesn't think I know about her little scheme. She thinks I'm stupid. I'm glad I'm away from Boston. I couldn't stay there and watch her spend all my dad's money."

Bobby was almost in tears. "That's the saddest thing I've ever heard! I can't believe that witch actually arranged it so that her stepson had to move out of the state. What a tramp! Hey look, Darl, what I said sarcastically this morning about loving a 'close' family, I didn't mean it. I'm sorry. I was just joking. I guess sometimes I joke too much."

"Don't worry about it, Bobby. I know you didn't mean it."

"I tell you what, Darl, to show that I'm sorry, I'm going to drop the first rule about not talking to me, and this weekend you can come over and watch the Davis Cup match with me, Destin, and Mike."

Darl looked confused. "Davis Cup? I've never heard of it."

Bobby started laughing to himself. "It's a very brutal sport," he said. "It was invented by Lord Davis in the 18th century. Two guys stand at opposite ends of a court, wearing nothing but a large protective cup over their groins. When the whistle blows, they take off running at one another with their hands tied behind their backs. The object of the game is to knock the other guy on the ground, but what really makes the game interesting is that they are only allowed to hit with their cups."

Darl was grimacing at the thought of it. "That sounds painful."

"It is. Sometimes they collide so hard during the initial run

Jim P. Sandras, D.D.S.

that pieces of plastic fly all over the spectators. It's not a pretty sight, Darl, like going to a Gallagher concert. It's a cross between sumo wrestling and a demolition derby, only worse. It's real popular in Europe, but the only place you can see it in the United States is on late night cable TV, or in downtown Detroit on Saturday nights."

"I think I'm going to pass on the Davis Cup," he said. "I'm not into violence, but thanks anyway. Maybe we can get together and watch some N.B.A. I love the Celtics."

"I doubt it, Darl. I can't stand basketball. Not enough contact." Bobby noticed that everyone in the class was working as they talked. "You need to get busy, Rose. You have a lot of work to do, so you better quit talking."

***

Across the lab Mike was sitting at his desk by himself, trying to figure out what he was supposed to be doing. His partner, Lewis, was in front of the class explaining to the instructors an experiment he invented. About an hour later Lewis came walking over to their desk where Mike was hopelessly looking into his microscope. "How's it going, Mike?"

"Not good," he answered while rubbing his eyes. "I'm not sure what I'm supposed to be looking for in this dumb microscope. It's been six years since I took Microbiology in college. Do you know what I'm supposed to be doing?"

"Sure, this is easy," he replied. "All you're supposed to do is identify the different forms of bacteria, such as rods and cocci. You can't tell exactly what kind they are by just looking at them. You must do more definitive testing and staining to tell its species. Watch, let me show you." Lewis looked in the

Dental School Debacle

microscope and started pointing out the different types of bacteria. Lewis was a very kind person, and was taking his time with Mike, making sure he completely understood what he was doing. In no time Mike was catching on.

"I can't thank you enough, Lewis. I was about to have a nervous breakdown."

"Any time, Mike." Lewis sat down and continued with his work. Fifteen minutes later, Lewis stopped, looked around the lab, and then grabbed his napsack and pulled it near him.

"Mike, are any of the instructors looking this way?"

Mike carefully scanned the room. "No, why?"

"I'll tell ya later. Just keep an eye out and let me know if any of them look this way." Lewis unzipped his bag and started filling it with petri dishes and various types of growing mediums. Mike was in shock. He couldn't believe the number one student in the class was stealing lab supplies.

"Nobody's looking, huh?" asked Lewis.

"No, not yet. But I think one of the graduate students is headed this way. Hurry up."

"OK, I'm finished," said Lewis, as he closed it. "This ought to be plenty enough."

"What are you doing?" asked Mike curiously.

"These petri dishes happen to contain the best substrate for growing Latripicus Psilocybinis."

"What the heck is that?"

"Ever hear of psilocybin?"

"You mean mushrooms?"

"Yep. Magic mushrooms."

"I thought they grew in cow manure?"

Jim P. Sandras, D.D.S.

"That's the North American species. I've collected some spores from the Amazon Basin, which grow twice as fast and are three times as strong. I have a lab in my apartment where I grow them. It's easy. The hardest part is finding the ingredients to make the substrate. But with these petri dishes it'll be easier than a sixth-grade science fair project."

Mike was in shock. "Wait a minute, Lewis. You're telling me that you, Mr. Genius, do mushrooms?"

"Not really," he said. "I used to do them a lot when I was in high school, but I grew out of that stage. Now I only eat them once a year, and that's for Mardi Gras."

"Then why do you grow them?"

"Profit."

"Profit? What are you talking about?"

"I have contacts across the country who will pay $240 per ounce, and they'll buy as much as I can grow. I can produce about five to eight ounces each month. How do you think I pay the car note on my new BMW? I don't know if you've noticed, Mike, but dental school doesn't pay very well."

"Aren't they dangerous?"

"Not at all. They're totally organic."

"What's it like?"

"It's hard to describe tripping on mushrooms," explained Lewis. "They're a *trip*. Some people call it the knowledge of the universe. Spores can travel through space and live up to 60 years. It's a known fact that the ancient Greeks used to eat them and hallucinate regularly. That's how they came up with mythology. No normal human being is going to see a seven-headed, one-eyed, female monster that sings to passing sailboats causing

Dental School Debacle

everyone aboard to lose their hearing."

***

The class finished their lab assignments and left for the day. Destin went straight home and rushed to the phone to call Candy. He couldn't wait to see what she looked like.

"Hello, can I speak to Candy, please? Hi Candy, my name is Destin Dufrene. I go to dental school with your brother, Joseph. He and I are lab partners, and he says so many nice things about you that I just have to meet you. Alright, he doesn't say nice things about you, but I still want to meet you. No, I didn't say friends, just lab partners. Yeah, he's a little boring. Yeah, like watching paint dry. Yes, he did tell me y'all were total opposites. That's why I want to meet you. Would you like to get together one night? I'll cook dinner, and we could watch Love Boat reruns. Really? That's my favorite late-night show, too. Gofer's the best. I think he should run for a political office someday, maybe the Senate. Yeah, I know. Isaac is a hard worker. Did you know he's the only bartender on the whole boat? So, what would be a good night for you? No, I'm not doing anything tonight. Sure, you can drive over here. I don't mind. Just take I-10 East to the Downman Road exit. I live in the trailer park on the left, lot number 70. So, I'll see you in a couple of hours? Great!"

Destin hung up the phone and waltzed with his broom while singing the Love Boat theme song. He got dressed and ran to the gas station across the street to purchase three bottles of MD 20/20 Plum Supreme. He rushed back, threw a couple of wine glasses in the freezer, and cleaned up his place for Candy. He was watching golf on his new favorite channel, ESPN, when he heard a knock at the door. He took his time answering, just to be

Jim P. Sandras, D.D.S.

cool, even though he was extremely anxious to see her. His heart was racing and his palms were sweating. Finally, he opened the door. There stood the most beautiful girl he had ever seen in person. She was wearing tight, straight-leg Levi's and an Adidas half T-shirt that came just above her navel revealing her thin, sexy waist. Destin stopped breathing and just stared at her face. She looked like she should have been on the cover of a Cosmopolitan magazine, not standing in a trailer park. In the awkward moment of silence, she introduced herself.

"Hi, I'm Candy," she said with her sweet voice. "You must be Destin."

His mouth was stuck open and had to force out words. "Uh, uh, I'm Candy, no, I-I- mean I'm Destin, you're Candy. Come in."

Destin politely reached for her hand and helped her up the wooden steps into his mobile home. "I'm sorry for acting like a fool," he said. "But I wasn't expecting Joseph's sister to be so beautiful."

"Why, thank you," she said with a smile. "Everyone tells me I look nothing like the rest of my family. My brothers and sisters are considered dogs by all human standards. I'm just glad my mother fooled around before she had me."

Destin started laughing. "Not only are you beautiful, but you're funny, too. How 'bout a glass of wine?"

"I'd love one, just don't tell Joseph. We Mormons aren't supposed to drink."

Destin took out the two frozen glasses, grabbed the bottle from the fridge, unscrewed the cap and started pouring, smiling at her the whole time.

"What kind of wine is this?" she asked.

Dental School Debacle

"It's called Mad Dog. But don't let the name scare you. This is what the Catholic priests drink. So, Candy, Joseph tells me you're going through some hard times right now."

She chuckled. "Oh yeah, real hard. I stay up all night and sleep as late as I want. Then when I get up, I usually go to my friend's house and lay out by her pool until the sun goes down."

"That sounds like hard times to me," said Destin, trying not to stare at her.

"Joseph is just jealous because he has to work all the time."

Destin handed her a full glass. "Here's your wine," he said. "Let's make a toast."

"Sure, but what to?"

"To the oral cavity."

Candy looked at Destin a little weirdly and then reluctantly toasted. "To the oral cavity." As soon as she tasted the wine her eyes watered. She put down her glass and started massaging her throat.

"WOW!" she said, as she wiped tears from her eyes. "That's some strong wine."

"Good stuff, huh? They call it 'The Wine of the Century'. I like to swish it between my teeth, although some people use it to clean their floors."

Candy regained her composure and picked up her glass. "I like it. It must be expensive."

"Very, but you get what you pay for. Are you hungry? I can make us some tacos."

"No thank you, I ate last night." Candy started walking around, checking out Destin's mobile home. "I've never been in a trailer before. It's a lot nicer than I thought it would be."

Jim P. Sandras, D.D.S.

"I call it my mobile condominium," he said proudly. "I love it! It holds a lot of memories. People don't realize there are many advantages of living in one."

"Like what?"

"To start off with, it has shock absorbers, you can shoot a pellet gun through the walls, and when the weather's bad, it rocks you to sleep. Plus, you don't have to put a quarter in the bed to make it vibrate. All you have to do is turn the washer on the rinse cycle. And best of all, if I ever get kicked out, which happens from time to time, all I have to do is get a truck with a trailer hitch and move it down the street. No packing."

"Do you live here by yourself?"

"Yep, just me and my Steely Dan collection."

Her whole face lit up. "Steely Dan? That's my favorite group! *Gaucho* or *Aja*?"

"*The Nightfly*," he replied.

"Nice." Now she was really interested. "Are you dating anyone?"

"I dated this one girl off and on for years, but she broke up with me this summer—left me stranded in Jamaica."

"Oh well, her loss. You're very handsome, Destin." Candy held up her glass. "My turn to make a toast. To Joseph. If it wasn't for him, I wouldn't be here."

"To Joseph." They were staring into each other's eyes as they tapped their glasses together. Candy slowly and cautiously took her second sip while Destin finished his glass and filled it up, again. Destin was so excited to be with such a beautiful girl that he wasn't paying attention to how much he was drinking. Besides, it was helping him relax. Candy sat on the couch while Destin

Dental School Debacle

drank his second glass, filled it up again, and went to sit next to her.

"You know, I've never been out with a dental student before. I didn't know what to think. Joseph tells me stories about all the sick things y'all do at school, and about those crazy parties y'all have. Is all that stuff true?"

Destin sat up straight and gave her a serious look. "All the rumors are true. And if it hasn't happened yet, it will. I'll see to it."

Candy laughed and placed her hand on his leg. "I like you, Destin. You're funny. And to think, I was scared of you at first."

The two were drawn together like magnets. The next thing they knew they were kissing.

When Destin woke up the next morning he immediately sat up in bed. He didn't remember falling asleep, much less what happened to Candy, who was nowhere in sight. He yelled out her name, but there was no response. When he stood up, he realized he was only wearing a bathing suit and a necktie. Then he stumbled around looking for her, but she was nowhere to be found. He looked in the driveway and noticed her car was gone. Destin was bummed. He had no recollection of what happened to her. He opened the refrigerator to get something to drink and found a note taped to the liter of Diet Coke. Destin ripped it off and started reading:

Jim P. Sandras, D.D.S.

Dear Destin,
Are all dental students jerks like you?
After the Love Boat was over and you
finished the third bottle of wine and threw
it across the room, I knew I was in trouble
and should've left then. I enjoyed our
adventure under the trailer and was
having a good time until you started
chasing me with a can of yams and bit me
on the arm. That's when I punched you
out. I just wanted to write you a note to
say that if I were you, I would quit
drinking that wine.
Thank you for not calling,
Candy
P.S. What the hell is an Oral Athlete?

Destin was extremely disappointed. He didn't remember a thing and blew a chance to have a beautiful girlfriend. Now, he had something else to deal with. He felt horrible, like there was a cobra in his ear eating his brain while trying to make its way down to his colon. He grabbed his head with one hand and his stomach with the other and cramped over in pain. He instantly concluded that he had a Class III hangover. He grabbed the bottle of orange juice and rushed to his medicine cabinet. He opened the liter bottle and added two Alka Seltzers, four packs of B.C. powder and half a cup of Worcestershire and shook it up. He downed the entire mixture in less than 30 seconds. He was just starting to feel a little better when he realized the time.

Dental School Debacle

"OH CRAP!" he yelled. "It's 7:30!" Destin had 30 minutes to get to the Microbiology lab. He quickly dressed and ran to the bathroom to brush his teeth. As he was putting the toothpaste on his brush, he remembered that he couldn't. He was grossed out—his mouth tasted like pigeon droppings mixed with brake fluid. In a mad rage, he threw his toothbrush against the wall and raced to school. On his way, he rode with his head out the window and his mouth open, hoping to catch a few bugs to improve the taste in his mouth. He was also hoping that Candy didn't tell Joseph about last night. It was 8:10 when he walked into the lab and sat next to Joseph, who already had everything set up for today's experiment. Dr. Fagen had just finished clearing his throat and was getting ready to lecture. Destin slowly glanced over at Joseph and smiled. He politely smiled back. Now he could relax.

"I hope everyone remembered not to brush their teeth," said Dr. Fagen. He could tell by the looks on the students' faces they were uncomfortable. "This is always an interesting morning. Just please, don't get too close to me. The first thing we will do this morning is remove samples of plaque from the tongue side of your partner's lower first molar. If you noticed, we put two packs of sterile scaling instruments on every desk. Be careful when you open these packs. The instruments are brand new and are extremely sharp. Place the plaque on the slide and use the appropriate staining solutions to identify as many organisms as possible. I know there are many different types, but this will give you an idea of what you will be up against everyday as practicing dentists. You can use your notes, textbooks, charts, or anything else that might help you. A few graduate students and I will be walking around if you need any assistance. Again, don't get too close to me."

Destin looked over at Joseph. "I'm sorry I'm late, but a state employee fell from the back of a truck and the lawyers were lined up across the interstate giving him their business cards."

"That's OK, Destin," said Joseph meekly. "It gave me time to get everything ready. By the way, how did it go last night with Candy?"

"Uh, uh, everything went fine. You didn't talk to her?"

"No. I was sleeping when she came home. Why? You didn't try anything on her, did you?"

"No way, Joe. We just sat around talking, and then watched the Wizard of Oz...I have the video. My favorite part is when the flying monkeys attack the Scarecrow."

Joseph tensed his face and leaned forward. "You didn't give her any alcohol, did you?"

"Just a chocolate Yoo-hoo."

"Did you talk to her about finding herself?"

"We talked a lot, Joey. She's a very sweet and modest girl. You're fortunate to have a sister like her. My sister rides on a broom. Professionally speaking, I believe Candy is just going through the normal adolescent-to-adult adjustments. Give her a few years, she'll find herself. And if she doesn't, call me. I'll try again."

Destin could tell Joseph was genuinely concerned about his sister. "Do you really think she'll be alright?"

"Positive," he replied. "Now let's get busy. We have a lot of work to do. You go first."

Joseph carefully unwrapped the sterile instruments and moved toward Destin, who was sitting with his eyes closed and mouth

Dental School Debacle

open. As Joseph put the instrument in Destin's mouth he hesitated. The hair in Joseph's nose receded up his nostrils. He held his breath and quickly backed up.

"My Lord, Destin. What did you have for breakfast?"

"A glass of orange juice. Why?"

"Not to be mean, or anything, but your breath is horrendous. The smell reminds me of something my dad once made me bury."

"Believe me, it tastes even worse. I'd shoot my leg to be able to brush my teeth. If I had known we had to do crap like this, I would've gone to law school."

"Let's try this again," said Joseph. Destin closed his eyes and opened wide, again. Joseph took a deep breath of fresh air, held it in, turned his head to the side and squinted his eyes and quickly peered in Destin's mouth. Trying to hurry, he accidently nicked his gums with the sharp instrument. Destin let out a scream that could be heard throughout the lab.

"OWWW!" He grabbed his face and started applying pressure. "What the heck are you trying to do? Gum surgery?"

Joseph felt bad and apologized. "I'm sorry, Destin. It was an accident. That's what I get for trying to hurry."

Destin leaned over the sink and spit out blood. "That's what YOU get? You mean that's what I get!"

"I told you, I'm sorry. It's your breath—it's making me nauseated. But I did get a large sample of plaque."

"Thank God," replied Destin. He went to the front of the lab to grab some gauze and applied pressure to his gums. Ten minutes later they quit bleeding.

Destin then proceeded to get a sample from Joseph. The two

began staining the plaque samples and put the slides under their microscopes. After only a few seconds of focusing, Destin was seeing thousands of organisms. He was amazed. "Man, Joe. You have Red China living in your mouth."

Everything was going smoothly for Destin. He was quickly identified the organisms and even planned to finish early so he could go straight to the locker room to brush his teeth during the entire lunch period. Meanwhile, Joseph had been focusing for over 20 minutes while intensely moving his slide, but still could not identify anything.

"How's it going over there, Joey?" asked Destin. "You're being so quiet."

Joseph backed away from the microscope and began rubbing his eyes. "Not well. I can't find anything in here—only a couple of objects that look like hub caps, and that's it. Maybe I didn't stain it properly." Joseph flagged over a nearby instructor. He was a young, Hispanic graduate student working on his doctorate. He graciously smiled at Joseph and walked over.

"Need some help?" he asked with a strong Spanish accent.

"Yes sir. I can't find anything normal on this slide. I'm wondering if I stained it wrong."

"Did you soak the plaque with saline solution before staining it?"

"Yes sir."

"How long did you put it in the methanol?"

"Five minutes, sir, then 12 minutes in the Giemsa stain."

"That's correct. Let me look. Maybe you're not focusing right." The instructor took his glasses off and looked into the lens. He adjusted the knobs and moved the slide around for

Dental School Debacle

several minutes with no luck. He put his glasses back on. "I can't find anything in here either, only a few inanimate objects that resemble hub caps. Let's take another plaque sample and use a different stain." The instructor picked up the scaling instrument and told Destin to open his mouth. It only took a second for his breath to encompass the instructors face. He dropped the instrument on the floor, covered his nose and stepped back. He then spent the next several minutes saying something to Destin in Spanish, and then made the sign of the cross over Destin's head and rushed straight to Dr. Fagen. The Hispanic instructor was talking fast and making lots of hand gestures, pointing at Destin as he explained the situation. The two walked over.

"This is the one," said the instructor, while pointing to Destin.

"There has to be an explanation for this," said Dr. Fagen. He leaned over to pick up the scaling instrument on the floor, wiped it off with his clinic jacket, and handed it to Joseph. "Get me another plaque sample. And here, use this." He reached in his pocket and tossed Joseph a surgical mask.

"This should help."

"Thank you, sir," he said. Then he tied the mask around his head and looked at Destin. "Open wide."

Destin was freaking out. His gums were just starting to feel better from the first experience with Joseph, and now he was doing it again with a dirty instrument he got off the lab floor. But Destin wanted to brush his teeth so badly that he would've done anything. He opened his mouth, but this time he didn't close his eyes. Right as Joseph was putting the instrument in his mouth, Destin grabbed his hand and looked into his eyes.

"I swear, Joseph, if you cut me again, you'll be waking up with tubes in your nose."

Joseph took Destin's threat seriously and was careful not to hurt him. Meanwhile, Dr. Fagen leaned over and whispered into the graduate student's ear.

"I have no idea where the dean gets these students."

Seconds later Joseph was finished. He removed the mask and smiled at Destin. "Now, that wasn't so bad, was it?"

"Now I know how a hooked fish must feel," he replied.

The Hispanic instructor looked at Joseph. "Muy bueno. I almost passed out. His breath reminded me of something my dad once made me bury."

Joseph could relate.

Dr. Fagen sat in Joseph's chair and proceeded to stain the new plaque sample from Destin. He put the slide under the microscope and commenced to focusing and moving the slide. This went on for five minutes. He stopped, reached into his pocket, pulled out a small bottle with no label, added a few drops of it to the slide, and started focusing again. After five more minutes of searching, he sat up and looked at Destin.

"In 20 years, I've never examined a slide so void of living cells," he said. "You must have a chemical imbalance in your saliva making it impossible for anything to survive. What did you drink last night, bleach?"

Destin tensed up and nervously glanced at Joseph, and then back to the instructor.

"MD 20/20."

Now Joseph was listening very intently.

Dr. Fagen's eyes popped open wide. "MD 20/20? You mean people really drink that wine? My neighbor keeps a bottle around,

Dental School Debacle

but he doesn't drink it. He uses it to remove tar and bugs from his car."

Dr. Fagen looked back into the microscope, examined the slide for another minute, and then gave up. "That wine completely killed every organism in your mouth. Microscopically, you're dead."

Destin slowly turned his head and looked at Joseph, who was so mad his ears turned red. "So, you did give my sister alcohol?" Everyone in the lab heard Joseph yell and looked that way.

"I can't believe I trusted you, Destin!" He stood up and punched Destin in the nose, and then jumped on him, knocking him to the ground.

"HELP!" screamed Destin. "Somebody get this maniac Mormon off of me!"

The entire class ran over to see what was going on. Brick and Dr. Fagen quickly pulled Joseph off Destin, and then Mike walked over to help him up.

"Are you OK, Destin?" asked Mike.

Destin started nervously shaking his knees while loosening up his shirt collar, acting like Rodney Dangerfield. "I'll tell ya', I get no respect." He was trying to make light of the situation, not realizing his nose was bleeding.

"What is going on here?" asked Dr. Fagen.

Joseph worked his way loose from Brick and started pointing at Destin. "This heathen got my sister drunk and seduced her!"

Destin put his head down and didn't say a word. He felt terrible. He knew he must have really upset Joseph for him to react like this. Kate walked over to Destin and wiped the blood from his lip with a Kleenex.

Jim P. Sandras, D.D.S.

"I don't know, or care to know what the problem is between you two," said Dr. Fagen. "This is Microbiology, not the World Wrestling Federation. You two follow me. I'm going to let the dean handle this."

The two students followed him out of the lab, into the elevators, and to the dean's office on the second floor. Dr. Fagen explained the situation to the receptionist. She shook her head at the two students and called the dean on the intercom.

"Excuse me, dean. Dr. Fagen is here to see you. There's been a fight in the Microbiology lab."

There was a moment of pause before the dean replied.

"Send him in."

Dr. Fagen went in by himself while Joseph and Destin waited in the receptionist's office. Joseph stared at the wall, not saying a word or even looking at Destin. His eyes were now starting to tear up. Destin felt sorry for him. He was thinking that this was probably the first time Joseph had ever been in trouble, and he was only trying to protect his sister. Destin quickly came up with an idea to get them both off the hook. Ten minutes later Dr. Fagen walked out and looked at the two.

"The dean wants to see you."

Destin stood up and smiled. "I hope you put in a good word for us, doc." He ignored the comment and went back to the lab. The dean was standing against the front of his desk with his arms folded when the two walked in.

"Have a seat," he said. "What is your class trying to do? Set a record for the most visits to my office? This incident has me upset for two reasons. Just yesterday I told your whole class that I didn't want to see any of you for disciplinary reasons. Maybe you

Dental School Debacle

didn't hear me."

"No sir," replied Destin. "We heard you."

"Second of all, I have an 11:00 tee off time at the Metairie Country Club. I was SUPPOSED to be playing with the deans from the rest of the medical center. We've had this planned for over a month. Now it looks like I'll have to catch them on the back nine." He turned and looked at Joseph.

"Mr. Smith, Dr. Fagen informed me that you punched Mr. Dufrene, knocking him to the ground? I know Mr.Dufrene is a little warped, but that doesn't give you the right to hit him, no matter what he did. This is a professional school. We will not tolerate behavior like this, and I will..."

Destin quickly interrupted. "That's not what happened, sir. Joseph didn't punch me. I was walking to my desk, and someone tripped me. I think it was Sherry Custard—she was the only one around. As I was falling Joseph tried to catch me, but instead he fell on top of me. Joseph is the gentlest person I've ever met. He would never punch me, or anyone else." Joseph was in awe. He couldn't believe Destin was taking up for him.

The dean was leaning against his desk thinking. Destin could tell that he was more concerned with making it to the golf course than this confrontation.

"Excuse me, dean. Did you say that you were playing at the Metairie Country Club?"

"That's correct."

"Wow! That's an awesome course. I played there this past Sunday."

He now had the dean's full attention. "How were the greens?"

"Very fast, probably around a 13 on the Stimpmeter."

The dean smiled. "That's fast."

"Especially #3 and #16."

"I know those holes well."

"What kind of clubs do you play with, sir?"

He quickly walked to his closet and pulled out his bag." I just bought them. It's a new brand—Callaway." He removed the driver from the bag and started swinging it in the office. "I can't wait to use them; the shafts are graphite."

"Smooth," said Destin, "but sir, your grip is wrong, and you're holding the club way too tight. Let me show you." Destin walked over and gave the dean a few helpful tips.

"Yeah, that does feel better," said the dean as he continued swinging. "Thanks for the tip, Mr. Dufrene. I'll tell you what, guys. Let's just forget about this whole ordeal. It's obvious there was some type of mistake, although I WILL have a talk with Miss Custard tomorrow. If I leave now, I could possibly catch them on the third hole." The dean grabbed his clubs and rushed out the door.

Joseph looked at Destin, let out a sigh of relief and smiled. "Thanks, Destin. I guess I underestimated you."

"Don't worry about it, Joey. It was my fault. Just put in a good word for me with Candy.

Plates

The sophomore students had completed several courses and were more than half finished with Microbiology when they started a new course—Removable Prosthodontics, where they would learn how to make dentures. After weeks of instructions and practicing on mannequins, they were ready to make dentures on a real live patient. They were now in their last lecture before seeing their first toothless human. Dr. Hernandez, an elderly Latin gentleman, was the instructor for the clinical part of the course.

"It's not easy to make a set of well-fitting dentures," Dr. Hernandez explained. "It involves a series of multiple impression techniques along with an accurate jaw relationship. A properly made denture will not need tape, powders or adhesives to hold them in. I know you've heard of these dentists and lab technicians who advertise a set of dentures for $250 in only one appointment. They have the philosophy that three sizes fit all. We call those plates, not dentures. Their patients walk out of the

Jim P. Sandras, D.D.S.

office and go straight to the drug store to buy Fixodent to hold their cheap plates in. Here at the dental school, we make dentures, not plates. We take a series of impressions, face and jaw records, and accurately reproduce the correct bite on an articulator. Now *that's* a denture. And I don't want to hear you call them plates, especially in front of me. I also have to warn you about denture patients at the dental school. Most of them are over 60, low-income, with no family and few friends. I don't know why; it just seems to work out that way. So, expect to treat them a little differently than the average dental patient because you will spend a lot of time working with them. And believe me, they love all of the attention. They always get very attached to their students. You have to be nice to them, but at the same time keep your distance. Otherwise, they'll come in every day complaining about sore spots as an excuse just to visit. It gives them a good reason to get out of the house. If you don't know how to handle them it could cost you a lot of valuable time. Not all denture patients fit into this category. There are a few young denture patients out there who lost their teeth from other things, such as car wrecks, systemic diseases, military service, drugs, or bad dentistry. These patients aren't as hard to manage and should present no problem, unless they're ashamed of having dentures. We rarely get that type of patient here at the school, but they represent a big percentage of denture patients in the private practice, so keep that in mind. We've scheduled denture patients for each of you at 9:00 this morning. Dr. Boozer will stand by the door passing out charts with your assigned cubicles. Make sure all of the medical records are up to date before taking the preliminary impressions. Use your best judgment on how to

Dental School Debacle

handle your patient. Take your time and treat them the way you would want to be treated, and simply do everything the way we showed you in the lab. If you need any help, ask me or any of the other instructors that will be walking around. We'll see you in the clinic. Good luck."

The students lined up by the door to get their charts from Dr. Boozer, an elderly dentist with a large red nose with protruding blood vessels: like W.C. Fields. He looked like he had been drunk every day for the past 30 years. He took his time walking to the door with the box of charts, gently sitting it on the floor, and gradually taking out the charts. Then he slowly walked over to Mike, who was first in line.

"Hey, Dr. Boozer," said Mike. "You got any rich widows in the stack, preferably with a bad heart?" Dr. Boozer didn't find it amusing. He handed Mike the top chart and said, "Move on."

Bobby was next in line. "Dr. Boozer," he said. "Someone told me there's a 19-year-old girl in the stack. Do you think I can use, I mean work, on her? That has to be the perfect date, don't you think? A 19-year-old girl with no teeth."

But just as before, the old instructor acted as if he didn't hear him. Bobby waited for some type of response, but Dr. Boozer gave him a chart and said, "Move on."

Terrance was next in line, watching all of this. He knew he could get the man's attention. "You have got to calm down, Dr. Boozer," he so bravely said. "All of these perverted jokes, the dancing, the booze, the women—it's time for you to quit acting like a comedian and start acting like a doctor. Remember, you're supposed to be setting an example for us students."

Dr. Boozer grabbed Terrance by the tie and pulled him up to

his face. The class came to a silence.

"Don't mess with me, son," he grunted. "I'm in the middle of a freakin' divorce, and my ex-wife's attorney woke me up this morning to tell me I have to pay her $10,000 a month. I swear to God, before I give her a dime, I'd give my nephew, Pauly, $100,000 to have her wiped off the face of the Earth." He let go of Terrance's tie, pushed him backwards, and then stared at the rest of the class, who were motionless after his comment about hiring a hit man. "The next person that messes with me will be making dentures for themselves."

He looked back at Terrance, who was almost catatonic. "Here, take your freakin' chart." Dr. Boozer threw Terrance's chart on the floor. The remainder of the students picked up their charts saying only, "Thank you, sir," or "Have a good morning, sir."

They rushed to their lockers to get their equipment before going to their assigned cubicles, which were small, open, 10'x10', half-walled-in areas containing a dental chair, cabinets, and a sink. Denture patients required more equipment than the regular patients. The students needed things like Bunsen burners, butane torches, articulators, hot water baths, tons of multi-color wax, a high tolerance to drool and old senile people, strong smelling chemicals, and about $50 worth of impression material. It took the students at least 20 minutes to get ready. They were all a little nervous. Most had never seen a person with no teeth before, at least not up close. Now they had to look into their mouths and feel their gums. They were hoping they wouldn't start laughing at the sight of some old toothless woman, whose chin touches her nose, trying to hold a conversation. When they finished setting up their instruments, they went to the waiting room to call their

Dental School Debacle

patients. Most people in the waiting room this morning had some type of aid, whether it was walking, hearing or visual. And no one had teeth. Mike was one of the first ones to call his patient.

"Mr. Arthur White." Seconds later an elderly, overweight black man stood up, walked towards Mike, and stuck out his hand.

"That's Reverend White. And you are?"

"Mike, Mike Williams. Nice to meet you, Reverend." They shook hands. "Follow me to our cubicle so we can get started." The Reverend followed Mike to the chair, took off his hat and sat down.

"I've been waiting over a year for y'all to call. I thought y'all forgot about me."

"No sir, we wouldn't forget about you," said Mike being polite. "The school has decreased the number of students they accept each year due to statewide financial cutbacks. Governor Edwards has been losing a lot in Vegas lately. "

"Yeah, I heard. I've been praying for the Governor. In the meantime, I'm getting good at catching my plates when I'm preaching." While he was talking, he had to continually push up on his loose upper denture that was falling out. "They've been flying out a lot lately, especially when I really get preaching. It's affected my sermons. I can't get as excited as I used to, and nobody sits in the first two rows anymore. I've tried all of them adhesives, from Fasteeth to Polygrip to Elmer's Glue, and nothing holds them in anymore, although it has improved my eye-hand coordination."

"When did you have these dentures made?" asked Mike.

Jim P. Sandras, D.D.S.

"Oh hell, I had these things made back in the 40's when I was in the service. Them military doctors yanked all my teeth before I knew what happened. Then they took impressions on me all day, every day for a week. When they were finished with me, I could swallow a sword."

"That's why they won't stay in anymore. Your jaws and gums shrink over time after your teeth are gone. You should reline your dentures every five years to keep them fitting properly."

"Well, you see, I didn't know that Dr. Williams. That's why I'm here. I'm going to put my whole dental soul in your hands. I will entrust my entire aesthetic and functional well-being to you. I know you will show me the way to take proper care of my plates and gums. I will follow you down the aisle of everlasting oral health and you can..."

Just then the Reverend's upper denture flew out of his mouth. But before it hit the ground the Reverend snatched it out of the air with the speed of a frog's tongue.

Mike started laughing. "I bet you'd be good at ping pong, Rev."

***

Destin was in the waiting room staring at all the sickly, toothless, old people staring back at him. He dreaded the thought of putting his fingers into one of their mouths. But he knew there was no way out of it, so he called for his patient. "Miss Dolly Landry," he announced loudly.

"That's me," said an old, skinny, bleached-blonde woman putting out her cigarette and blowing out her last puff. Judging by the numerous deep wrinkles in her skin, she was easily a three pack a day smoker. Destin also concluded she was Roman

Dental School Debacle

Catholic, like most people in the city of New Orleans, by her tattoo of the Virgin Mary on her forearm.

"Are you my doctor?" she asked with a raspy voice, like that of an elderly, sick man.

"Ma'am, I'm not a doctor, yet. I'm just a student, but I will be the one working on you. My name is Destin Dufrene."

"Can I call you Destin?"

"Sure, that's what my mama calls me. So, where are you from, Dolly?"

"The Parish."

"The Parish?"

"Yeah, St. Bernard, dawlin," she replied proudly. "Let me ask you something, Destin. Can I charge these false teeth on my daughter-in-law's credit card?"

"I don't think that'll be a problem," Destin replied. "When we get finished today, I'll take you to the business office to handle the finances."

Destin escorted her into the clinic to his assigned cubical, sat her down and washed his hands as he tried to make conversation with the woman. "So, are you ready for some new teeth, Miss Landry?"

"You damn straight."

"How old are the ones you have now?"

"I can't remember," she said, and then started to count out loud using her fingers. "You know, its hell gettin' old. I know I had them before Eisenhower was president."

"So, in other words, a long time?"

"Yeah, these are all cracked, and I'm missing several teeth, but they still fit. The only reason I'm getting a new set is because I

Jim P. Sandras, D.D.S.

lost my bottom denture. I'm a waitress at Port-O-Call, and I worry about how I look with no teeth."

Destin reluctantly asked the big question. "What happened to them?"

"I flushed them down the toilet."

Destin was expecting an off-the-wall answer, but not like this. "How did you do that, throwing up?"

"No, I was cleaning them off," Dolly replied, and then turned her head and went into a coughing fit.

"In a TOILET?"

"That's all I have. Ever since Hurricane Camille pushed my house five feet to the right that's the only plumbing that works, for some damn reason. No one can figure it out. I have to clean my dishes and my clothes in the toilet, even wash my face."

"Hurricane Camille was almost 15 years ago!"

"No crap," she replied, getting aggravated with the questions. "Right after that storm, I talked to a few plumbers, but dem no-goods just wanted to take advantage of me. My sista down in Delacroix lost her whole freakin house, so I felt blessed by Gawd. Besides, I ain't got much money. After I flushed my bottom denture down the toilet, I spent over a week digging through my septic tank with a rake looking for it. Then one day my daughter-in-law and grandchildren came over and saw me leaning over my septic tank with a crab net. She asked me what I was doing, and I told her. She gave me her credit card, and then left with my grandchildren and said they weren't coming back until I got new, clean teeth."

"That's a very touching story," said Destin. "Thank you for sharing it with me."

Dental School Debacle

"I have plenty more," Dolly quickly replied. "I used to be a showgirl and danced at the Moula Rouge in Westwego."

"I'd love to hear your life story, but I'll be graduating in two years, that's if I finish today. Why don't you take your top denture out and let me look at it?"

Dolly popped her teeth out using her tongue, and handed the wet, smelly object to him. Destin backed up, put on gloves and let her place it in a paper napkin. He then examined it. The entire denture was black from at least 40 years of cigarettes. It was missing three teeth and was cracked in six different places, held together only with Crazy Glue.

"I know it's a little dirty," she said, "but I washed it really good this morning in my toilet."

Destin dropped the nasty thing in the stainless-steel sink, causing another tooth to fall out. "She'll never miss it," he said to himself, and then continued with his work.

***

Meanwhile, Bobby was one of the last ones to finish setting up his cubicle. He walked out to the waiting room to call his patient. "Sergeant Steve Thomas," he said.

"Right here, Mr. Pubix," said a stern voice from behind him. He turned around to see where it was coming from. There in the doorway leading to the clinic stood a middle-aged, bearded man dressed in camouflage clothes and black Saigon-mirror sunglasses. "What kind of name is that, and what took you so long?" he asked unpleasantly. "I've been waiting here since 0-800." He had his arms folded and was inspecting Bobby from head to toe.

"How did you get past without me seeing you?" asked Bobby.

Jim P. Sandras, D.D.S.

"Better yet, how did you know my name and that I would be the one seeing you today?"

"I have ways of finding out these things," he said. "It's obvious you're susceptible to enemy attack. I hope you are a better dentist than you are a warrior."

Bobby started thinking to himself, "Who did they assign me to, a psycho Chuck Norris having military flashbacks?"

Follow me to our chair," said Bobby nervously.

"We're assigned to B-7, in the corner," said the Sergeant.

Bobby freaked out. "How did you know?"

"I always check out everything before I get involved. The last time I didn't, I spent seven years in Vietnam, and the last three were in a P.O.W. camp. That's how I lost my teeth. Charlie wouldn't let us brush. When I finally escaped, the dentist who examined me said I had severe periodontitis, so he rendered my gums smooth. I've been really busy since then trying to make sure all our boys were out of 'Nam. I've been back and forth nine times since, and every time I go back, I get in a gun fight just for the sport of it."

Bobby worried that the Sergeant was getting excited as he talked. "This is the first chance I've had to get some teeth made. Someone informed me that the best dentures in the state were made at this clinic, so here I am."

Bobby brought the Sergeant to the cubicle and sat him down. The Sergeant looked at Bobby like he wanted to head-butt him. "Did you register for the draft?" questioned the Sergeant.

"Na, I don't believe in war. I'm a lover, not a fighter."

"What are you, some type of sissy?" The Sergeant sat up in the chair.

Dental School Debacle

"No, I love women."

"You seem like a big sissy to me. How did you put yourself through college, as a manicurist?"

"No, I'm a bartender."

"Even worse, I bet you'd break easily under enemy interrogation. I refuse to let a bartender put his hands in my mouth. There's no telling what type of diseases you have. I know your kind. Is there another student around here who can make me a set of dentures? Someone with testicles?"

"Sure, I'll get you some testicles. You scare the heck out of me, anyway." Bobby walked out of the cubicle. "And Sarge, don't chew on my equipment while I'm gone. Oh, I'm sorry, I forgot... you don't have any teeth." Bobby laughed and quickly walked away.

"You little tooth fairy!" yelled the Sergeant across the clinic. "I ought to knock your teeth out and let you see how it feels to eat mashed potatoes all the time!"

All the nearby students overheard the conversation and were too scared to even look in the area of the Sergeant. Bobby walked around the clinic looking for someone to switch patients with. Then he saw Destin in his cubicle talking to this skinny old lady with two-tone hair. Everything looked like it was going smoothly for him.

"He's in a good mood, I'll ask him," said Bobby to himself, and walked towards him.

"Destin, can I see you for a second?" he asked nicely.

"Sure. I'll be right back Dolly." Destin walked over to the side with him. "What's the matter, Bobby?"

"You have to swap patients with me."

Jim P. Sandras, D.D.S.

"Why, what happened, your patient tried to gum ya?"

"No, he's driving me crazy," replied Bobby. "All he wants to talk about is making money. Money, money, money. That' all he talks about, how to make money."

"Sounds interesting, but I have a 75-year-old woman who is cracking me up. She's a trip."

"You have to swap with me," begged Bobby. "Come on, Destin, you'd get along good with this guy. He keeps telling me how to make tons of money in real estate. I don't have money to invest like you."

"If this guy is so rich, what is he doing at the dental school?"

"He heard we make the best dentures in the state. Plus, he took the thousand dollars he saved and put it in stocks."

"My type of man. Alright, I'll switch, but you owe me one."

"Thanks a lot Destin, you won't regret it." Destin walked over to Dolly and put his hand on her shoulder. "Miss Landry, I mean Dolly, I have some good news and some bad news."

"Tell me the bad news first," she said.

"There's been a mistake," he said. "I've been assigned to a different patient. It looks like I won't get a chance to work with you."

"I'm sorry to hear that. I like you, Destin. So, what's the good news?"

"You've been assigned to a good friend of mine. Dolly, this is Bobby..."

"Bobby Ewing," he interrupted quickly.

"Bobby, this is Miss Dolly Landry, but just call her Dolly."

"The pleasure's all mine, Dolly," said Bobby, as he took her hand and kissed the back of it.

Dental School Debacle

"It's nice to meet you, Bobby Ewing," she said. Then she looked up at Destin. "I like him already, Destin. Where do all these good-looking dentists come from?"

"You're a sweet lady, Dolly," said Destin. "I'll come visit you the next time I'm in Chalmette."

"You better."

"I promise. Well, I have to get to my new patient. Bobby, do you have his chart so I can look over it?"

"No. I left it in the cubicle, I'm sorry. Just go to B-7. It should be on the counter."

"What's his name?"

"Steve. He's a real nice guy. Hey, thanks again Destin."

"No problem. This better be on the level, Bobby. I know how you are."

Destin naively walked over to the corner where he saw this G.I. Joe looking guy sitting by himself with his arms folded, and he didn't look too happy. "How are you doing this morning, Steve? My name is Destin Dufrene. I've just been assigned to you. Bobby tells me you are into real estate. Let me ask you one quick question before we get started. How much equity do I need in order to buy commercial property in New Orleans East?"

"What the hell are you talking about?" he yelled. "For one thing, I hate real estate, unless I'm blowing it up. And another thing, it's Sergeant Thomas to you. I was in the jungles of Vietnam defending myself with my bare hands while you were playing with dolls, boy, and don't you forget it!" The Sergeant shook his head in frustration. "This is great, they take away Larry and give me Moe. Who's the real doctor around here, Curley or Shemp?"

Jim P. Sandras, D.D.S.

"Speaking of the doctor, let me see where he is." Destin took off running toward Bobby with fire in his eyes. When he got there, he could hear Dolly giggling. Then he looked and saw Bobby tickling her palate with his finger—a trick he learned in Oral Diagnosis. Destin grabbed him by the arm and pulled him away from the chair.

"Excuse us for a second, Dolly. We have a little matter to discuss."

Destin pushed him against the wall. "You traitor! You lied to me! You're not supposed to lie to friends, you lie to girls, remember? Why did you take advantage of me like that?"

"I'm sorry, Destin, but I had to. The Sergeant was about to kick my butt. He called me a sissy. Then when I told him I was a bartender he refused to let me put my hands in his mouth."

"That was brilliant!" said Destin, still aggravated. "You can't tell patients stuff like that."

"I don't want the Sergeant. He scares me," said Destin. "I want Dolly back."

"Sorry, Destin. I already have my trays ready to take impressions. Anyway, she said she likes me more. She told me so herself."

"I don't believe it," said Destin.

"It's true. I told you I have a way with toothless women."

"We'll let Dolly decide who she wants. The other one has to work on the Sergeant. Deal?"

"Deal." Destin walked up to Dolly and put his hand on her shoulder.

"Hi Dolly, I told you I wouldn't forget about you. I came back to make sure you are alright. Is Bobby taking good care of you?"

Dental School Debacle

"Aww yes, he's very nice."

Destin gave her the biggest smile he could. "Who would you rather have to make your teeth? Me or Bobby?"

Dolly thought for a second. "Well, both of you are very handsome young men, and are both real sweet, but I think I'm going to stick with Bobby. He has beautiful teeth. I want some just like his."

Destin gave him a dirty look. "I'll get you for this, Pubix. I promise."

Bobby smiled, showing his pearly whites. "See you later, Destin. Tell the sarge I said hello."

Dolly looked at Bobby and frowned. "That mean boy, Destin. He called you pubic hair."

Destin took his time walking back to B-7, where he found the Sergeant still sitting with his arms folded. "Where did you go?" he grunted. "Read your instructions on how to make a denture? I've been here for over two hours and haven't had a thing done to me, yet. At this rate I should be getting my teeth around the turn of the century."

"I'm sorry it's taking so long, Sergeant," apologized Destin. "But I had to report Bobby to the head instructor for not giving you the proper respect you deserve. Bobby also gave me the wrong information about you. He told me you were in the real estate business. That's why I asked you about property in New Orleans East. He really ticked me off, and he thinks it's funny. He's the one who told me to call you Steve. I'm really sorry about the way you've been treated, Sergeant. I swear, I'm going to get him for this."

"I'll give you a hand," said the Sergeant. "He upset me, too.

Jim P. Sandras, D.D.S.

He laughed at me for not having teeth."

"Yeah, we'll get him," said Destin. "He thinks everything's funny."

"He told me he was against war. War is what keeps this country free."

"I agree," answered Destin proudly. "God bless the military."

"Are you a republican, Destin?"

"I have a statue of Ronald Reagan in my trailer."

"I'm impressed. I can see we are going to get along fine. You seem like a hardworking young man. How did you pay your way through college?"

"My dad pays."

"Even through dental school?"

"Yes sir, he even gives me credit cards and an allowance every week."

"That's awfully nice of him. He must be well off. What does he do for a living?"

"He owns a textile company."

"Really? My family's in the textile business, too. What's the name of your father's company?"

"Sanitizo," said Destin. "He sells and rents linens to hotels, hospitals and restaurants all across Louisiana and Mississippi."

"I've heard of it," said the Sergeant. "Sanitizo is our competition. My family owns Cinico."

"Wow," Destin was impressed. "Cinico is huge! It makes my family's business look like a corner grocery."

"It's nationwide," replied the Sergeant proudly. "My grandfather started it."

"Why don't you work there?"

Dental School Debacle

"I did, until I got drafted. After I got out of Vietnam, I had no interest in money. You don't know what it's like seeing your best friend step on a landmine, and then get hit in the face with his guts. And for no reason. Believe me, it'll change your whole outlook on life. Nothing seems to matter after that. How old are you, Destin?"

"24."

"24... the prime of your life. When I was 24, I was a POW in 'Nam. They used to tie us up and make us watch as they tortured us. We were all the same age. We should've been out chasing women; instead, we had to pick leeches off each other before we went to sleep. Imagine you and your friends in a place you've never even heard of, where people are trying to kill you, and for reasons you don't understand. It just isn't fair—the young have to fight the wars for the old. I have a hard time getting my mind off of it." The Sergeant was getting emotional.

Destin felt sorry for him. "First of all, thank you for your service, Sarge. I can't imagine what you went through, and I know it probably destroyed some of the best years of your life. But don't let it destroy your whole life. You can't let them do that to you; you're better than that. You have at least 40 more years of life to live, so enjoy it. You owe it to yourself, and America owes it to you."

"You're right," replied the Sergeant. "I'm getting tired of all this fighting stuff, anyway, and these camouflage clothes are starting to get old. Do you realize that I haven't been on a vacation since I was in high school?"

"What you need is a trip to the Bahamas on one of those singles' cruises, where there's nothing but available women onboard. It makes The Love Boat seem like a Jehovah's Witness picnic. Believe me, I've been on several. All you smell is perfume. You have to take penicillin prophylactically a week before the trip—federal regulations. But first, let me make you a nice set of dentures with some white, white teeth. They'll look good with your tan."

"I could use a trip like that. Maybe that's what I need to get my mind off everything and start thinking about my future. Thanks for the advice, Destin. You know, you're a lot smarter than you look."

***

On the next aisle, Mike was almost finished with the preacher, and the clinic period was only half over. He was going as fast as he could, always keeping something in the Reverend's mouth so he couldn't talk, even if it was just a mouth full of cotton rolls.

"OK, that ought to do it for today," said Mike, but the Reverend could only mumble a few words back. Mike forgot he had filled the Reverend's mouth with rope wax.

"I'm sorry, let me take this crap, I mean this wax, out of your mouth."

"Ahh, that feels a lot better," said the Reverend, as he wiped the drool off his face and neck. "Can I talk?"

"Sure, we're finished."

"Let me ask you something, Mr. Williams. Is there any way I can get a gold tooth put in the front of my new upper plate?"

Mike stopped filling out the chart and turned around. "Yeah, but why do you want to do that?"

"I want to look good around the pool hall."

"Pool hall! I thought you were a preacher?"

Dental School Debacle

"I am, that's where I do my preachin', around pool halls and bars. I also pick up a few dollars on the side by hustling games."

"That's nice," replied Mike. "The church must be really proud of you. How about a gold crucifix on the tooth next to it?"

"No, but can you make me a gold pool stick with a diamond cue ball?"

"You've got to be joking," replied Mike. "I'm studying to be a dentist, not a jeweler."

***

Bobby, who had been wasting time joking around with Dolly, was preparing to take preliminary impressions. As he was mixing the material, she turned and looked at him.

"What are you doing?" she asked.

"I'm mixing the impression material."

"Oh no," she said. "The last time I had that crap in my mouth I got sick…real sick. I knew I shouldn't have ate that spaghetti this morning."

"Don't worry," said Bobby, as he loaded a tray with material. "This tastes a lot better than the stuff they used to use."

"It's not hard to improve on snake spit."

"Alright now, just relax and breathe through your nose. This stuff gets hard in about three minutes, OK? Open wide."

"I think I'm going to throw up," said Dolly, as Bobby put the tray in her mouth.

"Don't worry. The warm vomit will make the material set quicker." Her eyes opened wide as she grasped the arms of the chair tightly. Seconds later she started gagging. Bobby tried to ignore it, but then she started getting loud. Everyone nearby stopped what they were doing and watched. Dolly sat up and

Jim P. Sandras, D.D.S.

grabbed her throat, gagging louder than ever. A crowd gathered around the cubicle waiting to see the obvious outcome. The instructors walked over. Dolly couldn't hold it any longer. She threw up with the tray in her mouth, causing the stream of vomit to hit the wall, splashing the entire cubicle. Bobby was also getting sprayed as he struggled to get the tray out of her mouth. When he finally removed it, Dolly finished throwing up in the spittoon and then went into a morbid coughing spell. Both Bobby and the cubicle were covered with pieces of partially digested spaghetti. It looked like someone had dumped a can of Chef-Boy-Ardee all over him. Even the impression material had pieces of spaghetti in it. The disgusted spectators walked away holding their noses. It smelled like a three-month-old, rotten lasagna. Dr. Boozer walked up to the woman as she was wiping the noodles off her lips with the napkin around her neck.

"Woman, don't you know you're supposed to chew your food?"

"I got no freakin' teeth, you idiot." Dr Boozer just shook his head and walked away, leaving Bobby to deal with the mess.

***

A few weeks later they were finished with their impressions, face records and wax try-ins and were ready to flask and process the dentures, which they had to do themselves. The equipment was at school to do it, but most students took the dentures home and boiled the wax out on their stoves. After spending 10 hours a day at school they were ready to get away, even if it meant making a big mess in their kitchens. Destin and Bobby went to Mike's apartment to make the dentures while watching Monday Night Football. Mike borrowed the equipment from a senior

Dental School Debacle

student. Bobby brought a gallon of wine and three frozen pizzas to make a party out of it. By halftime, they were dizzy off the alcohol and the chemical fumes from processing the dentures in the small apartment. They were starting to act stupid. Mike juggled the new sets of dentures and was laughing at the Reverend's gold tooth. Bobby was scratching his crotch with the dentures while the other two were on the floor laughing. Destin took his shoes off and started clipping his toenails with the Sergeant's dentures.

"I got a great idea!" yelled Bobby, "Mike, don't you have a Polaroid camera?"

"I sure do."

"Let's take some really gross pictures with our patient's dentures," said Bobby, mischievously. "Then mail them the pictures a year after we graduate."

"That's a great idea!" said Mike. "I'm glad I came up with it."

"You two crazy fools can do it," said Destin, "But there's no way I'm going to mail the Sergeant a gross picture with his dentures, especially after he's been wearing them for three years. I treasure my life more than that. He'd sneak up on me and rip my heart out before I knew what happened. But if you want, I'll take the pictures."

"Great!" said Mike. "I know exactly what I want to do." He ran to his bedroom and came back with a Baby Ruth candy bar. Then he took the Reverend's set of dentures and went straight to the bathroom. Moments later he walked out drying his hands.

"Come take a picture of this, Destin," he shouted. Destin and Bobby walked into the bathroom and found the Reverend's dentures in the bottom of the toilet bowl holding the Baby Ruth between the teeth. Destin was laughing so hard he had a difficult time taking the pictures.

"I can't wait to mail the Reverend a picture of this," said Mike smiling. "Looks just like a turd."

"That's one of your better ones," said Destin.

"I know what I wanna do," said Bobby, as he ran out of the bathroom. A few seconds later he came walking back with his pants down, holding Dolly's dentures around his penis.

"Come on Destin, take the picture," said Bobby. Then he started singing:

"Hello, Dolly... I say hello, Dolly, it's so nice to have you back where you belong."

Destin stopped laughing just long enough to take the picture. When he finally did, he snapped several shots.

"I want a copy," said Destin. "I need to show my brother what I learned in dental school."

***

The students had delivered the dentures to their patients and were now making their 48-hour recall. Destin went to the waiting room to get the Sergeant, but he was nowhere to be found. He turned around to walk back to the clinic when he heard a familiar voice behind him.

"Destin, where are you going?" Destin turned around, but still didn't see the Sergeant.

"Over here!" came the voice again. It sounded like the sarge, but he didn't see him—only a young man in a suit.

"Can I help you?" asked Destin.

Dental School Debacle

"You don't recognize me?"

Destin looked the guy in his eyes. "Sergeant! I didn't recognize you. You shaved! And cut your hair! Look at you, all dressed up in a suit. Man, you look 20 years younger."

"I *feel* 20 years younger. And call me Steve, please. Can we go to your cubicle? I need to talk to you."

"Sure." The two walked over to Destin's cubicle and sat down.

"I'll tell you, Destin. These teeth really made a difference in my life. When I got home and looked in the mirror, I saw a different person. It's like a whole new me! I couldn't wait to shave. The only reason I grew a beard was to hide my collapsed face. And with these white teeth you gave me I feel like Robert Redford."

"Now that you mention it, you do look like him."

"And it feels so good to be able to chew again. I was getting tired of eating boiled eggs and weenies. The first thing I did after you gave me the dentures was go to Wendy's and order a triple cheeseburger. Then I went to Taco Bell and ate a half dozen tacos. It felt great, although my stomach was a little upset. I even called my father and asked him for a job."

"What did he say?"

"Get this, he was so happy I asked him for a job that he's making me manager of the Chicago plant and starting me off at $200,000 a year."

"That's fantastic!" said Destin. "If anybody deserves it, it's you."

"I'm flying up there this weekend, and I owe it all to you, Destin. If you ever need anything, please don't hesitate to ask.

Jim P. Sandras, D.D.S.

And if you're ever in Chicago, look me up. I'll get you tickets to any game you want, the Bulls or the Bears."

"How 'bout some Blackhawk tickets? I love hockey."

"Anything you want, Destin. I'll take care of you. Promise."

"I'll take you up on it. Good luck with your new job. I know you're going to kill'em dead."

"You should've been a comedian," said Steve, who then got out of the chair and shook Destin's hand. "You did an excellent job, Destin. These dentures feel great. This is the first time I've smiled in years. Now, I take these things out every night, right?"

"Right, and soak them in a glass of water with a little bleach," he said. "And it helps to brush them every now and then, too." Destin walked him out of the clinic and said good-bye. For the first time, Destin felt as if he had actually made a difference in someone's life.

***

Across the clinic, Bobby was sitting Dolly in the chair for the last time. "Dolly, your hair looks good. What did you do to it?"

"I washed it."

"I knew something looked different. You look five years younger."

"Thank you, Bobby. What do you want?"

"Nothing, I swear."

"It's these new teeth you made me. I feel young, again."

"When you smile you look just like Marilyn Monroe...before she died."

"Why thank you, Bobby. I also want to thank you for hooking my plates together with that little wire. I'll never lose them now."

"No problem. It's a little thing I invented just for you."

Dental School Debacle

***

Meanwhile, Mike had not shown up yet and was running extremely late. The Reverend had been waiting for over an hour when Mike finally came walking out of the elevator. He bumped into Sam, who had already finished his work and was getting on the elevator to go home.

"You're not just getting here, huh?" questioned Sam.

"Yep, I celebrated this morning. I had a bourbon and coke. This is the last time I have to listen to my patient. He says he's a preacher, but really he's a pool hustler with a gold incisor."

Just then the Reverend saw Mike standing by the elevators and walked towards him. "Mr. Williams, where have you been? I've been waiting here since 9:00."

"I'm sorry, Rev. But I stopped to help out two old nuns who ran out of gas on the Interstate."

"I'll see you later, Mike," said Sam as he got on the elevator that just opened. "Two old nuns, huh? You've been hanging around Pubix too long."

"Let's go sit down," said Mike, trying to ignore Sam's comment. He grabbed the preacher by the arm and rushed to his cubicle. The Reverend was having a hard time keeping up and was out of breath by the time they got there. It was obvious Mike wanted to get the appointment over with quickly.

"How are you doing today, Reverend?" asked Mike, as he put the napkin around his neck.

"I'm doing alright." The elderly man then paused a minute to catch his breath. "But I would be doing a lot better if these plates didn't hurt so much."

"Take them out and let me look."

Jim P. Sandras, D.D.S.

"You smell like you've been drinking, young man."

"I had to siphon gas for the nuns this morning."

The Reverend smiled showing his new gold tooth. "That was really nice of you, Mr. Williams. You're going to make a very good dentist." The Reverend took out his new dentures and carefully handed them to Mike, who turned around and tossed them in the sink. He began examining his gums. They were dark red and swollen.

"Now tell me, does this hurt?" Mike asked as he palpated the gums.

"Ow! Yeah, that hurts!"

"How about this?"

"Ow! Stop it! My whole damn mouth hurts! The only thing I can eat is potted meat. Can't you cut some of the denture away so that it doesn't hurt so bad?"

"Sure. I'd be happy to." Mike took the teeth back to the lab and grinded on them. A few minutes later he came back and put the dentures back in.

"How does that feel?"

The Reverend tapped his teeth together a few times while thinking. "Feels a little better. What about a cushion?"

"Cushions and adhesives are for wimps."

"If they start hurting, can I call you?"

"Sorry. We're off the next few weeks for Christmas holiday. Just take a shot of bourbon if they start hurting."

"I don't drink bourbon," replied the Reverend. "What about gin?"

"That'll work. Just tell your congregation at the pool hall that it's doctor's orders."

Dinner at Brennan's

The class returned after the holidays only to be welcomed with a whole semester of new courses. One of the easier ones was Dental Prophylaxis—the course where dental students learn to clean teeth. Even though most dentists have a hygienist to do it, they still must know how. First, they learned the various cleaning instruments and their uses. Then they practiced the actual cleaning techniques by scraping teeth on a mannequin. They were now SUPPOSED to be ready to clean one another's teeth. The class was gathered in the lecture auditorium waiting for their final instructions before going into the clinic.

To everyone's surprise, in walked a very attractive middle-aged woman in a white clinic jacket. She walked to the podium and clipped the microphone onto her collar. The guys thought she was too pretty to be teaching and should be married to a rich dentist, spending his money somewhere.

"Hello class, my name is Ms. Talamo. I'm in charge of the clinical part of this course." She spoke very eloquently. "By now, all of you should know the basic principles of performing a dental

Jim P. Sandras, D.D.S.

cleaning. It's not easy to clean teeth efficiently without causing trauma to the teeth and surrounding tissue. It takes a lot of practice along with using the right instruments. To facilitate the ease of tartar removal, you should always keep your instruments sharp. The sharper they are, the easier they remove tartar. Before we give you a starting check, we will test the sharpness of each instrument by trying to cut a piece of paper. If it does not cut the paper easily, you will not be allowed to start the procedure. If you are having any problems sharpening your instruments, just ask any one of us in the Hygiene Department and we'll be glad to help. And remember, every time you put a sharp instrument in a patient's mouth, you have to be extremely careful, especially when you're putting the instrument under someone's gums. You can rip the whole area with one slip. Last year a student needed sutures after this exercise, so be extremely careful until you get the hang of it. If the condition of the mannequins is any indication, this year is going to be even worse. I looked at them last week and some had cuts all the way to the metal. So be careful. We randomly assigned you into pairs for this afternoon. The first student has until 3:00 to be completely finished and graded, and the second student must be finished by 5:00. Two hours is almost too much time to clean someone's teeth, but we're allowing it so that you can take your time and not hurt anyone. The name of your partner and assigned cubicle is posted on the bulletin board outside the clinic. Get this information and then meet us in the clinic in 15 minutes. We will be walking around giving starting checks after we examine your instruments. If there are any questions, just ask. See you in the clinic."

The class got up and rushed to the bulletin board to see who their partners were. Destin caught up with Mike and Bobby waiting for an elevator. "You guys have any plans for tonight?"

Dental School Debacle

"No," Bobby answered.

"Not really, why?" asked Mike.

"My dad wants to take me out to eat tonight at Brennan's in the French Quarter. We never get to see one another. He told me to invite a couple of my friends, but they were all busy, so I'm asking you two. Whaaddaya' say?"

"Sure, that sounds great!" said Bobby. "I never pass up a free meal, even if it means I have to sit at a table with two Dufrene's."

"I'd love to," said Mike. "I've always wanted to eat at Brennan's. Everyone says it's the best restaurant in the area."

"Yeah, and we can go out on Bourbon Street after," said Bobby.

"I don't know about that," replied Mike. "Don't forget, we have Biomaterials lab tomorrow morning."

Destin was insulted. "Come on, Mike. Ten years from now we won't remember a thing from that class, but we'll probably still have scars from a night out in the Quarters. It'll be classic. Besides, I heard the Meters are playing at Tipitina's uptown."

They agreed that a night on Bourbon Street would be more memorable in the long run than a Biomaterials class.

The three got on the elevator and went to the third floor. There they found the rest of their class gathered around the list. One by one they let out sighs of either relief or despair.

"Aww no," Bobby grieved. "Brick's my partner. That jock is going to rip my gums out! I can see it already. He'll probably stretch my lips over my head trying to get his big fingers in my mouth."

"Don't feel bad, Bobby," said Destin reading the list. "Look who's my partner—my favorite person in the world, Sherry. I bet she checks my toes for plaque."

"At least you'll still have teeth when she's finished," said

Jim P. Sandras, D.D.S.

Bobby. "Brick's liable to knock my teeth out, and *then* clean them."

"Yeah, but I bet Sherry shoves her instruments all the way to my jaw to make sure she doesn't miss anything. You know she's going for an 'A'."

"Look who my partner is," said Mike. "Mr. Quiet himself, David Foster. That guy hasn't said two words to anyone since we started dental school, except maybe to his cadaver."

"That guy's weird," said Bobby. "He chain-smokes Camel non-filters. I bet he only uses one match a day, and that's in the morning. He must live with a constant head rush. You know he's never been to any of our class parties?"

"I talked to him for a while not too long ago," said Destin. "He said he's not doing well in school; he barely passed the freshman year. I don't think he likes dentistry."

As they were talking, a dozen attractive hygiene instructors came walking their way. "Hey fellas, here comes the beef," said Bobby with a gleam in his eyes. "I'd let any one of them probe my pockets, especially that little, short blonde with the overbite."

"We better go to our cubicles," said Destin. "It's almost time to start."

When Bobby got to his cubicle, Brick was intensely sharpening his instruments. "What are you doing, Brick?"

"My sister's a hygienist in New Jersey. She showed me a trick to get my instruments sharp enough to break out of jail. Right now, these babies could amputate a leg." Brick took a pencil out of his pocket and sliced it in half with one stroke.

Bobby looked at the halved pencil on the floor and swallowed. "Brick, why don't you let me clean you first, that way I can enjoy my gums a little longer."

Just then the short blonde with the overbite walked over. "Hi,

Dental School Debacle

my name is Debbie. I'm the instructor for this row." Bobby's heart started fibrillating.

"Nice to meet you, Debbie." Bobby shook the woman's hand. "My name is Bobby, and this is James, but everybody calls him Brick."

"Nice to meet you," she said with a smile. "Are you ready to get your instruments checked?"

"Sure," said Bobby. "You can check anything of mine."

Debbie picked up Bobby's instruments and successfully cut the piece of paper. "Good job, Bobby," she said, and then signed off his grading sheet.

"Thank you. Maybe later on I can show you my technique." Debbie just ignored him and picked up Brick's instruments. Right as she grabbed one, she screamed, pulled her hand back, and started sucking her bleeding finger.

"Owww! That thing cut me!" she yelled. "I've never seen instruments this sharp before. I barely touched it, and now I'm bleeding!"

"I worked on them all night," replied Brick proudly. "My sister's a hygienist. She gave me this special sharpening stone she bought when she was in Japan. It's what the Ninjas use."

"Your instruments don't have to be that sharp," she said. "You're only using them to clean teeth, not to clean fish. You'd better be REALLY careful, James. One slip, and you could cut off his tongue."

She looked at Bobby and shook her head. "I'm glad I'm not you." She was still applying pressure to her cut as she walked away.

Bobby swallowed, again, and looked at Brick. "I don't feel so good."

"Don't worry, Bobby. I'll be careful. I only cut the

Jim P. Sandras, D.D.S.

mannequin's gums seven times."

"This is just great," said Bobby, nervously. "Now I know why so many dentists are alcoholics. They all started drinking when they were guinea pigs in dental school. Just promise me one thing, Brick. When the Periodontist comes to suture up my gums, make sure he doesn't use cat gut. I don't want any part of a cat in my mouth."

Brick sat down in the dental chair and prepared to have his teeth cleaned. As Bobby was about to put the instrument in his mouth, Brick grabbed his hand and looked him in the eyes. "There's something I forgot to tell you, Bobby. If you hurt me, you're dead." Moisture formed on Bobby's upper lip. Not only did he have to worry about getting his teeth cleaned with razor-sharp instruments, now he had to worry about an ex-professional linebacker punching his lights out if he messed up.

***

By the time Destin got to his cubicle, Sherry already had her instruments neatly in order and was reviewing her notes for the 17th time that day. She was always afraid of missing something.

"Hi, Sherry," said Destin with little enthusiasm.

"Do you floss regularly?" she asked without saying hello.

"Yep, every Easter, whether they need it or not," he replied seriously.

"Oh no, let me see the lingual side of your lower incisors."

"Why?"

"I want to see how much calculus you have on your teeth. If you have a lot of build-up, I want to point it out to the instructor, so I won't lose any points."

"Whatever turns you on," said Destin, opening his mouth. As Sherry put her fingers in his mouth, he licked them.

Dental School Debacle

"Oh gross. That was disgusting!" She quickly washed her hands.

Destin had been wanting to ask her a question for a long time, and felt the time was right. "Sherry, when was the last time you went on a date?"

"My junior prom."

"What happened to the senior prom?"

"I was taking a speed-reading course that night."

"Don't you read anything besides textbooks?"

"One time I read a Cosmopolitan, but all they talked about was sex."

"And that's not important?"

She tensed her face. "I don't let my loins run my life."

"So, you do have loins. Bobby told me you were congenitally missing them."

"Bobby would lie to his dying mother," Sherry replied, and put down her notebook. "Are you ready to get started? I want to make sure I have enough time to do a good job. Why don't you clean me first?"

"Why?"

"That way I can see how the instructor grades you. If I know what she's looking for, I can definitely make an 'A'."

"You selfish broad! Did anybody ever teach you how to make friends?"

Just then Ms. Roux, their row instructor, came by. "Are you ready for me to check your instruments?"

"Yes Ma'am," said Sherry. "Mine are lined up in numerical order on the tray ready to be checked. And Ms. Roux, I wanted to tell you that I've really enjoyed your lectures. They're always very organized and informative. Will you be grading me today?"

"I'll be grading this whole row," said the woman, as she

examined the instruments. Sherry picked up her large book bag and pulled out a brown paper bag.

"Here, Ms. Roux, I made this just for you." Sherry handed her the bag. "I hope you like it. It's chocolate chip cheesecake. It's my own recipe. By the way, did I tell you how much I like your perm?"

"That's very sweet, but I don't eat carbs."

"Go ahead and take it," said Destin. "Just do like all the other instructors do, throw it away."

Ms. Roux smiled, and then put down Sherry's instruments. "These instruments are fine. Where's yours?"

"Right here," said Destin.

Ms. Roux took one of the instruments and purposely cut out a chunk of her fingernail. Destin couldn't believe it. But all of her fingernails were cut up, obviously from checking instruments.

"These look fine, too," she said. "Call me when you're ready to get graded." Ms. Roux left the cheesecake and walked away.

"Thank you, Ms. Roux," said Sherry. "I forgot to tell you how much I like your shoes."

"I can't believe you, Sherry," said Destin, shaking his head in disbelief. "How stupid do you think they are? Don't you know the instructors talk to one another? They're worse than students when it comes to gossip. And believe me, they all know that you're the biggest brown-noser that ever walked through the front doors of this school. Believe it or not, Sherry, that just makes it harder for you, both with the instructors and your classmates."

Sherry, who wasn't listening, sat in the chair and put the napkin around her own neck as Destin continued. "Do you know that two students in our class got married last semester, and you were the only one who wasn't invited to either of the weddings?"

Dental School Debacle

Sherry, who still wasn't listening to a word he said, was lying in the chair feeling the backs of her teeth with her fingernail. She finally realized Destin was talking.

"I'm sorry, what did you say?" she asked.

"Never mind. Just sit there and be quiet. And if you move, I'm liable to cut you bad, and enjoy it."

Destin sat in his chair and picked up his instruments. "By the way, Sherry, did I tell you I have epilepsy? Oh no, that reminds me, I forgot to take my Dilantin this morning. If I start shaking, grab my tongue."

Sherry ignored him, closed her eyes, and opened her mouth wide. While she had her eyes closed, Destin cleaned under his fingernails with the instrument, wiped it off on his clinic jacket, put his gloves on, and then put the dirty instrument in her mouth to begin.

***

Meanwhile, Mike and David had their cleaning instruments checked and were ready to start.

"Do you want to clean my teeth first?" asked Mike.

"It doesn't matter," said David with a depressed expression. "I'm going to fail anyway."

"David, if you keep talking like that, you will fail for sure. And you better not fail in my mouth!"

"I just don't care anymore," he said. "I'm not cut out to be a dentist. I hate saliva and blood."

"You better not see any blood in my mouth!"

"Don't worry, I'll be careful."

"If you don't like dentistry, why don't you quit? Don't waste your time in dental school if you don't like it. But I guarantee it'll be more fun after we graduate and start making money."

"I doubt it. I don't want to put my hands in people's mouths

Jim P. Sandras, D.D.S.

for the rest of my life, no matter how much money I make."

"Then why did you apply to dental school?"

"I had no choice. My father's a dentist, and he forced me into it. He told me the only way he would pay my way through college was if I went into pre-dentistry. It was either college or work, and I surely didn't want to work."

"God forbid."

"And besides, I can't let my mother down. All she talks about is her son, the dental student. My father would kill me if I quit. He's 6'3" and weighs 280."

"I see what you mean. I wouldn't want to get him upset, either."

"I'm terrible with my hands," said David. "Remember last year when we had to carve teeth out of blocks of wax? All mine looked like jagged shark teeth. The only reason I passed was because my dad went to dental school with the course director."

Mike grabbed his forehead. "And you're putting sharp instruments into my mouth? Where's the drugs when you need them?"

"Don't worry," said David. "I only cut my mannequin once."

"Yeah, but it probably went all the way to its neck. So, what else do you want to do?"

David looked at him and hesitated. Then he bent over and took a pack of Camel filterless cigarettes out of his left sock.

Mike looked at him like he was crazy. "You can't smoke in the clinic."

"I don't care. All them wussy hygienists are in the lounge drinking coffee and talking bad about our class. Besides, it's the only thing that relaxes me. You want one?"

"What the heck," said Mike. He took one out of the pack and lit it. "I might as well have bad breath, too." Mike took one

Dental School Debacle

drag and immediately got dizzy and had to sit down.

"David, why do you smoke cigarettes without filters?"

"Do you drink your beer through a sponge?"

"Good point. So, what else do you want to be?"

David blew out a big ring of smoke. "I'm a musician. I want to start a band."

"A musician? You, Mr. Quiet?"

"The only reason I don't talk to anyone around here is because they only want to talk about dentistry. That's why I don't go to any of our class parties. I hate talking about teeth."

"You got it all wrong, David. Only a few people talk about dentistry at our parties. Most talk about cool things, like cars, guns, the Saints, things like that."

David was looking at Mike with a long face, just listening. "You ought to come to our End-of-the-Year Party at Destin's beach house," said Mike. "Last year was a classic."

"Maybe."

"What instrument do you play, David?"

"Lead guitar. I used to play in a band in high school, until my dad made me quit. We were pretty good. He just hated the idea of me not being a dentist like him. It would kill him if I failed out or quit. All he does is brag about me, the dental student, to his friends at the country club. I can't go on much longer with this pressure."

"Did you try talking to him, telling him how you really feel?"

"I've tried, several times, but he doesn't want to hear it. Let's not talk about this anymore. It gets me depressed."

"Are you ready to get started?" asked Mike. Then he put his cigarette out in the sink.

"Sure," said David, and then did the same with his.

"You'd better clean me first," said Mike, as he laid down in the

Jim P. Sandras, D.D.S.

dental chair. "I'm still dizzy from that Camel." David put the napkin on Mike and then sat down next to him and picked up an instrument.

"Here goes nothing," said David. "Open wide and tell me if it hurts."

"Don't worry about that," replied Mike. He clasped down on the arms of the chair and closed his eyes. David put the instrument in the back of his mouth and started cleaning around his last molar. About the fifth time he scraped the tooth, he pulled out the instrument with a piece of his gums hanging on the tip. Mike grabbed the side of his face and yelled.

"I just found a piece of ground meat between your teeth. You should start flossing more," said David. Then he flicked the meat against the wall. "God only knows how long it's been there."

"That wasn't ground meat—that was my gums!" Then he sat up to spit blood into the spittoon and looked at David. "I think you'd make a good musician, David."

***

Across the clinic, Bobby was finished cleaning Brick's teeth and was nervously lying in the dental chair waiting for his turn.

"Alright Brick, PLEASE take it easy on me," he pleaded. "Remember, I didn't hurt you, not once."

"I know, you did a good job, Bobby." Then he picked up an instrument and started sharpening it again.

"What are you doing?" questioned Bobby.

"Just sharpening my instrument a little more."

"You got to be joking, Brick! You're just cleaning my teeth, not chopping down an oak tree. Stop that! You're going to cut my mouth wide open."

"I like the sound it makes," said Brick, and then put the sharpening stone down. "Alright, are you ready?"

Dental School Debacle

"I guess so," said Bobby turning pale. "I should've become an engineer."

"OK, open wide."

Bobby took a deep breath and opened his mouth. He was stiff as a board lying in the chair while tightly gripping the arm rest. The perspiration was starting to show through his light blue clinic jacket. Brick was cleaning his teeth skillfully, as if he had done it many times before, and was being extremely gentle. Bobby couldn't believe how well Brick was doing. Halfway through the procedure everything was still going smoothly. Finally, Bobby started to relax and forgot that a 260-pound maniac had a razor-sharp instrument in his mouth. It was going too well; Brick's mind started to wonder. Then suddenly it happened without warning. He nicked Bobby's gums with the instrument. It scared Bobby more than it hurt, but he jumped in the chair, which scared Brick, causing him to shove the razor-sharp instrument into his palate, making an incision right down the middle. Bobby let out a scream that could be heard outside the building.

"OHHH! What did you do?" yelled Bobby. He quickly sat up and grabbed his mouth. "My palate's laying on my tongue!" Bobby was trembling and his eyes were watering up in pain.

"Why did you jump?" asked Brick. "You scared me, and then I jumped. It can't be that bad. You're overreacting, as usual. Sit back and let me take a look."

Bobby, who was now crying, leaned over and spit a mouth full of blood into the spittoon. "No way, Brick! You don't know what you're looking at. Go get me a doctor, or anyone who can give me some Lidocaine! My palate is killing me!"

"Alright, first let me take a quick look." Brick pushed him back in the chair and examined his mouth while he was moaning with pain. "I can't see a thing with all this blood." He took the

Jim P. Sandras, D.D.S.

suction tip and cleaned out his mouth, and then started examining. "Wow, I think I see bone. Cool. I just did a perfect full thickness flap."

"I'm not worried what you did," cried Bobby. He was now in a lot of pain and hemorrhaging badly. "Please go get a doctor before I bleed to death. And tell him to bring some Morphine!"

Just then Debbie walked over to the side of the chair to see what was going on. "Is everything alright? Who screamed?"

When Bobby saw her, he dried his tears and tried to act cool, like nothing happened. He didn't want her to know that he was in a lot of pain. It wouldn't be manly.

"I'm fine, Debbie," he said trembling. "Brick just nicked my gums a little." He tried to smile, but when he did, blood trickled from the corners of his mouth onto his clinic jacket. Debbie saw it and took off running to get a periodontist. She knew that this was not normal following a cleaning.

***

Sherry finally finished cleaning Destin's teeth. She had been diligently scraping them for over an hour while he was grunting and giving her evil eyes the whole time. She had been extremely rough and was ignoring his pleas to ease up. But what really made Destin mad was that she didn't care.

"That ought to do it," she said after checking over his whole mouth one last time before getting graded. "I don't think there's an atom of plaque left on your teeth."

"Yeah, but do I have any enamel left?" he asked. "That was worse than getting my wisdom teeth out! Now I know why you wanted me to clean you first. After what you just did to me, I would've cleaned your teeth with a coal miner's pick."

"I'm sorry if I hurt you," she said, as she picked up her instruments, not looking at Destin. "You should've told me

Dental School Debacle

something."

He sat up in the chair. "I did! Seven times!" Destin then gave her a psychopathic look. "But you were too worried about your stupid grades to listen to me. Now, thanks to you, I won't be able to drink anything cold until I draw social security." He then acted as if he was going to throw his rinse cup on her, but didn't, even though he desperately wanted to.

Sherry jumped back against the wall of the cubicle and covered her face. "You're insane!"

"You haven't seen anything yet, girlfriend." Destin gritted his teeth. "Go get Ms. Roux so I can get the hell out of here. And bring me back some Advil; my mouth is killing me."

Sherry backed out of the cubicle while keeping her eyes on him, and then took off running. As soon as she was out of sight, Destin sprinted to the candy machine in the nearby dental assistants' lounge and purchased a pack of Oreos. He threw the entire contents into his mouth and quickly chewed them on his way back to the chair. Then he sat down and acted like he never left.

"This is going to be sooo satisfying," Destin said to himself. A few minutes later Ms. Roux came walking into the clinic followed closely by Sherry. The woman washed her hands, sat down next to Destin, and picked up a mouth mirror.

"I think I did an outstanding job," bragged Sherry, looking over the hygienist's shoulder.

"Open please," said the woman with coffee on her breath. She looked around Destin's mouth for a few minutes without saying a word. Then she put the mouth mirror down and looked at Sherry, who was waiting for a compliment.

"Did you really clean his teeth, or is this a joke?"

"Yes, I did it myself. It's pretty good for a dental student,

Jim P. Sandras, D.D.S.

huh?"

"This is the worst cleaning I have ever seen in my life. There's still food debris in his mouth. Did you even polish his teeth?"

Sherry quit smiling. "Yes Ma'am, three times, and I scraped his teeth for over an hour."

Ms. Roux picked up an explorer and pulled a piece of cookie out of Destin's mouth. "How do you explain this?"

Sherry was dumbfounded. "I-I-I don't know what that is! I checked his whole mouth, twice."

"Well, you missed it, and a bunch more. His mouth is filthy!"

The woman looked at Destin lying there enjoying himself. "Did she even attempt to clean your teeth?"

"I don't know what she was doing in my mouth, Ms. Roux, but it felt like acupuncture. I kept telling her it hurt, but she didn't listen."

Destin then got close to Ms. Roux and whispered in her ear. "To be honest, Sherry spent most of her time in the bathroom. I think she's been snorting something. I can tell. She keeps sniffing and rubbing her nose."

"I don't know what she's on," said Ms. Roux, as she stood up. "But she's going to be repeating this course over the summer. I'm giving her a 'D', which is just as good as failing."

Sherry was in such shock that she lost her breath. But still she forced herself to speak. "Something happened. His mouth was almost sterile a few minutes ago."

"Well now his mouth would be cleaner if he would've just rinsed. I'm disappointed in you, Miss Custard. You should worry about your performance as much as you worried about baking cheesecakes for the instructors. I'm also going to recommend that you undergo random urinalysis for the rest of the year. I'll see you this summer." Ms. Roux walked away.

Dental School Debacle

"Better luck next time, Miss Custard," laughed Destin, as he stood up. "You must hate summer." He rinsed out his mouth, took the Advil, and rushed off.

***

By the end of the afternoon, they had tied a class record for the most casualties in one clinic period. Out of 69 students, six needed over-the-counter analgesics, two needed prescription analgesics, and one, Bobby, needed sutures. He was in so much pain that he was prescribed narcotics. Even though Mike's and Bobby's mouths were killing them, they still met Destin's father at Brennan's Restaurant that night. When the three arrived, they couldn't find Destin's father, so they sat at a table for four and ordered a round of drinks while they waited. Thirty minutes later, Mr. Dufrene walked in.

"There he is," said Destin. He stood and started waving. "Over here, Dad!"

A very fit, middle-aged man with a slight touch of gray turned around and rushed over. "Destin, how've you been, son?" The two embraced.

"Great, Dad, you're looking good! How's Mama?"

"She's doing fine, son. Just worrying about how you never come home on weekends anymore."

"I've been busy, Dad."

"I know. I get the credit card bills every month. You haven't been renting anymore suites at the Hyatt Regency, have you?"

"Dad, I want you to meet some friends of mine," said Destin, trying to change the subject. "This is Mike Williams and Bobby, Bobby, what name are you using this week?"

"Dupont," he answered. The right side of Bobby's face was swollen from the oral surgery, but he didn't care at this point. He was on heavy pain meds and had been drinking scotch on the rocks. Bobby was sitting there with his shirt halfway unbuttoned, and blood-shot eyes that were randomly gazing, not feeling a thing.

"Guys, this is my father, Mr. Neil Dufrene."

"Nice to meet you," said his father as he shook their hands. "I'm sorry I'm late. I was in a business meeting across town, and we ran overtime." He sat down and put his napkin on his lap. "Destin has told me a lot about you two. Weren't you guys at my home in Pass Christian when those Mexican drug lords broke in?"

Bobby started banging on the table in laughter. Destin's heart came to a stop. He was afraid Bobby would give him away.

"Yes sir, Mr. Dufrene, it was a tragedy," Mike quickly answered. "Those guys came out of nowhere. It was like a movie. They jumped out of their boat and ran towards the house carrying rifles in one hand and bottles of rum in the other. Everyone took off running for their lives. We had no choice."

Bobby busted out laughing again, and then finished the rest of his drink.

"That's probably why the house still smells like a bar," said his father. Destin could tell by his dad's response that he knew the whole story was a lie.

"So, dad, how's business?" asked Destin, trying to change the subject, again.

"Business is great! This oil boom in Louisiana is keeping everyone busy."

The waiter walked up to the table. "Can I get you something to drink?" asked the feminine man in a tuxedo.

"Bring us a bottle of champagne," replied Mr. Dufrene.

"Make sure it's a big bottle," slurred Bobby.

"So, Mike and Bobby, how do you like dental school?" Mr.

Dental School Debacle

Dufrene asked.

"I like it a lot," answered Bobby. "But I also like bed sores."

"What have you guys learned so far?"

"I've learned a lot," replied Mike as he sipped on his third drink. "I can spot a transvestite a mile away. I can make a denture with a gold tooth. And I make the world's best Dead Juice."

"I can spot a tomato in someone's mouth," said Bobby. Then he started laughing so hard in the quiet restaurant that he was drawing everyone's attention.

Mr. Dufrene tensed his forehead, and then leaned over and whispered in Destin's ear. "What kind of friends are these? They're not like Fred and Boulon, are they? Now those two were losers."

"No, Dad. They're alright. We just had a bad day. We cleaned each other's teeth today in clinic, and we were all injured. But Bobby got it the worst; he was paired up with an ex-Green Bay Packer. You ought to see this guy, dad. We call him Brick. He's so big he barely fits two fingers in your mouth. Anyway, while he was working on Bobby the instrument slipped, so he says, and he accidentally removed a large section of Bobby's palate. A specialist had to take a piece of tissue off his cheek to place over the wounded area. He's on prescription drugs for the pain."

The waiter interrupted them with their champagne. "Bring us another one of these bottles every time you walk by, sweetie," said Bobby to the waiter. His eyes were now pointing in different directions.

After dinner they were drinking coffee when the waiter came by with a telephone.

"This is for you, Mr. Dufrene."

"Excuse me for a second, fellows," his father said, picking up

Jim P. Sandras, D.D.S.

the phone. "Hello. Yes it is. Yes. Are you sure? OK. I'll be there." Mr. Dufrene then hung up the phone. "I'm sorry fellows, but something important has come up; I have to leave."

"Is everything alright, Dad?"

"I have to be in Jackson first thing tomorrow. Our plant manager had a heart attack and was rushed to the hospital. I have to leave tonight. I'm sorry. Here's the key to my suite at the Royal Sonesta. Why don't you and your friends stay there tonight so you don't have to drive."

"Are you sure, Dad?" asked Destin, after quickly snatching the key out of his dad's hand.

"Be careful," he said. "It has a balcony over Bourbon Street. I don't want you falling off. I'm sorry I have to leave, Destin, but if I don't get there before the plant opens, there's going to be chaos."

Mr. Dufrene stood up and shook their hands. "I enjoyed meeting you, Mike and Bobby. Study hard. It'll all be worth it. Believe me, before you know it you three will be graduating."

Mr. Dufrene pulled out his wallet. "Here Destin, put this meal on my credit card. I'll get it from you later." He tossed his American Express Gold Card on the table.

"Sure, Dad, no problem." Destin looked at the card lying on the table and saw new golf clubs written all over it.

"Come home to see me and your mother, and not just when you need money."

"I will, Dad. I promise."

"See you later, son." Destin stood up and hugged his dad.

As Mr. Dufrene walked away, he paused and looked back at the boys fighting for the credit card.

"You three better be good, and don't tear up the hotel room. I know the owner." He quickly walked away.

Dental School Debacle

"I like your dad," said Mike. "It looks like he works hard."

"Somebody has to pay the bills around here," answered Destin.

Bobby started moaning while massaging his right jaw. "Destin, my mouth is starting to hurt, again. We have any Vicodin left?"

"Sure, we have lots more." Destin reached into his pocket and pulled out a prescription bottle full of pills. "Here, take two— one for good luck. Just don't operate heavy machinery. Here Mike, it looks like your gums are starting to hurt, too." Destin gave each of them two Vicodin. Then he took one himself for preventive reasons. They didn't know what they were doing; they had already taken a few pain pills, and then accidentally got drunk.

"Destin, I need something to swallow these with," said Mike. "My glass is empty."

"I agree. Waiter!" yelled Bobby across the quiet restaurant. Everybody turned around and looked. "Get your butt over here," he shouted. "We need something wet!" He was making a spectacle of himself and didn't know it. The only one who was embarrassed was the waiter.

"I'm sorry I didn't check on you sooner, sir," said the waiter politely.

Bobby looked at Destin and Mike and smiled. "I just love it when an older person calls me sir."

"What can I get you, sir?"

"Is your mama still alive?" Bobby asked seriously.

"No, sir."

"Then bring us a bottle of Don Perigon and three large cups to go, stat!"

"That means right now," added Mike.

"And while you're at it, bring us the check," said Destin.

Bobby took the expensive bottle of champagne and poured it

into 16-ounce Styrofoam cups. Destin paid the bill, leaving a huge tip. He felt sorry for the waiter.

The three left the restaurant and walked straight to Lee Circle to catch the streetcar uptown. They got off at Napoleon Avenue and walked down to the river to Tipitina's, one of their favorite places to hang out. They were only there a few minutes when the manager recognized Bobby from the Tavern and asked them to leave before a fight broke out. Bobby was extremely upset and wanted to fight but was too sedated to put up a struggle. Destin agreed and had the manager call them a taxi. In just a few minutes they were pulling up to the Royal Sonesta. Due to various legal and ethical reasons, their attorney advised them not to talk about things that took place on Bourbon Street that night. They exist only in the partial and hazy memories of three former dental students.

High Speed Fun

It was the week before starting Clinical Operative Dentistry, the last class of sophomore year. They would drill and fill their first tooth on a real live patient—the kind that screams and bleeds. They had completed their Local Anesthesia lecture course and were about to go into the clinic to give their first shots...on one another! This time they were allowed to choose their own partners. Even though they were working on friends, the students were still afraid of the abuse they would endure. No one likes needles, much less a shot by a sophomore dental student who's doing it for the first time. They were about to play the part of a human pin cushion.

"This morning you will be using all of the techniques of local anesthesia that you have learned in the lecture part of the course," said Dr. Salvagio, the professor of Oral Surgery. "I know it's harder to give a shot to a human than an orange, but just take your time and administer one drop every second to numb the tissue before the needle gets there. A painless injection should take a full minute. I promise you, giving a painless injection can make the difference between a mediocre practice and a very lucrative one. Today, I want you to start off with local infiltration of the upper arch. Then go to the inferior alveolar mandibular nerve block, and then try the Gow-Gates Technique. And don't forget everyone's favorite—the palatal injections. I know these are the most painful, but it's important for you to try all of the techniques on your partner. This is your last chance to experiment. Next time you do this will be on a real patient. If you have any problems getting profound anesthesia, ask one of the instructors walking around the clinic. Don't forget, there is a limit on the amount of anesthesia you can give a person. Use the formula we gave you in class to figure out the maximum dosage your partner can handle."

Dr. Salvagio smiled. "Take it easy on your partners. They have to do the same thing to you."

The students paired up and nervously started giving one another injections. You could hear the moaning throughout the clinic. They felt like experimental monkeys. By the end of the period each student had received at least eight shots, and some as many as 12. They were numb from the neck up. After clinic, the students went to the cafeteria and attempted to eat lunch, although it was difficult. Their food and drinks ran down their faces onto the floor. They tried to laugh, but no one's face was cooperating. They couldn't even communicate, only mumble and drool. Some made the mistake of drinking coffee out of a vending machine, causing nasty third-degree burns. They were scorching their lips and tongues and didn't realize it, at least not until the anesthesia wore off. Supposedly, they were now ready to give a painless injection, although a few students never got the hang of it.

***

It was 12:30 the next day, shortly before they saw their first

Dental School Debacle

operative patient. The students were excited and nervous at the same time. Sure, they had seen patients before, but only to take x-rays; they didn't have to deal with pain or fear. Now they had to give a shot and put a high-speed drill in someone's mouth. They knew it was easy to cause a lot of damage to a person with just one slip. There were a lot of things to get in the way—lips, cheeks, tongue. But the fact they were students and could not be sued made it a little easier. They got to their cubicles half an hour early to set up their instruments and get everything ready. Mike and Destin were assigned cubicles next to one another and were leisurely waiting for 1:00.

"I hope Dr. Hebert isn't grading our row," said Destin.

"Why? I've never heard of the man," replied Mike.

"I was talking to a Junior the other day," said Destin, "and he told me that he was like a drill sergeant. He gives all of his students a hard time. They say never joke around with him; he doesn't think anything's funny. And he's very religious, too. Southern Baptist, I think."

"Did you know Brick is in the cubicle across from us?"

"Oh Lord," Destin replied. "I mean, I like Brick and everything, but he gets mad at his patients too easily. He thinks he still in the NFL. Did you ever see him with a patient?"

"No, but I've heard about it."

"You ought to see him, Mike. He flexes his chest and then stares at them like he's about to inflict pain. Never says a word. Just stares."

"That's what I call chairside manners," laughed Mike.

A few minutes before 1:00, the instructors walked into the clinic and went to the row they would be grading. Dr. Hebert walked toward Mike and Destin, and then passed them by.

"Whew, that was close," said Destin, breathing more easily.

Jim P. Sandras, D.D.S.

"For a minute there, I thought he was coming over here."

"Look where he's going," said Mike, "To Sam's row. Hey, I've got an idea." Mike looked over at Sam, who was cutting his cuticles with a dental instrument. Mike called him over. "Hey Sam, come here!"

"What do you want Sam for?" questioned Destin.

"I want to warn him about Dr. Hebert. I wouldn't want to see him mess up."

Sam innocently walked over. "What can I do for you, Mike?"

"You don't look too busy over there."

"My patient told me she'd be running a little late today. I accidentally told her on the phone that this was my first filling, ever. Then she told me she was going to have a few drinks to relax before she came in."

"At least she'll be sedated," said Mike, looking at Sam sincerely. "Do you know you have Dr. Hebert for your row instructor?"

"Is that his name? I've never seen him before."

"He's a real cool guy," said Mike. "He loves to joke around with students. If you tell him a joke and he likes it, you're almost guaranteed good grades."

"Really?"

"Really, he has a great sense of humor."

"I don't know any good jokes," Sam replied.

"I do. Dr. Hebert is into real estate. I heard he owns a bunch of rental houses. In fact, it's his passion. I have a good real estate joke you can tell him. He'll love it." Mike pulled Sam over and whispered in his ear.

Sam started laughing. "I like that one," he said. "Are you sure Dr. Hebert's going to like it?"

"He'll pee on himself, I promise. Go tell him right now while he's not doing anything."

Dental School Debacle

"Alright. Hey, thanks a lot, Mike. I'll talk to you later." Sam walked away to look for his instructor.

"What did you tell him?" asked Destin.

"Just watch."

Sam walked over to Dr. Hebert with a big smile on his freckled face. The man was sitting in an empty cubical reading the monthly issue of Dental Economics magazine.

"Hi, Dr. Hebert, my name is Sam Adams. I'll be working under you."

The man put down his magazine and looked up at Sam with little emotion. "Yes, what can I do for you?"

"Do you know anything about real estate?"

The man smiled and sat up in the chair. "As a matter of fact, I do," he said. "I own 16 rental houses. Why?"

Sam spread his legs open, grabbed his crotch with both hands, and looked at his instructor. "Is this a lot?" he asked, forcing himself to laugh. "You get it, a-lot?"

The man was in shock. He stood up and stared Sam in the eyes. "That's disgusting! I've never seen anything so filthy! You need help!"

Sam stood there with his mouth wide open. At this point he knew he was on the bad end of a practical joke. He looked over at Mike and Destin who were banging on the counter laughing. Then they ducked when they realized Sam was looking.

"Only the devil could come up with something that perverted," continued Dr. Hebert. "Young man, you need to come with me to the revival at our church tonight so the minister can pray over you and anoint you with oil. You need deliverance!"

Sam tried to explain. "B-B-B-But sir. You don't understand."

"I do understand," interrupted Dr. Hebert. "You need help,

Jim P. Sandras, D.D.S.

and the only way you're going to get it is at a Southern Baptist revival."

"But sir, I'm Catholic."

"I don't care if you're Jewish. You'd better be at the First Baptist Church on Canal Blvd. at 7:00 tonight, or I'll make life very difficult for you."

"But sir, someone told me to tell you that joke," said Sam in desperation.

"His name was probably Lucifer. Be there or else. By the way, why aren't you busy? Where's your patient?"

"She's running a little late, sir."

"You'd better get on the phone and call to make sure she gets here. If you don't get any work done today, you're going to be in trouble. Now get on the phone and call her!"

"Yes sir," said Sam humbly. As he walked to the phone on the wall he was cursing under his breath. "I'll get you for this, Mike!" he kept saying.

***

Across the clinic, Bobby and his young, black, male patient were laughing together as they watched Darl across the aisle trying to give his patient a shot. He would pick up the syringe and turn around to put it in his patient's mouth. But, when he would get about a foot from her face, his hands would start shaking so badly that he had to put the syringe down. After four tries, he still didn't get the syringe in his patient's mouth. Darl took off his fogged glasses and wiped the sweat from his forehead. His patient was so nervous she had tears running down the side of her face.

"He's never going to give her a shot," said Bobby to his patient.

"Look how he's sweating," said Bobby's patient. "He's

Dental School Debacle

soaking wet."

"The patient's so scared her knuckles are white!" laughed Bobby.

"Yeah, and she's darker than me," said Bobby's patient. "Look at him; he's trying again."

They were both watching intensely as Darl put his glasses back on, and then stared at the loaded syringe on his cart.

"I bet you he doesn't do it," said Bobby.

"I bet he does," said his patient. "I can tell by the look in his eyes, he's determined."

"I bet you $10," said Bobby.

"You're on," replied his patient.

The two gamblers turned all of their attention towards Darl, who now looked like he was ready to go. He picked up the syringe with one hand and used the other hand to stabilize it.

"Go baby, go. You can do it," whispered Bobby's patient.

Darl turned towards his patient, who was sitting there petrified with her eyes closed and mouth open, gripping the arms of the chair so hard she was warping the plastic. Using both hands, Darl slowly moved the two-inch needle towards her open mouth. He was doing fine, until he got six inches from her face. Then his hands started shaking again and sweat was dripping off of his forehead.

"Come on, you're doing great," said Bobby's patient. "Don't stop now."

"He's going to choke," said Bobby. "Why don't you just give me the $10 now so we can get started."

"No way, he's going to do it, I can tell."

Darl finally started moving the syringe forward, again.

"He's gonna do it, I told ya," said Bobby's patient.

Darl then put the shot in the woman's mouth.

Jim P. Sandras, D.D.S.

Bobby slapped his leg. "I can't believe he did it."

Bobby took out his wallet and gave two $5 bills to his patient.

"This is great," said the guy, as he put the money in his pocket. "I'm getting paid for going to the dentist."

Just then there was a loud scream followed by another loud scream. They turned around and saw Darl hopping on one leg in the middle of the aisle while holding the other. Then they saw his patient sitting up in the chair holding her cheek with blood running between her fingers and down her arm. Bobby jumped up and ran towards Darl.

"What da heck happened?" he asked.

"I accidentally shoved the needle through the woman's cheek and into my thigh," he said rubbing his leg. "Now it's numb."

"Good job, Darl," joked Bobby, as they watched Darl's patient jump up, still holding her cheek, and run out of the clinic, down the stairs.

***

By this time most students were busy drilling on their patients. Destin was ready to start when he overheard Brick yelling at a little old lady who weighed about 90 pounds. His hand was easily twice the size of her head. He was holding the syringe in her face as he talked.

"Quit whining!" yelled Brick. "You won't feel a thing, unless you don't cooperate. Then it could get messy."

"How long have you been giving shots?" asked the petite, white haired woman nervously.

Brick looked down at her with his large brown eyes. "Two days."

"Oh my God!" she said. "Can you please get a real doctor to come give it to me?"

"Don't worry, I practiced all night on grapefruits."

Dental School Debacle

The woman looked up at the ceiling, made the sign of the cross, and started praying. "Jesus, Mary and Joseph, please don't let this young man kill me."

"Relax, you won't feel a thing." Every time Brick tried to put the shot in the woman's mouth, the old lady would lock her lips and grab his hand. Brick looked at Destin and shrugged his shoulders. Destin jokingly clinched his fist and made a motion to punch her out.

Brick liked the idea and nodded.

"Well, Mrs. Bergeron," Brick said with a smile. "It's obvious you don't want me to give you this shot."

"Now you're using your big head," she answered

"We have a new type of anesthesia we can try."

"How big is the needle?"

"There is no needle," Brick replied professionally. "It's very popular in Australia. It's something like hypnosis."

"If there's no needle, I'll try it."

Brick laid her all the way back and started talking softly. "OK, Mrs. Bergeron, I want you to close your eyes and relax, breathe deep and relax, just relax…"

The woman was doing what he said and was starting to relax.

"You are about to lose all sensation," he said. "Just relax. You won't remember a thing, I promise." As Brick was talking, he made a fist and cocked his large arm back. Destin, who was watching, put his hands over his eyes—he couldn't look.

"Just relax," he repeated, again, and then punched the woman in the back of her right ear. Brick coughed out loud at the same time he punched her to cover up the noise.

After a moment of total silence, Destin peeked through his fingers.

"Is she still alive?"

Jim P. Sandras, D.D.S.

Brick put his mouth mirror under her nose to see if it would fog up. "Yeah, she's breathing."

"Brick, I was just joking. I didn't want you to really punch her."

"It was in her best interest," he said. "I had no other choice. Now she's sleeping like a baby. I ought to get a lot done today."

Brick started whistling as he pried opened the woman's mouth and shoved a rubber wedge between her teeth, and then began drilling like a man on a mission.

***

It was 3:30 and Sam's patient still wasn't there. Dr. Hebert had just finished grading a student's work and walked past Sam, who was just sitting in his cubicle making a house out of cotton rolls. Dr. Hebert looked at Sam and then looked at his watch.

"I thought you had a patient this afternoon, Mr. Adams?"

"I do, she's on her way. I just called her office and they said she left to go to the dentist a couple of hours ago. I think she stopped to have a drink on the way here."

"Well, for your sake, I hope she comes. For now, at least look busy, and quit playing with those cotton rolls."

"Yes sir," said Sam. As Dr. Hebert was walking away, he turned around. "And don't be late tonight."

Sam angrily knocked down his cotton house and mumbled to himself. "I swear, I'm going to get Mike for this, if it's the last thing I do." He stood up and looked over at Mike, who was busy drilling on his patient.

"Now's my chance," Sam said to himself. He quietly snuck around the clinic and tip-toed up behind Mike like a Shaolin priest walking on rice paper. Mike could not hear him over the sound of the drill. Sam stood directly behind Mike, and using his two index fingers poked him under his arms and yelled.

Dental School Debacle

"WATCH IT!"

Mike jumped out of his chair, knocked over his instruments and let go of the drill, which was still spinning in the man's mouth. Mike turned around to see what happened. He was breathing rapidly, and his eyes were pulsating. He found Sam bent over laughing across the aisle. The veins on Mike's temples instantly bulged out. He walked over, grabbed Sam by his clinic jacket, and pulled him up.

"What the hell are you doing?" Meanwhile, his patient was struggling to get Mike's drill out of his mouth. Fortunately, he was numb and couldn't feel a thing.

"I was just getting you back for making me tell Dr. Hebert that stupid joke," said Sam. "Thanks to you, I have to go to a Baptist revival tonight and get anointed with oil."

Mike was still breathing rapidly. "Couldn't you see I had a high-speed drill in my patient's mouth? Now it's stuck in his tongue!"

"If you would've had proper hand positioning and finger rest, this wouldn't have happened."

This made Mike furious, but his patient started kicking and fighting to get the drill lose. Mike sat down in the chair and smiled at his patient like he had everything under control. Following a small struggle, and with the aid of a scalpel, Mike was able to remove the drill out of the man's tongue.

"Sorry about that, Mr. Plaisance. Something flew in my eye and made me jump."

The man sat up and started feeling for his tongue while trying to ask questions but was too numb to be understood. Mr. Plaisance panicked when he noticed the blood on his lips.

Just then the instructor walked over. "What's going on over here? Who screamed?"

Jim P. Sandras, D.D.S.

"I'll see you later, Michael," said Sam, as he quickly walked back to his cubicle. "Call me tonight." Mike gave him a look to kill, and then looked back at the instructor.

"I had a little accident here, sir," explained Mike. "My drill slipped, and I accidentally nicked my patient's tongue—it's bleeding a little."

The instructor made light of it and chuckled. "Don't worry, son. This kind of thing happens when you're learning. It's called nerves. Let me take a look." Mike handed him the mouth mirror, and then he leaned over to look in the patient's mouth.

"Mr. Williams, I thought you said you nicked his tongue? It's cut in half."

When Mr. Plaisance heard the bad news, he grabbed his heart and began praying in French.

"Calm down, sir. It's going to be alright," said the instructor as he put his hand on Mr. Plaisance's shoulder. "The tongue heals fast." Then he looked at Mike. "Run to the supply window and get me a surgical kit."

Mike took off running like an Olympian.

***

In the meantime, Sam was still sitting in his cubical staring at the clock on the wall. It read 4:05, and his patient still wasn't there. Every time he looked over, Dr. Hebert was looking back at him. Just as he was starting to pick up his instruments and sneak out, the receptionist came over the loudspeaker.

"Mr. Sam Adams, your patient is here."

He couldn't believe it. "Better late than never," he said to himself, rushing towards the waiting room. But Dr. Hebert waved him over to where he was sitting.

"It's now after 4:00, Mr. Adams. You must be finished, graded, and out of the clinic by 5:00. So, if I were you, I wouldn't

Dental School Debacle

waste any time."

"Yes sir." Sam went back to his cubicle, picked up his loaded syringe, put it in his jacket, and ran to the waiting room. Sitting in the corner by herself was a young, nicely dressed lady with crossed eyes, and her head was wobbling back and forth.

"You must be Ms. Valance," said Sam, as he approached her.

"Am I late?" slurred the woman as she tried to focus on Sam.

He could smell liquor on her breath. "A little," he said. "So, let's get going, we have a lot to do."

"Are you the one who's going to be working on me?" She was so intoxicated she was spitting as she talked.

"Yes Ma'am. My name is Sam Adams. I'm the one you talked to on the phone the other night."

"Oh yeah, I remember," replied the woman. Then her eyes rolled up in the back of her head.

Sam was shaking his head in disbelief. "I thought you were joking when you told me you were going to have a drink before you came in."

"I had to," she slurred. "That's the only way I can let a dental student drill on me. I also did a blue Valium my sister gave me. I don't want to remember anything that happens here this afternoon."

"That's a good idea," said Sam, smiling wickedly. "Look, we're kind of pushed for time here. Can you open your mouth so I can see what tooth I need to work on?"

"Sure." Then she closed her eyes, opened her mouth, and put her head back. Sam took the syringe out of his pocket, rammed it in her mouth, and quickly injected the anesthesia, all in a matter of three seconds. The woman was so drunk she didn't know what was going on. The people sitting in the waiting room could not believe what they were witnessing.

Jim P. Sandras, D.D.S.

"OK, I see which one I want to work on," said Sam, and put the empty syringe back in his pocket. "Let's go to my cubicle. We're running out of time."

The woman stood up and fell back in her chair. "I think I'm gonna need some help," she mumbled.

Sam grabbed her by the arm, pulled her up, and then quickly escorted her to the cubicle. He sat her down, put the napkin on her with one hand and started drilling with the other. He was going so fast that he didn't even take the time to turn the water spray on, causing pieces of tooth and smoke to come out of her mouth. The smell of burnt tooth quickly filled the area. When Sam finished drilling there was a layer of enamel dust over the woman's face. He stood up and called Dr. Hebert over.

"Are you ready for a starting check, Mr. Adams?"

"No sir, I'm ready to get graded," said Sam, handing Dr. Hebert his mouth mirror and explorer.

"Already? What did you do, give her the anesthesia in the waiting room?"

Sam smiled. "As if."

Dr. Hebert sat down and started looking at Sam's work. "Uh huh, uh huh... uh, huh. Not too bad, Mr. Adams. Just remove two more atoms of enamel. Then smooth off that dentinal tubule and fill it."

Sam did just exactly that and miraculously finished before 5:00. He then went home, showered, and headed for church, grunting the entire time. The only thing that kept him from injuring someone was the fact that the Second Annual End-of-the-Year Party was this weekend.

Second Annual End-of-the-Year Party

After finishing their sophomore year, and with only three weeks off before starting the dreaded junior year, everyone eagerly anticipated and prepared for the Second Annual End-of-the-Year Party on the beautiful Mississippi Gulf Coast. They nominated Terrance to take care of the details, again, since he did such a good the previous year. Besides using up the remainder of the class funds, he collected $40 from each student. This covered all the drinks, food, beer and fireworks that could possibly be needed in one weekend. This year they decided it would be easier to get canned beer instead of kegs. Terrance and Destin went to Schwegmann's and bought 125 cases of Old Milwaukee and $500 worth of assorted wines, and a few six packs of soft drinks for Sunday. They were expecting a bigger turn out than last year, so Destin borrowed his brother's Winnebago

Jim P. Sandras, D.D.S.

motor home and parked it on the side of the house where the single girls could sleep. Most drove straight there Friday after class and continued to arrive until Saturday. David Foster got a few of his old band members together to play at the party. They called themselves "The Loose Teeth". It was a beautiful, cloudless weekend in June. They were all having a great time swimming and water skiing in Bay St Louis. Friday evening, as the bright red sun was setting over the water, The Loose Teeth began playing on the beach. Everyone gathered around the band screaming and dancing to the music. The
sophomore year was now just a bad memory.

Terrance walked up to Destin and yelled over the ear-splitting music. "They're awesome," shouted Terrance into Destin's ear. "I didn't know David could talk, much less sing and play the guitar."

Destin turned his head and began yelling back in Terrance's ear. "David's a cool guy," he yelled, "although he hates dentistry. Mike told me he wants to be a professional musician, but his dad wants him to be a dentist."

"What a drag. He's an excellent musician."

They both stood there jamming to the music, when Destin got an idea and yelled to Terrance. "Do you like boiled crabs?"

Terrance stopped dancing and got serious. "I LOVE boiled crabs, why?"

"When I was pulling people skiing earlier, I saw crab traps everywhere. Later tonight we can get in the boat and go rob a few. I bet we could fill up two ice chests with crabs in no time."

"Isn't that against the law?"

"Yep, extremely," replied Destin calmly. "The crabbers can legally shoot you."

"Excellent! Then I'll do it. I'm in the mood for something

Dental School Debacle

illegal."

Right after midnight, Destin, Terrance and Brick got in the 22-foot Cigarette speed boat and took off to search the dark Gulf waters for crab traps using a flashlight. After a half hour of searching, they found a whole row of traps tied to floating plastic milk jugs. In no time they filled up the two large ice chests and were now throwing crabs on the deck.

"I think we have enough crabs for everyone," said Destin.

"Not yet," said Terrance leaning over the side of the boat pulling up a trap full of crabs. "Let's get some more, a lot more. This is fun."

Brick was cautiously watching the crabs crawling out of the full ice chest onto the deck towards his feet. "But Terrance, we're out of room. Anymore and they'll be eating us."

"Alright, this is the last one."

Destin was intensely scanning the dark water for any signs of the Coast Guard, or even worse, crabbers. As Terrance was dropping the last trap back into the water, Destin spotted an approaching green and red light.

"Awe crap," yelled Destin as he pointed. "Here comes a boat!"

"I can hear it," Brick said.

Destin panicked. "Let' get the heck out of here!"

Instinctively, he pushed the throttle all the way down. Terrance, who did not have a clue as to what was transpiring, fell from the back of the boat into the dark water without the other two knowing. Terrance was treading water as he yelled for his two friends, but they couldn't hear him over the noise of the racing engine.

"HELP! DESTIN! BRICK! HELP!" It was his worst nightmare come true. Not only did Terrance dislike the dark, but

Jim P. Sandras, D.D.S.

he wasn't that good of a swimmer. His life was flashing before his eyes.

Meanwhile, back in the boat, Brick finally realized they were missing a passenger.

"Where's Terrance?" yelled Brick over the roar of the engine. Destin quickly turned around and saw that he was missing a passenger.

"AWE NO! He must've fallen out!" Without slowing down, Destin made a 180 degree turn and headed back to the area of the crab traps, while keeping a close eye on the green and red light. Brick stood on the bow of the boat with the flashlight, searching the dark water for his friend and president of their class.

After only a few seconds of searching, Brick spotted the splashing water and started jumping and pointing. "LOOK! There he is, Destin! Over there!"

"I see him. But look, that boat is still coming this way."

Destin went as fast as he could to retrieve Terrance without running over him. When they finally got to him, he was struggling for his life.

"HELP ME! I'M DROWNING!" he yelled as he spit water.

Brick leaned over the side and easily lifted Terrance out of the water, into the boat. "What happened to you?" Brick asked. Then he looked down and crushed several crabs that were about to bite his feet.

"I don't know. I was putting the crab trap back in the water, and the next thing I knew I was swimming next to it."

Just then, they heard a gunshot that hit the side of the boat. All three students instinctively hit the deck. Destin slowly peeked above the side only to see two more bullets hit the front of his brother's boat, destroying the blue and white fiberglass. Now they

Dental School Debacle

could hear a man screaming at the top of his voice.

"THOSE ARE MY CRABS!" Then another shot hit the windshield.

"Let's get out of here," said Destin, "before he uses us for bait." He crawled to the throttle and pushed it all the way down from the floor and steered the boat with his eyes just high enough to see over the bow. In no time the speed boat was out of range of the crabber's rifle.

Terrance finally settled down and was breathing regularly. "We need to do this more often, Destin."

But Destin wasn't paying attention to what he was saying. He was too busy looking at the holes in his brother's boat and trying to come up with a story to explain them.

"Benedict is going to castrate me. Look at his boat! It's full of holes!"

"Don't worry about it," joked Brick, after squishing two more crabs. "Just tell your brother that those Mexican drug lords had so much fun last year they came back."

Destin steered the boat away into a series of bayous to make sure the mad crabbers could not follow them to his house. Almost an hour later they pulled up to the pier. When they arrived, the pier was full of people nervously waiting for them. Sam ran to the boat and threw them a rope.

"Where have you been?"

"We were worried to death," said Sarah. "I was about to call the Coast Guard."

"What happened to you, Terrance?" asked Bobby. "You're soaking wet."

"We couldn't find any crab traps," Terrance replied. "So, I had to jump into the water and catch them suckers with my bare hands. Do me a favor, Bobby. Throw me a beer. This saltwater makes me thirsty."

"Sam, can you get us another ice chest to put these crabs in, although Brick smashed half of them."

"Don't worry about those smashed ones," said Sarah as she scanned the boat. "I'll make a gumbo with them."

They loaded up the crabs and carried them to the house, where the party was in full swing. The Loose Teeth had just started playing again and had everyone dancing on the beach. Meanwhile, Destin and Terrance had set up the propane boiler and were seasoning the water for the crabs. At 3 a.m. they were throwing the steaming hot crabs on the tables. Everyone ate themselves full, and there was still plenty left over. Soon after, almost everybody passed out. It had been a long last day of the sophomore year.

***

The whole house was awakened early the next morning by a guy screaming. Destin opened his eyes and laid in bed listening. Then he smiled and thought to himself: "I bet the poor guy woke up and found Trog sleeping next to him." He stretched out, yawned and rolled over, only to come face to face with Trog. Destin screamed and leaped out of the bed. Then he began spitting on the carpet. After he wiped his tongue with the curtain, he put on his Nautica shorts and rushed out of the room.

"I hate it when that happens," he said. Then he walked downstairs, around the large house, stepping over people everywhere, trying to find where the screaming was coming from. He walked into the kitchen where he found Mike pouring cans of beer into an empty milk jug.

"Are you just getting here?" asked Destin, with his eyes half

Dental School Debacle

open.

Mike smiled and nodded at Destin, and then took a long swig out of the jug and screamed again.

"Calm down. You're giving me a headache. And why are you so happy?"

"I didn't tell anyone, but I almost failed the year," replied Mike.

"Why? I thought you had good grades?"

"I did, except for one class, Occlusal Equilibration. I failed the final by two points.

"Yeah, that was a hard test."

"Two days after I got the results," Mike continued, "I ran into Dr. Shawky in the elevator. It was just me and him. He looked at me and said, 'Sorry about your final grade, Mr. Williams'."

I asked him if there was any way I could retake the final. He shook his head no. Then I mentioned that I met his daughter, Niki, at Augie's DeLago a few weeks ago, and even got her number."

Destin's eyes finally opened all the way. "What did he say?"

"Shawky looked very concerned. When the elevator doors opened, he pulled me aside and agreed to give me a make-up exam if I promised not to call her."

"I understand his concerns," said Destin.

"So, last week he let me take a remediation test, which was even harder. I didn't find out til this morning that I passed."

"Well congratulations," said Destin, as he grabbed a beer. "Let's celebrate."

As they were toasting, a loud destructive noise came from the living room facing the water. They ran to the room and discovered the back door was gone—it had been ripped off its hinges. Destin could not believe his eyes. He ran onto the porch

Jim P. Sandras, D.D.S.

and spotted Brick running down the pier carrying the door and drinking a beer.

Destin yelled. "Brick! What the heck are you doing with the door?"

Brick slowly stopped running, turned around and tried to focus on Destin, but the morning sun was in his eyes. "We're going to pull it behind the boat," he replied. "I'm going to put on a water-skiing show, like Cyprus Gardens. It's going to be awesome! Get your cameras ready."

It was way too early in the morning for Destin to worry about his dad chewing him out for the missing, custom-made door. He was about to lose his temper.

"You idiot!" he screamed. "My dad's gonna kill me!"

Brick looked at the wooden door under his arm, and then wiped the foam off his mouth and tried again to focus on Destin. "I'll put it back when we're finished."

Sam, who was sitting on the porch in his bathing suit eating a bowl of Captain Crunch, gave Destin some advice.

"You better let Brick do what he wants," Sam said. "He's been up all night practicing this skiing routine—him, Bobby and those two girls. Then Brick started drinking hot beer at around 5:00 this morning. I bet he's already drunk a case of hot beer. He claims it goes down easier."

Destin looked back at Brick, who was now foaming profusely from the mouth like a rabid dog and decided not to argue with him.

"Be careful with the boat," Destin yelled. "It's messed up enough. And don't kill yourselves. You have two more years of school."

Brick nodded, crumbled up the can like it was paper, and

Dental School Debacle

tossed it in the water. Then he took off running down the pier with the expensive door under his arm and jumped into the water, followed by the two girls. Bobby threw Brick the ski rope and he tied it to the brass doorknob. All three held onto the door as Bobby raced off around a bend, out of sight. Ten minutes later the boat was back in sight, this time Brick was standing on the door with two girls standing on his shoulders. Everyone in the nearby houses was so impressed they ran to the beach applauding and taking pictures. As they passed in front of their pier the girls on Brick's shoulders were waving nonchalantly as if they had done it many times before.

Destin was amazed. "How'd he do that?"

"Brick can do anything he wants when he puts his mind to it," said Terrance, as he walked out of the house with a cup of coffee in his hand.

Sam walked over to Destin while pointing to an approaching sailboat in the gulf. "Destin, I've been watching that sailboat for almost an hour, and I swear, it looks like it's heading straight for your pier."

"I noticed that, too," Destin said, and then ran inside to get his high-powered binoculars. "I can't read the name of the boat," he said while focusing. "I think it's Spanish…now I can see it…it's definitely Spanish…hey, now I see a Cuban flag on the mask. What's going on here? Wait a minute…I don't believe it…It's Bart Lucas!"

"It can't be," said Terrance. "The dean told us he was locked up, remember?"

Destin handed Terrance the binoculars. "Here, you take a look."

After focusing the binoculars for a few seconds, Terrance's

mouth dropped open. "That's Bart—he grew a beard! Let's go help him."

They all raced down the pier to greet him as he single-handedly took down the sail, started the small outboard engine, and steered to the pier.

"What are you doing here?" yelled Destin. Bart killed the engine, ran to the front of the sailboat, and skillfully threw him a rope.

"You didn't think I was going to miss the party, did you?"

"We heard you were in a Cuban prison," said Terrance.

"Actually, it was a mental institution," he explained, while standing barefoot on the front of his sailboat. His lips and face were extremely red and chapped, and both his hair and beard were to his shoulders. "After last year's End-of-the-Year Party I was so pumped up and full of adrenalin I felt adventurous. So, I took this sailboat, which I thought was my uncle's, but wasn't, and sailed towards Key West. All I took with me was a gallon of rum, a few cans of Vienna Sausage, four Jimmy Buffett tapes, and a few limes, you know, for scurvy. Around the third day a storm blew me off course. I didn't know where I was. Two days later I was picked up by the Cuban Navy. Them idiots thought I was a spy."

"What did you tell them?" asked Mike.

"I told them I was an Oral Athlete. They immediately threw me in the mental ward."

"That'll do it every time," said Destin.

"It wasn't that bad," Bart explained. "I had my own bedroom with a window facing the Gulf. There was a beautiful white beach with a gorgeous view of a volcano, the food was excellent, everyone was so nice…it was like Club-Med, only free. I decided

Dental School Debacle

to plead insanity so I could stay there a while. I needed a break after that freshman year. I even learned how to play the guitar. Then I remembered that this was the weekend of the Second Annual End-of-the-Year Party. So, I escaped last weekend, stole this boat, and here I am." Bart jumped off the boat onto the pier and shook everyone's hand.

"It's good to have you back," Destin said. They all walked back to the house where the party was just starting up again. Everyone was glad to see that Bart was safe. The guys started barbequing and hitting golf balls into the water. Brick made Darl get in the water, then they hit balls at him like he was a flag. Brick also told him he was responsible for finding the balls. They spent the day playing volleyball, water skiing and laying out on the white beach while drinking ice cold beer.

***

That afternoon Lewis Tripper volunteered to cook for everyone. He claimed to have a secret recipe for mushroom spaghetti. He said it was out of this world, literally. Lewis made a five-gallon pot of spicy, red gravy, and when no one was looking he added five ounces of his own illegal Amazon Basin mushrooms. Everyone ate the spaghetti and loved it. Just as they were finishing, the doorbell rang. Kate was getting up for her third helping and answered the door with an empty plate in her hand and red gravy on her extra-large shirt. She walked back to the dinning room looking for Destin.

"There's two girls at the door looking for you, Destin," said Kate, and then belched. "They said they're hygienists from Slidell. They heard about the party from their cousin and want to know if they're welcome."

Destin was leaning back in his chair wearing only his wet

Jim P. Sandras, D.D.S.

Nautica shorts, with his bare feet propped on the imported dining room table, flossing his teeth. "Are they good looking?" he asked.

"They're not ugly," Kate said, and then went on her merry way to the kitchen. Destin tossed the used floss onto the table and went to front door while trying to comb his hair with his fingers.

Destin greeted the two well-dressed brunettes with a big smile as he opened the door. "Hi, I'm Destin. Welcome to my humble abode."

Both girls appeared to be in their mid-thirties, attractive, and most importantly, were not wearing wedding rings, which is what Destin always checked first.

"Hi, I'm Roxy and this is Kim. We work for a dentist in Slidell. My cousin works at the dental school, and she told us about this party."

"Everyone's talking about it," added Kim.

"We just happened to be on the coast and decided to stop by to see if the rumors were true. I hope you don't mind."

"Are you kidding?" Destin replied. "Anyone who works in saliva all day is a friend of mine."

As Destin was escorting the two girls inside to introduce them to everyone, Brick walked in from the back porch soaking wet and spotted the two new faces. Without giving it any thought, Brick took off running at the two girls and tried to tackle them both. With his double vision, he only hit Roxy, just barely missing Kim. Brick slammed her against the wall like a hockey player and then fell on the floor on top of her. Sarah ran over and grabbed Brick by the hair and pulled him off the innocent girl. She was the only one who could control him.

"Come on, Dick Butkus," said Sarah as she lifted him up. "This isn't the NFL. I think it's time for you to go nighty-night."

Destin and Kim rushed to Roxy and checked her vital signs.

"Her pulse seems normal," said Destin, "but her eyes are rolled back."

"She's breathing kind of slow," said Kim. Then she took a pillow off the couch and elevated her feet.

"Is she alright?" asked Sarah.

"I think so," replied Destin. "I can see her pupils now."

Slowly but surely, Roxy regained consciousness and eventually sat up and looked around to see a crowd of people gathered around her.

"What happened?" asked Roxy, dazed and confused. "I think I was struck by lightning."

Kim was angry and raised her voice at Destin "What's that dude's problem? He could've killed her!"

"I apologize for Brick," said Destin. "He's been up for the past 48 hours trying to see if he can drink a six pack of hot beer every hour, and so far, he's doing it. The only thing he's eaten in two days is a dozen crabs."

As Sarah was escorting Brick out of the room, he knocked her arm away and tried to look at her, but only one eye would open.

"Leave me alone, woman," he demanded while wobbling side to side. "I'm OK, I'm just thirsty." He stumbled out to the porch for more hot beer.

Sarah shook her head. "Does anyone have an elephant gun?" She went to the kitchen and grabbed a large cast iron skillet. Then she went straight to the porch and smacked Brick in the back of the head. He fell face first into an ice chest. Terrance and Bobby were sitting on the porch smoking cigars watching.

"Sarah, you're my type of woman," said Terrance, as he puffed on his cigar. "You knocked him out."

"It was for everyone's safety," replied Sarah. "He was getting out of hand."

Bobby laughed with the cigar in his mouth. "You didn't mess up Mrs. Dufrene's frying pan, did you?"

The three dragged Brick to the side of the house in the shade, covered him with a tarpaulin and left him alone to sleep. In a matter of seconds, he was snoring.

Inside the house, Destin and Kim were helping Roxy to her feet.

"Come on, Roxy," said Kim. "I think it's time to leave."

"Yeah," replied Roxy as she rubbed her shoulder. "This party is worse than I thought."

"No, don't go," Destin pleaded. "You just got here. I promise Brick won't touch you again. Besides, you haven't met the rest of the class. They're semi-normal. Let's get something to drink and take a walk on the pier."

"Alright, we'll stay a few more minutes," Kim said.

"Just promise you'll keep that big ape away from me," said Roxy.

"Scout's honor."

"I've never been on a pier before," said Kim as she walked around observing the exclusive mansion and expensive furniture. "This house is gorgeous. I've never been in a house this big before. Whose is it?"

"My dad's," Destin replied.

"Wow, he must be rich," said Roxy. "What does he do for a living?"

"He owns a company that makes glass eyeballs for horses on merry-go-rounds," he said with a serious face.

Dental School Debacle

Kim looked confused. "Gee, I didn't know there was such a company."

"Somebody has to make them," he said, and then escorted the girls to the back porch. "Let's go outside and get something to drink."

While they were standing on the porch, they heard a girl yelling from above. Destin looked up and saw Kate standing on the third-floor balcony preaching with no clothes on.

"I am mother nature," she yelled while looking at the sky. Her eyes had a mysterious twinkle. "I created the wind and the fire. I soar with the eagles. I am Trog—The Empress of All Dairy Products."

Destin shook his head in disbelief. "Trog's losing it. I think dental school is finally getting to her."

"Either that, or she's having a cholesterol seizure," said Bobby.

Just then Mike walked up to Destin while staring at his hands. "I'm feeling weird, Destin. I've just realized how nice it is to have hands, and they're so convenient—right here at the end of my arms."

Destin, Roxy and Kim backed away from Mike and walked back to the house, only to find Sam wearing a life jacket, goggles and diving fins. Destin noticed that neither Sam nor Mike had pupils in their eyes—only a mysterious twinkle.

"Where are you going, Sam?"

"I'm going to look for a lost treasure chest," said Sam seriously. "I just remembered I hid it in the bay during a previous life right after the French Revolution."

"OK fine," replied Destin, as he moved to the side so Sam could pass. Then Darl came running out of the house with a shovel.

Jim P. Sandras, D.D.S.

"Where are you going?" asked Destin.

"Fishing," he replied. He didn't have pupils either, only that mysterious twinkle.

"With a shovel?"

"I'm going after the big ones."

"Good luck," said Destin. "Watch out for Sam, he's treasure hunting."

Then in the back yard three hygiene students came running by the house acting like they were riding horses. When Bobby saw this, he ran down the steps and began chasing them riding his make-believe motorbike. They ran right past a student sitting on the ground having a conversation with a pine tree about posterior composites. Kate was the next to come running out of the house, still without clothes, only a twinkle in her eyes.

"I'm free, I'm free," she repeated as she skipped down the pier and jumped into the water. Out of nowhere, Sarah came running from the side of the house twirling a nylon rope and looked up at Destin on the porch.

"Where did that wild boar go?" she asked, with the same twinkle.

"It jumped into the water at the end of the pier," replied Kim.

Sarah smiled and waved. "Don't worry, I'll catch it."

Kim looked at Destin. "I didn't know dental students were so weird." Kim realized Destin was thinking about something else and not listening. Then she noticed that now, he too, had the same mysterious twinkle in his eyes.

"You know, I've never caught a trout with my teeth before," he said. "But for some strange reason, I feel as if I can right now. Excuse me, I'll be right back." Destin ran down the pier and jumped into the water with the rest. The two girls looked around

Dental School Debacle

and noticed that everyone had the same look in their eyes and started to panic.

"What should we do?" asked Kim.

"I don't know, but I'll tell you one thing. When I get home, I'm gonna call my cousin and curse her out."

Just then, Lewis walked out of the house drinking a Diet Coke and introduced himself to the two guests. He was the only one around without the twinkle in his eyes and acting normal.

"Would you ladies like something to drink?"

"What's going on here?" asked Roxy. "They all seemed normal at first, and then they started freaking out."

"Yeah, it's like a radioactive meteorite flew over," said Kim.

Lewis casually smiled. "Don't worry. They'll be back to normal in a few hours. I put five ounces of Amazon Basin mushrooms in their spaghetti without them knowing it. Right now, they're tripping their brains out. The hallucinations should decrease in about an hour, and then they'll start having fun."

"They won't drown out there, will they?" asked Kim.

"Nah, the tide's out," Lewis said. "It's only four feet deep out there right now."

While Lewis was getting them something to drink, Roxy noticed Brick sound asleep against the wall and pointed at him.

"That's the one who tried to kill me," she said.

"You should have seen him, Lewis," said Kim. "He dove through the air and tackled her."

"That sounds like Brick."

"I've got an idea," said Roxy. "Let's shave his whole body."

"That's a great idea," said Kim.

"I can't let you girls do that to Brick," he said. "Even though he gets a little rough sometimes, he's still my classmate and friend. Besides, he'd kill us…literally."

"Then what do you suggest?" asked Roxy.

"I have a better idea," Lewis said. "But we're going to need some help." Lewis searched the estate for a half hour before finding two guys whose eyes were not twinkling too badly. Along with the two hygienists, the five carried Brick to the beach, took his bathing suit off, and turned him onto his stomach, leaving his butt cheeks exposed to the elements.

"This was a great idea, Lewis," said Kim.

"Brick's been up for at least two days," he said. "I'm sure he'll sleep way past lunch. That should be plenty enough time for a good tan."

"That big fool won't be able to sit down for a week," said Roxy with a smile of satisfaction.

***

The morning sun came quickly. As soon as the rays hit her face, Kate opened her eyes. All she could see or hear were seagulls flying overhead. Kate didn't have a clue as to where she was, until she sat up and looked around. The first thing she saw was Destin sound asleep wearing a life jacket, with his head on her leg. Then she noticed that she was at the end of the pier and that there were several other people sleeping out there, also. She stood up and stretched, and then it hit her—she was naked. Kate screamed loud enough to wake up the people in the house.

"AHHHH! WHERE ARE MY CLOTHES?"

Destin woke up, raised his head and looked at Kate standing over him without clothes.

"Oh no," he said. "I've died and gone to hell." He covered his eyes and laid his head back on the wooden pier. Kate took the life jacket off Sam, tried to cover her private parts and ran to the

Dental School Debacle

house.

Mike sat up on the pier, forced open his eyes and saw Kate's rear end bouncing as she ran. "Now that's something you don't see every day."

"Where am I?" asked Sam as he sat up. "And why am I dressed like this?"

"I have no idea," replied Destin as he sat up with extreme difficulty. "But I bet we had fun last night."

***

The students helped each other up and walked inside. They were all feeling nauseated, especially after seeing vomit from some unknown source all over the back porch. Inside there were two lines of people— one for the soft drinks and one for the medicine cabinet. This year, they planned ahead for this Sunday morning. The medicine cabinet looked like that of a professional rugby trainer. They had muscle relaxers, sutures, bronchial dilators, Motrin, Vicodin, xylocaine with and without epinephrine, antiemetics, salt tablets, gauze, plaster of Paris, liquid skin, ice bags; and just for the heck of it, someone put a bottle of cat nip next to the Vicodin. After choosing their drug of choice, they stood back in line for the soft drinks so they could swallow the pills. Everyone in both lines was complaining about how their fingernails were hurting from opening so many cans this weekend. By lunch time their brains were beginning to function halfway normal. While everybody was cleaning up the house, a hygiene student came running through the back door.

"Everyone come look," she shouted. "You've got to see this and bring your cameras." She ran back outside followed by everyone else. There sticking out of the sand was a huge red butt. It was already burned from the intense ultraviolet rays reflecting

Jim P. Sandras, D.D.S.

off the sand and water, but Brick was still sound asleep.

Sarah, who had just finished loading up her car, noticed the crowd of people gathered on the beach and ran over to see what was going on. As soon as she saw the huge, dark pink buns facing the sun, she knew Brick needed help. She rushed over and slapped him in the face several times to wake him up before he developed third degree burns on his gluteus maximus. When he realized what was going on he jumped to his feet, ran down the pier, and dove into the water to wash off.

After all the excitement was over, the students continued cleaning and preparing to leave. The hardest part was picking up all the cans. There wasn't as much damage to the house as the previous year, thanks to the mushrooms. But there was still enough damage to justify filing an insurance claim. It took them until late that afternoon before the place was livable again. Kate was the first to leave. She was so embarrassed she raced off without telling anyone goodbye and went straight to Taco Bell. Then everyone walked to the end of the pier with Bart to see him off in the sailboat. They tried to talk him into going back to dental school, but he said he was still young and could try again later. Besides, he said the thought of getting up early every morning only to shave and go to work just to pay his taxes was something he wanted to put off as long as possible. While the girls were picking up the dishes, the guys helped David and The Loose Teeth load their van and thanked them for the entertainment. The remainder of the students told each other goodbye then left the estate to continue with their brief, but important time off before beginning the dreaded junior year.

Destin, Mike and Bobby slept there Sunday night so that they could wake up early in the morning and try to repair the broken

Dental School Debacle

door. After two hours of trying to fix it, they realized they were doing manual labor and immediately stopped. To keep wild animals and intruders out of the house, they pushed the refrigerator into the opening. The three good friends told one another goodbye and went on their separate ways. This year Destin had to go to both his dad's and brother's insurance offices to file claims. He decided that it was in everyone's best interest to tell the truth this year—that DEA agents,
who were looking for the Mexican drug lords, shot at the boat and busted down the door only to find harmless dental students listening to jazz and drinking pina coladas. The federal agents apologized and quickly left.

TO BE CONTINUED...

Boiling crabs at 2:00 a.m.

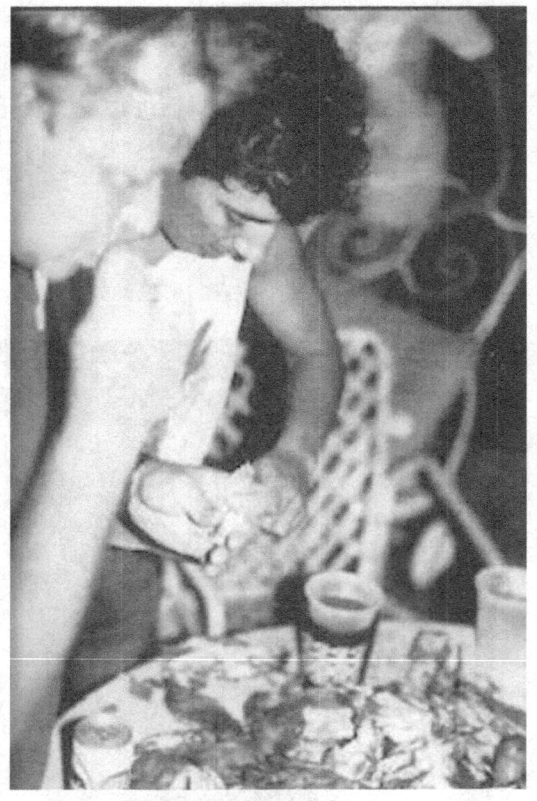
Eating crabs at 3:00 a.m.

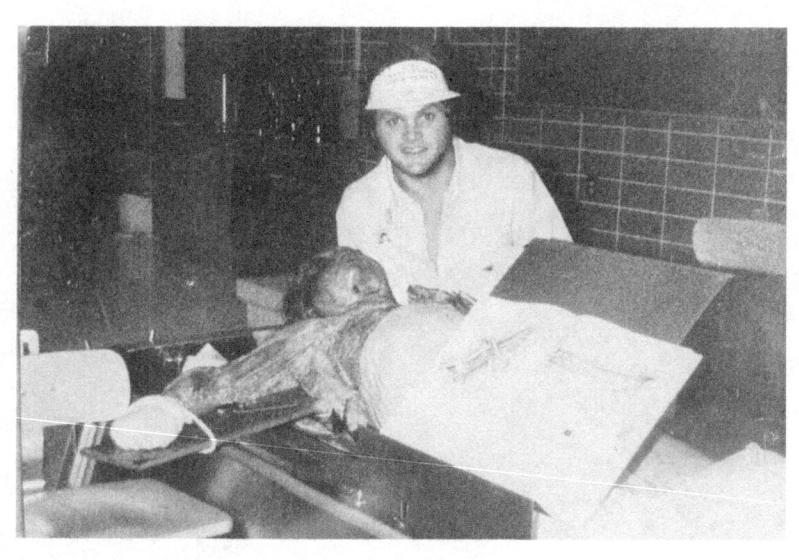

Made in the USA
Columbia, SC
13 December 2025